CLOSER
TO
HOME

BISEXUALITY

&

FEMINISM

ELIZABETH REBA WEISE

D0089339

The Seal Press

Cover art Jana Rekosh.
Design by Clare Conrad.

Library of Congress Cataloging-in-Publication Data

Closer to home : bisexuality and feminism / edited by Elizabeth Reba
    Weise.
        p.   cm.
      ISBN 1-878067-17-6
      1. Lesbianism. 2. Bisexuality. 3. Lesbians–Sexual behavior.
    4. Feminist theory. I. Weise, Elizabeth Reba, 1962-
    HQ75.5 C56 1992
    306.76'5–dc20

Printed in the United States of America
First printing, May 1992
10 9 8 7 6 5 4 3 2 1

Foreign Distribution:
In Canada: Raincoast Book Distribution, Vancouver, B.C.
In Great Britain and Europe: Airlift Book Company, London

Acknowledgements

First thanks go to the authors, the women across the country who sent in innocuous query letters and followed up with incredible essays, the women who write what we've been needing to read. I'm honored to have been able to assist in the process.

I want to give thanks to Lenore Norrgard, who first sat down with me and mapped out a book on bisexuality and feminism in 1988, and who has been a thoughtful and insightful reader and friend throughout. And strong praise to Amanda Udis-Kessler, whose mind I love, whose hours of phone calls from Boston make my heart glad, and who, as a reader and shadow-editor, helped me through the morass of post-modern thinking. Much love as always to Susan Zoccola, who has been hashing this all out with me for the last fifteen years.

Thanks to Lani Kaahumanu, who explained what madness it was to edit a book and then told me how to do it.

The women of Seal Press have been wonderful. Finally getting to know Barbara Wilson, my editor, has been one of the boons of this book. Holly Morris stayed calm and helpful during PageMaker madness. Cathy Johnson, proof reader extraordinaire, made this a much more coherent piece of work.

A year's worth of thanks to my housemates at Lambda Beta Lambda, Prithy and Kiser, who fed me potato masala and took me two-stepping when it all got to be too much.

Peggy Choe made the mistake of coming to Seattle to visit the month the copy-editing changes arrived and was utterly indispensable. She was also voted the woman we most want to live with by Lambda Beta Lambda. Please move back.

Linda Botich, Lizabeth Coller and Peggy Walsh answered my frantic call for typists to enter in all the non-computerized essays and in doing so made this process immeasurably easier. Anita Anderson, Peggy Walsh and Janine Gressel helped proof the final manuscript; grateful thanks for their eagle eyes.

Thanks to my seriously computer literate sister, Victoria Weise, who helped start this project by installing my new hard drive, and finished by figuring out how to transfer twenty-one different word processing formats to ones my computer could read.

A book isn't a real book without an index. Many thanks to Lise Kreps who gallantly volunteered to produce the index, something she does professionally and the science of which became apparent when she asked "Have you ever seen the word 'heterosexual' appear in an index?"

And finally to the women of the Seattle Bisexual Women's Network, who in 1986 created a place to come home to.

To the women of the Seattle Bisexual Women's Network

TABLE OF CONTENTS

Elizabeth Reba Weise

INTRODUCTION

Bisexuality is about choice. About living out the consequences of loving and desiring people of either sex. Very simple. But until the recent rise of a bisexual movement in several Western countries, it was difficult to find anyone, much less a vocal community, who could openly and proudly acknowledge the possibility of choosing bisexuality instead of the either/or of heterosexuality/homosexuality.

The notion of a bisexuality grounded in feminism, and contributing to its meaning, is more resisted and problematic still. Those of us who consider ourselves feminist are excited about the possibilities of a bisexuality informed by the understanding that sex and gender are classifications by which women are oppressed and restricted. We see bisexuality calling into question many of the fundamental assumptions of our culture: the duality of gender; the necessity of bipolar relationships; the nature of desire; the demand for either/or sexualities; and the seventies' gay and lesbian model of bisexuality as a stage in working through false consciousness before finally arriving at one's "true" sexual orientation.

Those who trivialize our thoughtfulness and self-determination see bisexuality as a phase, an unwillingness to face the stigma of homosexuality, a cop-out. It's an inability to come out as lesbian, the result of overactive libidos, or just a bit of kinky weirdness. In lesbian and feminist communities, bisexual women have been portrayed as shirkers, women who want all the good of being with women without taking the heat it brings on. Women who won't stick around when the shit hits the fan.

Bisexuals are supposed to be people who can't make up their minds, or who are too afraid to. Because this culture presents sexuality as something *essential* to our make-up, something we're born with, the idea that it need not be so black and white is threatening. One major argument for gay rights has been, "We're born this way, so you can't discriminate against us because it's *not our fault.*" Suddenly, you've got a crowd of people saying, "Hey, we *choose* to be this way," and all those civil libertarian arguments fly out the window. We want the right to love whom we choose not because we're forced by our unrelenting biology to choose lovers of the same sex, but because we don't accept someone else's moral code that says loving women is wrong. As Queer Nation says, "Get used to it."

But it confuses people. They don't know where to put us. A friend's mother accepted her several-year relationship with her lesbian lover as a marriage. But when they broke up and my friend started seeing a man, her mother lost it. "All those years I treated Kelly like a daughter-in-law, and now I find out that you were straight all along!"

It's no easier from the lesbian perspective. I sat in my own living room and listened to my housemate and friend of over eight years drill one of the contributors to this book: "But once you've been with women, why *ever* go back to men? What's the point? When are you going to give up on men and just be a lesbian?"

There's no model, nothing to point to in our common cultural background that supports or even explains what it feels like to fall in lust or love or both with women *and* men. What do you do in high school when you like girls and boys? What do you do in a workplace when you talk about your past romantic fiascos and the pronoun-soup gets a little too confusing?

I know a woman who was a lesbian for seven years. Then one day she admitted that she desired men. My friend desired men, so she stopped being a lesbian and became a heterosexual. Whereas seven years earlier she had undergone a process of redefining her past through the model of false consciousness, she now did the same thing in reverse. Heterosexual society had wanted her to be with men. When she decided she wanted the company of women, the politic of the times demanded that she choose women over men in all things. What kind of true or false consciousness was this?

For each transformation, she rearranged her interior landscape of desire to conform to outside pressure, which she internalized to the extent that the pressure didn't feel like it was on the outside at all, but coming only from inside of her. She felt as if there were only two possibilities, so she *had* to fit all her feelings and desires into the narrow confines given her, like Cinderella's stepsisters cutting off their toes and heels to get the glass slipper to fit.

But desire will out. Which is what the voices of the women in this anthology are saying. We choose to acknowledge our desires and *then* find a way to live with them as feminists and as thoughtful human beings.

Bisexuality alone calls these assumptions into question. But as feminist women committed to a radical political theory that seeks to overcome oppression based on sex, we are constantly challenged by our being open to choosing men as our intimate lovers and friends despite the fact that men are the prime oppressors. Patriarchy is the problem, not individual men. However, men raised under patriarchy are often its servants. How do we reconcile those two seemingly irreconcilable facts?

A bisexual-feminist perspective embraces the reality that sexuality can be a fluid and changeable part of being human. It rejects the dichotomization of politics and desire. This embrace is not always an easy one. Our arms are unaccustomed to opening so wide. But for bisexual women that embrace is more honest. It means confronting culturally prescribed notions of duality and conflict. Being gay in a homophobic world can never just be a null-state. Being straight is the norm. Lesbianism can be tinged with meaning, danger, fear and no little exultation, but it's seldom an unthinking state. To be a bisexual-feminist woman means to live an intensely examined life.

The women writing in this anthology are working toward an understanding of what a bisexual feminism would look like. The essays describe feelings, duty, politics and love. They talk about a fierce desire to live ethically and to have our lives mirror what we believe. They also describe the reality of loving this woman or that man and struggling to create a language that allows us to talk about it.

These essays describe the varying realities of how we as bisexual women live our lives and try to make sense of them. Some are written from an intensely personal place, doing the truth-telling that will allow us to discuss what loving means at a level beyond politics. Some write the theory we need to understand how cultural expectations influence us. Each helps to define the pluralism that is our lives.

The questions we ask, and the answers we find, would not be pos-

xii *Closer to Home*

sible without the liberation movements that came before us, especially the feminist and gay liberation movements that we grew out of. Their analysis of sexism, oppression and heterosexism birthed the language that made this questioning possible.

Feminism is a radical political theory, a method of analysis, a call for revolution and change. Lesbianism is a practice, something that arises from desire. Politics and desire were, some of us found, unhappy bedmates.

In the canon of lesbian life, one was supposed to lead to the other. For many women, it did. Some were primarily attracted to women. Others made a conscious choice to be with women despite the fact that they also sexually desired men or perhaps only desired men.

Lesbian communities were extremely strict about this point in the seventies. Bisexuals were merely women who hadn't yet overcome the false consciousness of thinking they *chose* to be with men. By the 1980s, with the lesbian sex wars raging around us—could or should desire be politically correct, was it okay to wear lipstick? skirts? leather?—questions of desire got more play within women's communities.

As for heterosexual society, it saw bisexuals as swinging singles who would do it with anything that moved, pleasure-besotted nihilists on the model of David Bowie and Mick Jagger. Bisexuality was about sex. It wasn't about falling in love or dating or building relationships. We swung, we didn't buy houses with our lovers, especially if they were women.

But where were bisexuals during all of this? We were out creating our own movement. In San Francisco, bisexual groups had been meeting since the early seventies. The Bisexual Center (founded in 1976) ran support groups, rap groups and social functions for a large bisexual network. It helped bring together bisexual activists who played major roles in the formation of the more than thirty bisexual groups in the Bay Area today. The second West Coast flowering of bisexual activism began with BiPol, the bisexual, lesbian and gay political action group begun in 1983, and later the Bay Area Bisexual Network. Those groups grew larger and stronger throughout the eighties, and in 1990 they sponsored the first National Bisexual Conference in San Francisco. That conference brought together more than five hundred bisexual activists from across North America and several European countries.

It was a major milestone for the bisexual community in terms of organizing, networking and visibility. Bi-Net, the National Bisexual Network of the United States, was founded at the conference. It now publishes a newsletter and serves as a clearinghouse for information on bisexuality and bisexual groups.

On the East Coast, the foremother of all bisexual groups, the Boston Bisexual Women's Network (BBWN), was reshaping the women's community. BBWN had its beginnings in 1982 at a lesbian discussion group the night it tackled the topic of bisexuality. Some of the women who attended that discussion went on to start a bi women's support group, the BiVocals, and then BBWN. Ten years later there are a multitude of bi women's support groups and activities in the greater Boston area, as well as a men's group, a newsletter and an active East Coast Bisexual Network.

Since the early 1980s, other bi groups, both women's and men's, have emerged across the country. Some of the strongest are in Seattle, Los Angeles, New York, Washington D.C., Philadelphia, Santa Cruz and Chicago. There are also active groups in Toronto, Amsterdam and London.

The bi movement has been characterized by several different influences. Some bi groups have their roots in feminist and lesbian-feminist politics. The two largest women-only groups, Boston's and Seattle's, are both staunchly feminist-identified. Other groups have grown more out of a sexual liberation model. Those groups have tended to be co-sexual. San Francisco and Washington, D.C. are strong and active multicultural groups with a more representative showing of people of color. Most bi groups, however, are a white, middle-class phenomenon. College- and university-based groups have been in the forefront of transforming lesbian and gay groups into lesbian/gay/bisexual groups, or simply "queer."

Bisexual groups across the country have been calling for more inclusion of bisexuals in lesbian and gay communities and politics in reaction to our invisibility in a community that we are part of and active in but that often refuses to recognize us. Several of the authors in this book tell specific stories of pushing for bisexual inclusion and the results. Bisexuals have lobbied hard to include the "B-word" in lesbian and gay pride marches, conferences, newspapers and magazines, some with more success than others.

The bisexual movement is just beginning to feel its strength. The new emphasis on queer politics, as opposed to gay/lesbian politics, brings with it a sense of bisexual inclusion. Queer politics are bi-friendly. The whole notion of queerness and queerdom may finally evolve into the true inclusion of bisexuals in the greater gay and lesbian community. Because of growing numbers of out-bisexuals who are participating in queer discourse, it is being redefined.

This book grew from a history of seven years of bisexual organizing. For me, the founding of the Seattle Bisexual Women's Network in 1986 created a space where I could stop worrying about where I fell in some arbitrary designation of sexuality and start concentrating on what I was about. After a year in the group, Lenore Norrgard and I co-founded *North Bi Northwest*, SBWN's bi feminist newsletter, to discuss questions of what it meant to be bisexual.

One day Lenore called me and said, "We should write a book together about this stuff." We got together and sketched out a sixteen-chapter tome on the politics of bisexual feminism. We weren't the only ones thinking about it. Seal Press called a few months later to ask if I was interested in working on a book on the subject.

That was in 1989. There were many meetings over the course of the next year. Lenore decided to step back in the process and only consult. Seal and I decided that an anthology of writings by women on the topic of feminism and bisexuality would give voice to the greatest possible breadth of experience. We limited the book to writings by women because we wanted to address the unique situation of bisexual women caught between heterosexual sexism and the ideological purity of the lesbian community.

Three years later, the book you hold in your hand came into being. The twenty-one women writing in this book ask, and answer, some of the difficult questions that feminism and sexuality raise: how do we live honorably, how do we bring together our desire and love in the face of gendered dichotomies? They reopen a discussion that seems long gone from popular feminist discourse; how do we cope with sexism and heterosexism within relationships?

The women in this anthology give themselves many names. Bi-dyke, bi-lesbian, bi-feminist, lesbian-identified bisexual, bisexual, bi-affectional, lesbian, and formerly-lesbian bisexual. Anything but straight. As Margaret Mihee Choe points out in her essay, "identity is that which makes one recognizable to self and other." The plurality of names, and the combinations used, are all attempts, in our clumsy and woman-wordless language, to create this identity, to make ourselves recognizable. To indicate that we, as feminists and women who recognize the realities of sexism and heterosexism, embrace our queerness, our lesbianism, our woman-loving, and also claim and embrace our openness to men.

There are no good words for who we are or what we do. There is no easy shorthand to say what we mean. We are left with cobbled-together phrases, long introductory explanations, frustration, or a combination of these. "Dyke," which to me is a positive word meaning a strong, capable woman who loves women and who doesn't put up with stupidity from men, doesn't have a bisexual equivalent. Would that it did. As the bisexual movement grows, and as more and more people become open to the fluidity it encompasses, perhaps we will find the words we need.

We hope these essays will make you think, whatever your sex, gender, sexual identity or preference. We want them to cause a firestorm of controversy that will make people question their basic assumptions about sexuality. We want reading it to feel like sitting down at a dinner party with a group of strong-minded women who talk late into the night about what their definitions of self and sexuality mean, personally and politically. We hope it will strike a chord, make you shout out loud, "Hallelujah, somebody finally said it!" or throw down the book in disgust.

In these writings, and in our lives, we are rejecting the rule set out for us, the rule that says, "Choose only one." We are redefining the world and demanding to be accepted on our own terms. We are creating a place to come home to.

DEFINITIONS

Ruth Gibian

Refusing Certainty:
Toward a Bisexuality of Wholeness

Where are we going? Where are we going when our principles start to stunt our own growing? Looking for freedom—where is our freedom when we've broken old chains just to make new ones?
—Meg Christian, "From the Heart"

Walking home one August afternoon, savoring the aftertaste of the conversation I have just left, enjoying my giddiness, enjoying the sensation of my body in the hot sun, I go over the past hour again in my mind: how we sat in the shady courtyard at the Y, hunched over our knees talking about the outrage of the administration putting in new grass and fuchsia baskets when some staff haven't gotten raises in years. How intent we became on this very ordinary banter and on talk about a graduate program three thousand miles away, a new job starting next week, an animation festival playing downtown. How charged the words became, and the space between them. Crossing the field between the Y and my apartment, it hits me: what I'm feeling is attraction. And then my exhilaration mixes with fear, my anticipation with denial. *This couldn't be attraction, shouldn't be.* This is familiar. This is what I felt the first time I found myself attracted to a woman. This time, years later, out, proud and happy as a lesbian, I am attracted to a man.

Before that day, I had considered my sexuality static. When I came out as a lesbian, I, like many other women, felt I was giving voice and life to my true self, releasing what had remained stifled and denied for too long. Coming out for me was very powerful, the culmination of years of attractions that were paired with so much dread they immobilized me. Once I finally accepted my feelings and found my way to other lesbians, I soared. For weeks, months, I experienced elation so dramatic things tasted different, colors looked brighter, every sense was sharpened. I felt myself intensely, purely, it seemed. My journal from that period is filled with entries like *this is the truest thing I've ever felt.* I had broken through the constraint of what I thought I should feel and was positively ecstatic with the recognition of my own desires. Finally I had silenced every voice inside my head except for my own, and she told me, loud and clear, that I loved women. That simple. That marvelous. From now on, I promised myself, no more repressed feelings. No more shoulds. No more fear of what I felt. I would listen for that still, deep voice and let her be my guide.

And then I fell in love. With a man. And that old sense of dread competing with desire came rushing back. Fortunately, even though I had internalized the politics of a community that said by loving a man I was a traitor taking the easy—that is, straight—way out, I managed to sort out and hear that inner voice, who assured me: yes, you feel this. Yes, this is love, Yes, I will never repress feelings again, not for a woman, not for a man.

Other inner voices were plenty loud, too, mostly judges. Like the one that said, *see, this lesbian stuff was just a phase, nothing serious, nothing real.* A dangerously invalidating voice. And what if we do change? What if our feelings vary? Does that negate our previous experience, make it any less important? It certainly didn't negate mine. I still love women, feel attraction, desire. Those feelings couldn't be more serious or real, and I am still proud of and open with them. None of that changed when I began to love a man. But even if my attraction to and love for women does at some point ebb, why should that be a negative? If, in other parts of our lives, we don't strive to be static beings, but value growth, development and change, why should our sexual beings be any different?

Perhaps one reason is that the subject of sexuality is heavily charged in our culture. Establishing an identity of any kind is often a perplexing challenge; establishing a sexual identity requires that one grapple with an inner experience that for many—no matter what orientation—brings up shame, guilt, embarrassment or, at the very least, vulnerability. Because of the silence that often surrounds sexuality issues, it is not uncommon for a person to go through this process in isolation. It is far less daunting to invest in our search for sexual self-knowledge if we believe that our quest will end in a definitive, categorical answer: we will find out that we are *this*. Having risked so much, we want the truth we discover to endure.

This notion of sexual stasis is reinforced by the fact that we as a culture define sexual orientation largely in terms of current sexual behavior. We basically buy the notion not only that we are who we sleep with, but also that we are who we sleep with *today*. Lesbian communities accept and perpetuate this as much as the heterosexual world does. And what a narrow definition it is: it invalidates past actions, past feelings and present feelings. It doesn't allow conflicting feelings to coexist, denying the possibility of paradox and discouraging ambiguity. It says: you must stay still so we can see who you are. Like a snapshot, this definition is a lie, halting the natural motion of our lives. It says: you are the one thing we see most readily; your actions create concrete casts.

In Kafka's story "The Top," the main character, a philosopher, takes great delight in catching children's tops in spin, because he is hopeful that by understanding the spinning top he will understand all things.[1] However, each time he does catch one, he becomes disgusted with the piece of wood in his hand and throws it down, The disgust seems to come from his desire for a *spinning* top; as soon as he catches the top, it is no longer spinning but still. There is no way to fix the spin and have the top remain what it is. So it is with bisexuality. Any attempt to define it as static makes it something other than what it is, stops it in mid-spin.

The definition of a static sexuality is based on binary opposition. By tying sexual identity to a current relationship, it says loving women excludes loving men, and loving men excludes loving women. Even Alfred Kinsey's continuum of sexuality is based on binary opposition: pure heterosexuality is on one end, and pure homosexuality is on the other. Bisexuality falls in the middle, not pure anything, incomplete, a mixture. "Bi" is two, implying a split, two parts and no whole.

Indeed, our entire Western system of thought is based on binary opposition; we define by comparison, by what things are not. We understand healing because we know hurt, know darkness because we understand light and recognize its absence. We understand these as entities that exclude each other, and our understanding depends on this exclusion. This has been true throughout recorded history. In a discussion of the ancient Egyptian language, Sigmund Freud cites examples where two words with antithetical meanings form a compound word that then retains the meaning of only one of its elements; for example, "lightdark" might mean only "light."[2] Meaning even in this early language is formed by contrast, by the relation of two bipolar elements to each other.

The harm of thinking in opposites goes beyond the fact that it creates exclusion. Jacques Derrida critiques the use of polarities in philosophy, language and thought by pointing out that the common dichotomies that compose Western thinking, such as good versus evil, presence versus absence, truth versus error, identity versus difference, soul versus body, man versus woman, contain a hierarchy in which "the second term in each pair is considered the negative, corrupt, undesirable version of the first, a fall away from it. Hence, absence is the lack of presence, evil is the fall from good, error is a distortion of truth, etc."[3] Because of its hierarchical nature, binary opposition makes equality impossible. Living in a culture that defines sexuality in binary terms—man/woman, heterosexuality/homosexuality, monogamous/single—we are not only limited but oppressed.

French feminist Hélène Cixous moves Derrida's critique one step further into a feminist analysis, describing this ordering of opposites as patriarchal, privileging the masculine in each pair and thus defining the feminine as the absence thereof.[4] "Where is she?" she asks, listing familiar dichotomous pairs: activity/passivity, sun/moon, culture/nature, day/night, father/mother, head/heart, intelligible/palpable, logos/pathos.[5] "She" is relegated to a position that denotes lacking. These hierarchies, Cixous declares, create "lack-banks" and a repression of the feminine.[6]

So if repression and exclusion begin in the way we form our thoughts, in the way we work our language, then expression and inclusion can be created by inventing meaning without such dichotomies. Within such a framework, we can experience complexity without it becoming paradox and can live in a place other than the poles without being "between."

Happily, this is hardly a novel idea. Indeed, Cixous and other French feminists, particularly Luce Irigiray and to some extent Julia Kristeva, have sought to create a form of expression that does precisely this. *Écriture feminine*, often translated as "writing the body,"[7] grows from the premise that language is bound to sexuality and that feminine sexuality, rather than being narrowly focused and thus exclusive, is diffuse and nonexclusive. "Woman has sex organs just about everywhere," says Irigiray.[8] "If she is a whole," says Cixous, "it is a whole made up of parts that are wholes, not simple, partial objects but varied entirety, moving and boundless change, a cosmos where eros never stops travelling, vast astral space. She doesn't revolve around a sun that is more star than the stars."[9] Binary oppositions become irrelevant. Instead of meaning deriving from dualistic difference (black is not white), meaning derives from multiple difference (blue is not green or yellow or mauve or magenta). Everything exists in relation to everything else. It follows that *écriture feminine* takes as one of its trademarks a lack of closure in language.[10] Cixous posits that this openness is critical to inventiveness, that "those who change life cannot help but be stirred by anomalies—complementary or contradictory."[11]

It is in this context that Cixous talks about bisexuality:

Bisexuality—that is to say the location within oneself of the presence of both sexes, evident and insistent in different ways according to the individual, the nonexclusion of difference or of a sex, and starting with this "permission" one gives oneself, the multiplication of the effects of desire's inscription on every part of the body and the other body.[12]

This is a sexuality that doesn't strive for stasis or consistency. It "does not annihilate differences but cheers them on, pursues them, adds more."[13] This is a sexuality that is not threatened by inclusion but instead becomes larger because of it. Desire itself becomes multiplicitous. It does not try to stop the top; it *is* the top.

The French feminists are not the first to question the Almighty Power of Opposition. Even Freud's interest in the workings of the ancient Egyptian language sprang from his desire to understand the tendency for dreams to unify opposites and to express an idea by its opposite. He was fascinated to discover that, in addition to the compound words described earlier, certain words in Egyptian mirrored this kind of expression by signifying two opposing concepts. The same word that meant outside, for example, also meant inside. Freud does not challenge the notion that meaning is arrived at by the contrast of opposites—in fact, he appears to support it fully. But Freud doesn't interpret such a construction of meaning as privileging one part of the pair. Instead, he points out that, in dreams, opposites can represent a single idea or feeling without any appearance of contradiction.[14] Dreams refuse the certainty of "no"—any two things can exist in unison.

How do we refuse the certainty of "no" in our waking lives? How can we conceive of duality without inviting a split? How can parts be whole? As bisexuals, how can our various hearts exist in unison? What would a "yes" concept of sexuality look like? How do we apply our new conceptions to our daily lives?

One beginning is to see the wholeness of each thing we perceive. Darkness is not the lack of light, it is *darkness*. It is completely itself. Bisexuality isn't the exclusion of heterosexuality or of homosexuality; it is the inclusion of both as component parts. Bisexuality itself says yes: yes, I can love women; yes, I can love men. Nature often works in duality without excluding or ascribing favor to one side. Symmetry: the Rorschach whole of our bodies, an eye on each side, a hip, a shoulder, an arm. Two sides of a chin, a nose. Component parts, component hearts. The two equal halves of a leaf. And more, the power of perspective: the many faces of a globe as it turns.

We can also refuse the certainty of "no" by refusing the certainty of "yes" as well. When I came out as a lesbian, part of what I did was to declare my identity fixed, unified. And joyfully so. But I also imposed definition on what James Hillman calls my "many-sided soul,"[15] only to discover such definition meant limits not nearly as pliable as my soul. Certainty invites contradiction, and contradiction, confusion. If I see my Self as mixture and motion, then there are no contradictions or inconsistencies. Changes are not negative or positive. No judgment.

This way of perceiving the Self doesn't come without cost, however. Seeing ourselves as having fixed identities is comforting. We understand ourselves, can make generalizations, predictions about ourselves. We can make connections with other people like ourselves based on these generalizations. When we see ourselves as less rigid, we are faced with having to learn new ways to recognize who is "like us."

It can be useful, then, to understand *sexual orientation* as distinct from *sexual identity, orientation* being the entire complexity and multiplicity of our experience, and *identity* being the name we give to best fit that experience at any given time. The advantage of such a distinction is that a fluid and diffuse understanding of *orientation* gives a more adequate expression to our "many-sided souls," without necessarily having an impact on the more fixed, and thus comfortable, *identity* by which we describe ourselves.

To illustrate, consider the factors that compose orientation: attraction, behavior, fantasies, emotional preference and social preference.[16] Each of these factors moves and changes with an individual's growth and experience over time. Imagine if a person could describe her or his experience of each of these factors as a color. For example, attraction might be blue, with light blue representing exclusively opposite-sex attraction, and deep blue representing exclusively same-sex attraction. The level of intensity and personal significance of each attraction would also determine the exact color. A person's life history and dreams might be drawn in dozens of shades of blue. If each of the factors could be expressed in the same way using a range of colors—red for fantasy, green for emotional preference, for example—then the composite of a person's orientation could contain thousands of permutations, reflected as slight gradations in lightness, hue and saturation. Now imagine creating color composites for even a few hundred people, laying them out into a kind of quilt and taking a black-and-white photograph of all that color. It would give a black, white and gray approximation of what was there, enough so the photograph was representative of the pattern, but it would not be precise. Nor are the approximations *homosexual, heterosexual* and *bisexual* precise. With reductive names (or film), we lose the richness and depth of color.

Imprecise or not, identity is important. Among other things, identity is how community is formed—lesbian and gay communities, yes, and also religious communities.[17] People find safety in community as well as similarity, recognition and inclusion. We have power, voice, can make ourselves heard and felt in the larger world. We belong, a new and welcome experience for many of us who have felt out of place in mainstream culture. We can be openly ourselves, fully ourselves. No secrets. No editing.

But because community is based on certain fixed aspects of ourselves, those aspects must remain fixed, or else the community loses its cohesion, its definitions. To preserve itself, the community imposes rules. To belong, one must give up the freedom to be a paradoxical Self, to overlap labels, cross borders, scramble definitions. And, occasional rhetoric to the contrary notwithstanding, lesbian communities do judge "membership" according to present lovers. When one lesbian suggested to me that perhaps I was never a "real lesbian," she was thinking of my current partner, a man. She was not thinking of my affectional orientation, not asking about significant loves, not wondering where I am most comfortable, most at home. She, and others who would make similar judgments, are struggling to hold onto labels and definitions that shape the community that is their sanctuary and strength.

So bisexuality falls outside the thick black line that marks the boundaries of community, and perhaps that's why it's often viewed as shaking the durability of a self-sufficient, woman-loving culture. But it shakes our insides, too. It makes every one of us vulnerable to the possibility that it could happen to us. Before I thought bisexuality was a personal issue for me, a lesbian support group that I was in had a heated debate about a woman who had dropped in a few times. She considered herself heterosexual but had just ended what she called a two-year "affair" with a woman and didn't know where else to go to get support. Some of us were in favor of her coming to the group. After all, weren't we a support group for women who loved women? And wasn't she clearly a woman in pain who had lost the love of a woman? And where else *could* she go? Others in the group were firmly, even angrily, opposed to her inclusion in the group. She wasn't "really" a lesbian, they argued, didn't identify with lesbian culture or values, was in fact afraid of her own love for a woman. I talked to a separatist friend one day about this debate, as I fervently lobbied for a community that would support and include women-loving-women anywhere in their process. (At the time I was still adhering to the static she-just-doesn't-know-she's-really-a-lesbian-yet paradigm.) My friend thought for few moments before she suggested that a fear she understood was hard at work in my group. "On the straight/gay continuum, I'm over here," she said, drawing in the air and pointing beyond the imaginary end of the gay side, "and to think of myself even a little bit over here"—fluttering fingers towards the middle—"scares me half to death."

It *is* easier to deny what scares us half to death, to push it away, see it as "other" and not as our own. So the emotional motion of an individual is collectively echoed by a community, and we end up with more paradox. Lesbian and gay communities, experts by experience in being shunted off to the side, being denied and excluded, find it difficult to embrace our own fringes because of fear. Like growing up and discovering to our horror how much we resemble our parents, lesbian and gay communities are finding out how much we resemble heterosexist society. That which we are afraid of becoming we make sure isn't part of us.

Back to that day in August: I too was scared, found myself denying what I felt. What was so frightening? I find myself thinking now of my long and tumultuous coming-out process, and of one particular session with the counselor who finally brought me out of fear and into pride and confidence. I had been pouring out to her all the reasons why coming out was so terrifying. Chief among them this time was a fear of not fitting in. I mean, everyone knew how tough it was to be a lesbian, how much society made them outcasts. I was scared to identify myself as a lesbian and so claim myself as such an outcast. I imagined endless isolation and loneliness (and I hadn't even read Radclyffe Hall!). My counselor, bless her, nodded sincerely and empathetically and then asked, "When was the last time you felt you did fit in?" The truth was out: the womb, maybe?

The months that followed brought other revelations. Instead of feeling like an outcast, instead of feeling isolated, as soon as I claimed my identity as a lesbian, I felt more included, more like I "fit in" than I ever had before. Here were people who knew how I felt, who accepted me without knowing anything more about me except that I too celebrated my love for women. That summer I traveled alone across country and was embraced anywhere I found a women's community. Women put me up in their homes, fed me meals and told me I was welcome back any time.

To fall in love with a man, to be anywhere outside the center of my community, threatened my treasured sense of belonging. It confused the exhilarating feeling of pride that had blossomed when I claimed my lesbian identity.

There were other, more complex feelings, too. I felt more than pride in loving women. I felt proud to *dare* to love women, pride in the struggles I had and would continue to sustain. In my courage to stand up and stand out. My fear of falling in love with a man was, well, heterophobia. All kinds of internal voices began warring, many of them more concerned with principles than with feelings: *people will look at me, see me with a man, and they'll never know I love women. And if I truly loved women, why would I want to be with a man? Am I deserting my own feelings? I don't want to lose woman-centered culture. I haven't been a lesbian long enough. People will say I "went back to men." The lesbian community will think I've defected. I want to belong to the community. I want to belong.*

Some of the voices have proved to be right, and some dead wrong. The more I hear them replay, the more I recognize exclusive, oppositional elements and the more readily I can filter out my own truth. But some voices have been doggedly persistent. Many people do look at me with a man and assume I'm heterosexual. It's frustrating to have to continually educate. I can kiss my partner in public without fear of harassment. People guess our relationship if he picks me up at work. But I didn't desert my own feelings. I love my partner and know I would have been short-changing myself, my capacity for a mutually fulfilling and loving relationship, if I had denied my feelings for him in favor of a fixed lesbian identity. And heterosexuality, although it does carry certain privileges, is not necessarily easy. Feminist heterosexuality isn't easy, and feminist bisexuality is yet more complex. In this relationship we're continually reinventing, catching ourselves in and pushing against sexist roles and assumptions. In fact, excavating those roles and assumptions was easier in the exclusive company of women, where because no one was filling in with the corresponding male roles and assumptions, I found myself discovering daily the depth of my socialization. With my male partner, when bits and pieces of inequality make subtle intrusions into our relationship, it takes more vigilance to rout them out. There's something about the familiarity of patterns we learned when young that makes them more invisible to us, despite our best and most deliberate intentions.

Then there is the paradox of monogamy. Can the "mono"/one of monogamy coexist with the "bi"/two of bisexuality? Many bisexual stereotypes and much of what I read ascribe to bisexuals either polyfidelity or short-term serial monogamy. Surely bisexuals are in an excellent position to explore relationship possibilities beyond the conventional. But what assumptions do we accept if we reject monogamy? Does an acceptance of fluid and multiple feelings necessitate fluid and multiple relationships? Do we perceive a contradiction in terms in being both bisexual and monogamous? Do we feel we would lose facets of ourselves by relating to only one gender, that is, staying in one relationship? That would promote a closed definition of sexuality, a definition where identity is again bound to behavior. At this time, I choose monogamy, but I don't perceive my long-term relationship as encompassing the totality of my feelings. Learning to legitimate desire without necessarily acting upon it is a challenge any long-term monogamous relationship faces. To maintain a bisexual self-concept in a monogamous relationship, the challenge is imperative.

My concern about the approval of the lesbian community catalyzed other shifts as well. In anticipating community disapproval, I gradually stopped considering myself part of the community. Of course I still had lesbian friends and continued to make new ones, and I went to marches and events, but I stopped feeling and expecting to feel universal, unconditional support. I would catch myself internalizing what I perceived as community principles of inclusion and exclusion. Sometimes I even put a face on the internal judge, letting one lesbian, usually one I didn't know very well or whom I perceived as having clout in the community, represent morality for the entire community. As long as I believed in the polarity of "us and them," I could find no way to include myself. I mourned my loss.

In fact, as I told—and continue to tell—people about my involvement with a man, I have had very few experiences where people distance themselves or openly refuted my "right to belong." On the contrary, nearly every one-on-one experience turns out to be affirming, an exchange, a coming together. One lesbian friend tells me that knowing me and hearing me talk about my process has turned around her attitude toward bisexual women. Two others have become involved with men themselves. With still another, my coming out as bisexual has led to hours of passionate conversation about conceptions of sexuality, the power of secrets and, correspondingly, of truth, and the balance of paradoxes in our lives.

Much of the acceptance I've encountered is an indirect product of my dissatisfaction with the name "bisexual" as a descriptor for myself. True, it is accurate in that it describes those I believe could be my lovers, but it doesn't say enough about how I got here, what my feelings are, my beliefs. It's the black-and-white photograph of my vibrantly colored life. To compensate for the lack of an adequate label, which I know would have its limitations anyway, I find myself telling my story, or as much of it as the situation warrants. It gives people the chance to hear, not *defector* or *fence-sitter*, but process, struggle toward self-understanding, self-claiming. It gives them room to hear about feelings and to tell their own. It gives me—and all of us—room to be larger than a name.

From this I've learned a different kind of pride. My pride as a lesbian was a little bit more glorious: Wow! Look who I am! My pride now is somewhat quieter, more complex. I'm looking less for external validation and more for internal. I'm proud of my own growth, my courage and persistence to make individual choices, to find a life that fits me instead of trying to find a me that can fit the world and its many definitions. I find pride in my wholeness, in the complexity of my self.

Recently I received a letter from one of my first lesbian friends, a woman to whom I am indebted for infinite support and coaching through attractions, heartbreaks and a large chunk of my coming-out process. She thought I'd be interested to know that she's been doing work lately, artistic and personal, on healing false dichotomies.[18] On finding connections and patterns between ideas that have been artificially posed as opposites. On seeing nature, for example, not as separate from us, not as *out there*, but as inclusive—we are of it and it is of us. There is no boundary. In this process, she has found in herself a part that doesn't want to exclude men as potential partners.

Inclusion. Discovering oneness where we believed there was polarity. Healing false dichotomies.

It's true that I miss the more complete and intricate connections to community I once had. Groups and activities that I used to feel addressed my growth and experience now leave me feeling slightly off-center. I miss the calm satisfaction I felt when, seeing another lesbian, I knew that we were in a sense family. But my experience has given me pause: is community as solid as it appears? I have seen so much divisiveness and heard so many stories of feeling betrayed within communities that I've had to rethink my perceptions and expectations. I still believe in the strength of a united voice, and I remain committed to being a part of that voice. But I think the safety I perceived as universal and unconditional was naive, illusory, bound to crumble at some point. Now I think about "personal community," about building individual alliances based not on pat labels or conventions but on individual stories, or, as we called them in women's studies classes in the seventies, personal histories. It takes longer but is more enduring, truer to each person's unique journey. I think about building and rebuilding politics based on the reality of experience, about how we have used our personal histories to create the foundation of contemporary feminism: the personal made political.

Telling our stories is still important. As we change as individual women, our stories change, our needs change, and we make feminism as a movement grow. We have to stay in touch with each other without assuming we already know what direction our feminist struggles must take. In my mind a feminist approach to change still starts small, with one woman connecting to one woman, then another and another and another. This is where I understand the origins of strength and power. As women we look at who we are, we look at how we fit, and we envision and "re-vision" until the way we think has broadened to include our reality more completely. The values in feminist communities focus on the collective participation of all individuals. It makes sense to apply this to a changing perception of sexuality: inclusion of all parts is inclusion of the component parts, our component hearts.

Endnotes

Effusive thanks to Karen Parrish, whose feedback helped bring this essay into wholeness, to Sally White, who was the first to suggest I write this piece or something like it, and to Beth Ruml, Steven O'Dell, Diane Sarotte and the many others whose insights and reflections repeatedly sparked my own thinking.

1. I would like to acknowledge Anne Carson in *Eros: The Bittersweet* (Princeton: Princeton University Press, 1986) for drawing my attention to this story and to questions of desire and meaning.

2. Sigmund Freud, "'The Antithetical Sense of Primal Words': A Review of a Pamphlet by Karl Abel, *Über den Gegensinn der Urworte*, 1884," (1910) in *Collected Papers*, (New York: Basic Books, 1959), p. 188.

3. Johnson, Barbara, trans. *Dissemination*, by Jacques Derrida, (Chicago: University of Chicago, 1981).

4. Hélène Cixous, "Sorties: Out and Out: Attacks/Ways Out/Forays" in *The Feminist Reader: Essays in Gender and the Politics of Literary Criticism*, ed. Catherine Belsey and Jane Moore (New York: Basil Blackwell, 1989), pp. 101-116. Extracted from *The*

Newly Born Woman, trans. Betsy Wing (Minneapolis, University of Minnesota Press, 1986), pp. 63-64, 83-88, 91-97.

5. Ibid., p. 101.

6. Ibid., p. 104.

7. See Arleen B. Dallery, "The Politics of Writing (the) Body," in *Gender/Body/Knowledge*, ed. Alison M. Jaggar and Susan R. Bordo (New Brunswick and London: Rutgers University Press, 1989), pp. 52-67 and Jones, Ann Rosalind. "Writing the Body: Toward an Understanding of *l'Écriture feminine*" in *The New Feminist Criticism*. ed. Elaine Showalter (New York: Pantheon Books, 1985), pp. 361-377.

8. Luce Irigiray, "This Sex Which Is Not One," trans. C. Reeder, *New French Feminism*, ed. E. Marks and I. de Courtivron (New York: Schocken, 1981) p. 103.

9. Cixous, "Sorties: Out and Out," p. 108.

10. Cixous, "Sorties: Out and Out," p. 104.

11. Cixous, "Sorties: Out and Out," p. 103.

12. Cixous, "Sorties: Out and Out," p. 104.

13. Cixous, "Sorties: Out and Out," p. 104.

14. Freud, "The Antithetical Sense of Primal Words," p. 184.

15. James Hillman, *Re-Visioning Psychology*, (New York: Harper and Row, 1975), p. 213.

16. See Fritz Klein et al., "Sexual Orientation: A Multivariable Dynamic Process," *Journal of Homosexuality*, 11: 1/2 (1985), 35-49.

17. This connection by static characteristic is also, I believe, why a bisexual community has yet to flourish in the same way lesbian and gay communities have. Bisexual identity is more fluid than fixed, slipping more out of definition than into it.

18. My thanks to Greacian Goeke for introducing me to this term.

Margaret Mihee Choe

OUR SELVES, GROWING WHOLE

Not so long ago, a distinguished personage alit upon a university to accept an award. Besides presenting the winner with the award, the venerable institution provided several venues for the display of the object of its beneficence. Because the prize-winner was a woman, the university's Wymmin's Center was permitted to lease her for an event; because she was African-American, Black Studies booked her for a talk; and because she was a published author, the School of Arts stuck her on a discussion panel they happened to be having with a few other writers. To avoid the impression that the university was making her sing for her supper, as it were, the award acceptance was first on her itinerary. This ceremony took place in an auditorium packed with the kind of faces one seldom saw on this university campus, unless one happened to glance into a room where a janitor mopped the floor alone, or intrude upon a professor's outer office where his (and I do mean his) secretary was squeezed between her (and I do mean her) desk and filing cabinet. It was those sorts of faces that now watched with anticipation as the honoree approached the podium with more presence than one would have expected, even from a pair of broad shoulders and a six-foot frame (plus heels) like hers. At the podium she gathered her audience—of which I was a part—into the palm of her hand, paused as we got comfortable there, opened her mouth and let out a melodious, bluesy moan. The audience was stunned. The audience went wild. In my mind's eye I saw some scrawny, tweedy type paging frantically through a Filofax. Singing? Music? That wasn't scheduled for this slot!

To think about someone—one's self—as "feminist" and "bisexual" requires one to divide a whole identity into tidy slices, each slice marking off where the self begins and where the normal population fears to tread, each cut diminishing this self and distancing it from the world; each slice severing the connections to other parts of the self. When I speak "as a feminist" do I cease to exist as Korean-American? How does one isolate parts of one's self, such as bisexuality and feminism, for the purposes of definition, and disregard the rest, without warping one's self for the benefit of public clarification? How does one keep from singing when the schedule clearly states "Speech"? Answer: one can't. One can, instead, discuss how feminism and bisexuality interact and function within identity as a whole. In this essay I reflect on how my experience with race is bound up with my bisexuality and feminism. Feminism does women the favor of putting a name on "personal" problems and oppressors. One's failure to become a writer may be because one lacks 500 pounds a year and that elusive room of one's own. If one is bad in math or falls silent before large groups, it is not necessarily a personal flaw, but perhaps a social bias. We know now that we are not born "feminine"; we are guided into and then caged within femininity. Feminism rebuts patriarchy's assertion that the problem lies with the individual, who happens to be female. Now composedly, now passionately it loosens the underpinnings of patriarchy. It says, look: this is not "idiosyncrasy"; this is oppression, this is from without. Feminism, then, is this recognition of the systemic oppression of women and a call to dismantle this system. As a call to action it insists that women are entitled to options in life other than being vessels for the next generation. Feminism opens the world to women, but perhaps even more radically, feminism gives women access to women: to themselves and to others. Women can lay claim to themselves and to other women, not solely as oppressed sisters, but also as lovers and primary partners.

From here, the step to lesbian separatism is short. In separatism women dispense with men (or at least with the system they embody) entirely and replace men and masculinity with women and femaleness, with the latter usually manifested in an androgyny perceived as bold and liberating, empowering. Separatism is empowering, insofar as it enables women to experience life on both sides of the gender wall, and even to tear this wall down. It transforms femininity for itself, but it throws up its hands at men and nonseparatist women as incurable, looking upon them as immutable categories. Even if separatism attracted many more women than it did at its height, feminism would still be left with the task of overhauling the rest of society. Separatism, too, assumes a model of women's lives, characterized by the isolation of women from one another and from means of survival. This model seems too modern, middle-class and Western for separatism to have relevance for most women. This last reservation I have about separatism stems from my Asian perspective. The model does not fit most Asian women, who tend not to be isolated in nuclear families, split-level ranche houses and family station wagons, nor are they isolated from each other; indeed, feminist analysis might even perceive them to be ghetto-ized in their traditional communal spheres.

> I mixed Oriental pieces with country furniture...Because they're simple, they blend well.
> —homeowner Rose Tarlow, *Architectural Digest*

At this point it is necessary to discuss what it is to be Asian and Asian female in America.[2] I like to think of Asians as the first and last Americans. The first Americans crossed the Bering Strait from Asia and were here to greet Northern and Southern European explorers and African slaves. Modern-day Asians began to come to the United States in the mid-nineteenth century, but the concept of Asian-American, that is, the idea that "Asian" and "American" are not mutually exclusive terms had yet to gain acceptance in my childhood. Growing up Asian in areas with small, new or nonexistent Asian populations, I became the Asian. Whatever I did was measured against the prevailing white American rendering of the Asian. If I excelled at school it was because Asians were smart. If I spoke (or acted) up, it was atypical for an Asian. If I was chosen last for sides for some team sport, well, in the pre-Michael Chang world who had ever heard of an Asian-American athlete?[3] I decided that, in the absence of an actual Asian population, the media must be responsible for shaping these beliefs about Asians that I encountered. In the media I found the occasional proof of Oriental if not Asian existence. Here I use "Oriental" in the sense Edward Said has determined the term to have been used.[4] "The Occident" uses its Adamic prerogative to name and organize itself and the rest of the world to its taste: it makes "the Orient" its Eve. Orientalism dehumanizes and exoticizes, fictionalizes and romanticizes people, cultures and geographic areas deemed to be non-Western. It has the power to name and other-ize in racial and sexual terms as patriarchalism does only in sexual terms. Orientalism was originally developed as an academic subject, but gained political influence and still offers a facile framework for structuring a world view, as I found in my search for Asian-American presence in the media.

I came up empty or with grotesque, foreign, Orientalized versions: slant-eyed, buck-toothed, Coke-bottle-eye-glassed bombers of Pearl Harbor; napalmed gooks, panty-hose commercial China dolls; Caucasians such as Peter Sellers, Jennifer Jones and Linda Hunt playing Asians or Eurasians; statistically nonexistent "other" in sociological studies and newspaper opinion polls. Specifically female images were few and far between: one could opt between being a Dragon Lady like Yoko Ono, with tremendous destructive powers, or a shadowy Lotus Blossom, with a demurely downcast gaze and chastely upturned collar. Such images—when they appeared at all—I found repulsive, as they were designed to be, but I accepted them. There was no refuting voice as there was for sexist claims. Faced with the apparent choice to belong to the (white) American world around me or to disappear off the face of the nation, I gave myself up to America, not realizing that no matter how fluent I was in American culture, I would be understood ultimately as a foreigner, a member of a foreign race. Ironically, I am Asian in a very American sense of the word. In Great Britain, for example, Asian usually refers to South Asians, whereas in the United States, "Asian" is generally East and Southeast Asian. It is also Western to lump together peoples from a wide range of cultures, languages, climates and religions. It is unlikely that many Koreans feel solidarity with their former imperialist oppressors the Japanese, the way a Korean-American might feel with a Japanese-American. Although it is racism which joins us by tossing us into a one-size-fits-all category, like people dismissed for being queer, we can find strength in such a union.

Another irony of being the United States' most pointedly foreign race is that race is largely denied Asians. We are billed as the model minority—well-behaved and intelligent, rather like the ideal house pet. In America's black-or-white racial dialogue we have no voice. The racism of everyday life I met with was not racism: racism was having your house illumined by crosses burning in your yard; it was the "strange fruit" of Southern trees. In the America in which to be human is to be white and to be black is to be racial, Asians are simply not part of the picture. As any woman without a name for sexual harassment does, I mistrusted myself: I faced racism by looking inward: there is something wrong with me. Because I did not fit into a recognized racial category, the treatment I received could not be racism. I could not talk about it because, until recently "Asian-Americans" did not exist; I did not exist. I had to create myself and did so in the white mold. I sought to purge myself of the Asian taint. I shunned not only Korean food, but also all Asian cuisines—which at that time comprised Cantonese Chinese food where I lived—because if America could not differentiate between Asian cultures, certainly I wasn't going to start splitting hairs—Chinese, Japanese—what's the difference? I did not have to put a ban on the language; by the time I was conscious of language, I had lost Korean. I was proud to speak English "without" an accent, that is, with an American accent, and even, until New York rid me of it, a proper Bostonian accent; it was thus through language that I primarily sought to anglicize myself. As I grew, this purge came to influence all my choices, from clothes (conservative quasi-preppie) to books (Laura Ingalls Wilder, L. M. Montgomery and Frances Hodgson Burnett were among my favorite childhood authors) to companions.

The pull in both directions—"Asia" and "America"—was constant; Korean immigrant households were the stages of this messy drama. Those homes seemed chaotic in the way Korean and American objects and customs jostled each other: American running shoes, laces tied and backs bent down, stood in a bookcase placed at the door expressly for shoes removed upon entry; suffocatingly heavy comforters, designed with Korean home heating in mind, covered Western-style beds in stiflingly overheated New York City apartments; fried chicken—eaten for breakfast. To the Western sensibilities I strove to maintain (I was a dogmatic youngster), this was an eclectic approach on the wrong, that is, Eastern, terms. America almost clinically isolated the Orient and accepted its individual items only after extracting them from their cultural contexts and giving them an American gloss; clearly the litter of everyday Asian life was not acceptable. One might sit on the floor for a special *fête à la japonaise*, but certainly not for one's Thanksgiving dinner. I swallowed whole this separation into Occident and Orient, and the acceptance of the latter on the former's terms.

Eventually the banana I had become got out of hand. I slipped on the peel and came to. Although I make it sound sudden, it has been a painful process, a scene in slow motion replayed over and over again from countless different angles. I let my perm grow out, then found that I could not reconcile myself to my natural hair; I stopped trying to write like a nineteenth-century English aristocrat, but stopped writing altogether; I gradually overcame my acquired distaste for Korean and Cantonese cooking and discovered Japanese, Indian, Hunan, Szechuan, Vietnamese and Thai foods. I coaxed my Korean middle name out of hiding, but nobody calls me by it. I began to see stereotypes for what they are: shorthand caricatures for the perception-impaired.

That I came late to sexuality I attribute partly to my parents, whose culture emphasizes scholastics for children and young people to the exclusion of social activity, and partly to my having to expend so much energy on unacknowledged racial issues. To be a sexual being one must be able to desire; one must be able to say, "I want." One must have primacy in one's life; one must be able to live the body. Clearly, I was not ready. I came to sexuality and feminism at about the same time, though I was not aware of the two being closely connected then. After graduating from a women's college, I went to work in a male-dominated environment that aroused a dormant feminist zeal. I also met my first long-term lover (a man) and the first lesbian with whom I was to become close. The aspect of feminism that appears to have been most relevant is its insistence on the primacy of one's body and the importance of individual experience. I took feminism's message to be: want and then do what you want. Feminism, however, needs to be reminded occasionally of its own foundations, that, for example, the pro-choice movement is based on each woman's right to be sovereign over her own body, which includes sexuality and sexual expression.

But bisexuality has come to symbolize much more than sex in the feminist context in which we now speak. Bisexuality could even be seen to be lesbianism of post-feminism. Feminist bisexuality is a statement that says, "Loving women now is a given; we know we love women, we know we want to be with women; and now we're strong enough to love men. On our terms." In choosing a lover I use my own standards and reject dichotomization. As an Asian (formerly Oriental,) I've seen the necessity of taking control of my racial identity. As a bisexual feminist I seek to take control of my sexual pleasure.

Feminist bisexuality is still an individually forged identity, and as such it is problematic, for identity is that which makes one recognizable to one's self and to others. My not being black or white in America may make bisexuality easier. One could even say that bisexuals are the Asians of sexual America: you're not one or the other, so you're overlooked. Your sense of your own identity often does not match the perception that the society at large has of you. Lesbians and gays (blacks) think you're groveling at the feet of straights (whites), while straights (whites) don't want you living in their neighborhoods or marrying into their families, though you might be less repugnant to them than lesbians and gays (blacks). But just as "people of color" have changed the divisiveness of "non-white" into a statement of solidarity, so are "nonheterosexuals" transforming "queer" into a unifying term. We are beginning to, as Audre Lorde puts it, join "across sexualities" instead of using sexuality against each other.

> I cannot stay in the desert
> where you will have me nor
> will I be brought back in a cage
> to grace your need for exotica.
> I write these words
> at night
> for I am still a night creature
> but I will not keep a
> discreet distance
> If you must fit me to your needs
> I will die
> and so will you.[5]

Feminism and antiracism work to revise predetermined social identities. I am applying the same creative approach to sexual identity as well. It is a matter of starting with the being and describing it, rather than starting with a description and tailoring the being to fit the description; Mitsuye Yamada's poem "Desert Run," which alludes to the internment of Japanese-Americans during World War II, is apt here.[6] For me, little is gained by framing questions as "either/ors." Categories of identity—black/white, gay/straight—lack the flexibility necessary to describe the flux and multiplicity of reality.

When an individual rejects a culture's vision of herself, she may fall back on a subculture to provide her with a sense of identity, of community. Feminist "women's" culture, however, is often narrowly defined.[7] The solution need not be simply to turn one's back on a hostile or merely indifferent mainstream and cultivate otherness wholesale. Instead of defining myself by what I'm not—neither black nor white, a "minority," but not the one the word most commonly denotes, neither straight nor gay—I make it my responsibility to create myself whenever possible. A black/white world leaves me, as an Asian, nowhere. The gay/straight world would do the same, and I have lost interest in honorary citizenship. I am now at the point where I have grown tired of chopping myself up to order into tiny, less-than-human pieces. I'm going to let the cuts heal and let myself grow whole.

Now it occurs to me: could it be that that university might have been astute enough to realize that the recipient of its award was, as a whole person, too formidable a mouthful for those dentures to chew? Better to serve her up in courses, a representative and well-prepared serving of her sex, race and one of her professions, each in turn. But the university had neglected to take into account that its prize-winner was much more than it, even in its benevolence, gave her room to be: among the myriad other identities she possessed were activist, mother, editor, composer, dancer and singer. She declined to be pigeonholed, dissected and neatly compartmentalized. She would be what she wanted when she wanted. She sang in the lecture hall. She put on all her hats at once—even those the university had neglected—and then tossed them all out to us. Did she know, as she filled her lungs with air, that a hat worn too long sinks down to cover the face and becomes a mask? Did this prize-winner know, as her vocal chords pulled her out of these pigeonholes, that the further away you are from that white male ideal personhood, the less they know what you are and the less you can afford to sit quietly while they decide what you may and can be? I know. I know because she sang it to me.

Endnotes

The title of this essay, "Our Selves, Growing Whole," is most directly inspired by Diane Mei Lin Mark's poem "OurSelves," which appears in the anthology, *IKON* second series, No. 9, Asian Women United Journal Collective (1990.): p. 31. I would like to say *tack* to the editor for her patience with this essay and its author.

1. I make a distinction between "feminine," which is a set of characteristics that a monolithic "woman" is supposed to embody in any given culture, and "female,"

biological sex.

2. "America" refers to that which is perceived to be American. Among Korean immigrants I grew up knowing, "American" often denoted race (white), which reflects a generally accepted prejudice that "real" Americans and real American culture are white.

3. I would include the figure skater Kristi Yamaguchi if I were not so skeptical of the world of ladies' amateur figure skating, which, for example, mandates skirted skating attire for its performing competitors.

4. Edward W. Said, *Orientalism* (New York: Vintage Books, 1979).

5. Audre Lorde, "I Am Your Sister: Black Women Organizing Across Sexualities," in *Making Face, Making Soul=Haciendo Caras: Creative and Critical Perspectives by Feminists of Color*, ed. Gloria Anzaldúa (San Francisco: Aunt Lute Foundation Books, 1990), pp. 321-5.

6. Mitsuye Yamada, "Desert Run," quoted from Anzaldúa, *Making Face*, pp. 10-13.

7. Too often "women's" culture has been "white lesbian" culture.

Elizabeth McKeon

To Be Bisexual and Underclass

My mother wanted to be a doctor. Needless to say, lower-class rural women did not go to medical school in the 1940s. I, in her place, am the one to live out this dream—a dream of pain and wonder that pulls me from my working-class roots and sets me adrift in uncharted waters.

As a bisexual feminist, I am also drifting. Drifting between communities—lesbian and straight—neither of which is really home. This sense of drifting is both curse and blessing to bisexual women. We are doubly excluded, but we also doubly belong.

A white bisexual woman of mixed-class background, I was born into a family on the lower economic side of the middle class. My parents both grew up poor. My father became a teacher, so I grew up knowing educational privilege. But he got cancer when I was six and our family started to slip back into the working class it came from.

My mother worked as a dressmaker to support the family. My adult sisters—one an exotic dancer and prostitute, the other a service worker—helped raise me. I grew up in a world of welfare, biker gangs, prostitution and drugs. To pay the mortgage, my mother rented rooms to boarders. My sister (the exotic dancer), my mother and I shared a dirty and overcrowded living space with six or seven others. I was fluent in both standard English and an under-class dialect.

In our primarily white working-class and lower middle-class community, I did not hear much about lesbianism, let alone bisexuality. I knew that I liked women "more than I should," but I couldn't see a place for this desire. I envisioned myself marrying my high school dropout boyfriend and living out the rest of my life as the women of my neighborhood did. For a while, I even thought about becoming a stripper like my sister. She made good money and had a measure of financial and social independence. Maybe her fierce sexuality appealed to me. If I couldn't see a way to love women, at least I could be in charge of my own body and sexuality.

None of my early visions came to pass. I was offered a scholarship to attend an elite boarding school for two years, and I accepted it despite my family's confusion and resentment. I went to boarding school and learned that history and literature were beautiful things; I also learned there was an upper middle class that considered me inferior. I went to college and learned that other gay women existed; I also learned that many of them accepted me only to the degree that I assimilated into their class identity.

In college, while struggling with my dreams and my class identity, I finally saw a place for myself: as a doctor working with women and with low-income communities like mine. I felt that as a doctor I could bring technical skills as well as a much-needed sensitivity to underserved communities. It has taken a while, but I am now on my way to achieving that goal.

I only wish I could have gotten an education without feeling that I was becoming estranged from my family. I wish that being a bisexual, especially a working-class bisexual, were not so lonely. When properly channeled, though, loneliness can lead to insight and productivity. I hope to be of real service to communities that lack good health care, and I also want to join other marginalized women in making our voices heard in the feminist discourse.

To this end, I offer some observations about the special situation of feminists who are bisexual, working class or both, in various sexualities and cultures.

Bisexual and Working Class: Some of the Worlds We Move Between
Heterosexual Under-class Cultures

The dominant white working-class world is not very accepting of bisexuals or lesbians.[1] It tends to adopt the mainstream views spread by the mass media. In its defense, I will add that many working-class gay people are closeted more by the overclass than by their own class: some cannot afford to risk their jobs by coming out. Under-class bisexual women, especially if they have at least the appearance of a heterosexual relationship, may have little incentive to take the economic risk of coming out. Though this homophobia in the underclass may be encouraged by the overclass as part of a "divide and conquer" mentality, it has taken root on its own.

Bigotry in any form is inexcusable, but examining its different forms in various communities reveals differences in meaning. Many under-class families, for instance, are strict and lack exposure to certain liberal concepts of tolerance. Our families are unlikely to read feminist books or to go to family counseling to understand their bisexual or lesbian daughters. My blue-collar stepfather derives his ideas about homosexuality from the Bible and *Reader's Digest*, and although I do not excuse his attitude toward gay people, I see that even if he was predisposed to changing, he has never been exposed to information that would help.

Specific cultural attributes shape views of homosexuality in underclass communities of color. Differences in culture, language, class and immigration create different climates for homosexuality, for example in each Asian-American community. In some communities of color, there may even be pockets of acceptance. There was some acceptance of homosexuality, for instance, among African-American musicians in the 1930s. Today, Beth Brant describes both intracultural homophobia and the special place of lesbian and gay Native Americans as elders of their communities.[2]

The poorest sectors of straight-identified society manifest unique attitudes toward alternative sexualities: as one moves down the economic ranks, the concept of propriety changes and begins to lose its meaning. I knew a prostitute in my community who lived at one time with her man and another female stripper in what was rumored to be a three-way sexual relationship. And why not? Within a subculture of prostitution so closely allied with the drug trade, who cares if the prostitutes sleep with each other? The overclass certainly does not care either.

Straight Over-class Societies

The experience of lesbian and bisexual women is so foreign to the white overclass as to be almost inconceivable. Mainstream society usually ignores our existence (even more than it ignores the existence of gay men), recognizing us only to ostracize us or to exoticize our sexuality in straight men's pornography. Bisexual women in the "jet set" are sometimes considered chic and therefore escape the fate of their less fortunate sisters.

There are exceptions to this invisibility or ostracization in some mainstream feminist groups, but even so, these groups rarely raise their own consciousness about their homophobia or other oppressive behavior. They tend to wait for "outsiders" to educate them and set the political pace—women of color, lesbians, bisexuals or lower-class women.

Alliances between mainstream feminism and more oppressed communities have been uneasy because white middle-class feminism has refused to incorporate the agendas of marginalized women. Tensions of class, race and sexuality divide feminists. Within the black feminist movement, new class differences between African-American communities may cause similar tensions.[3]

I have met with blank stares when I asked a medical student women's group to work on issues of low-income women and women of color. I know there are many individual heterosexual feminists who do not change the subject when lesbians, bisexuals or women from other marginalized communities speak out, but many feminist groups are still on the whole unaware of the differences among women—differences that can seem more separating than womanhood is unifying. It is this lack of awareness that stands in the way of change, not the differences themselves.

Middle- and Upper-class Lesbian Worlds

For some of us, it hurts more to be excluded from the lesbian community than from the straight world. Oppressed groups often expect solidarity and support from other oppressed groups, especially when their oppressions are closely linked. Under-class women, women of color, bisexual women and others may expect more from the lesbian overclass than from the heterosexual world, even more than from heterosexual feminists. The lesbian community claims to be more sensitive. It also holds many resources for women who love women—cultural, economic and political.

With many individual and even group exceptions, the lesbian community still has work to do to stop excluding marginalized women, including bisexual women. Some have argued that since bisexual women can get needed resources from "the patriarchy," they should not drain support from the beleaguered lesbian community. To demand sexual purity in exchange for membership in lesbian circles, however, requires the assumption that all bisexual women have equal access to patriarchal resources.

Many members of the lesbian community fail to recognize that all bisexual women are not created equal in terms of power. Bisexuals of color, working-class bisexuals and others interested in creating social change may have scarce access to financial, educational and political resources outside the lesbian community. Other oppressed communities have their own work to do and may not be able to spare much for the struggle against heterosexism and homophobia.

By this argument, I do not mean to suggest that racially or economically privileged bisexual women do not have legitimate reasons for asking acceptance in lesbian communities. The main reason I seek connection with lesbian organizations and communities is that *I am gay, too.* If bisexual women are to live in the lesbian part of ourselves, we need to be among women who love women as we do. This need may not be one of "support" so much as one of exposure to lesbian cultures, of access to coalitions, of friendship if the spirit moves.

I believe we should all be able to be sexual with consenting adults without regard for what seems "politically correct." Heterosexual desire may be particularly poignant for bisexual women from less empowered groups when we choose to make alliances with "our" men. Is it reasonable to ask a bisexual woman of color to abandon her struggle against racism in favor of exclusive work against sexism or heterosexual oppression? And if she chooses to ally herself politically or sexually with men of color, is it reasonable to exclude her from the larger lesbian community?

Of course the answer should be no. Yet bisexual women feel these pressures constantly. As a working-class woman, I have found it ironic to be criticized for "sleeping with the oppressor" when the men I grew up with had little oppressive power beyond their white privilege. I have even been criticized on these grounds by an upper-class lesbian who lived on an "independent income," a patriarchal resource if I have ever heard of one!

More writing is emerging about classism, racism, anti-Semitism, ageism and other topics by lesbians and bisexual women of all backgrounds. More groups are talking about their differences and accomplishing related political work. Bisexual feminist groups are forming for mutual support and political action. These trends are encouraging, and I hope they will continue.

It should be noted that lesbians of all backgrounds, along with gay and bisexual people of both genders, have been at the cutting edge of social change in a heterosexist society. Along with some bisexuals, lesbians have carved out a place for sexual difference because there was no choice in order to survive. Bisexual women owe to lesbians many of our gay rights as well as a large measure of our own identification as "non-heterosexuals." We need to recognize the essential ways in which lesbian separatism has contributed to feminist thought, not the least of which has been to show that women who so choose can live without men and even exclude men entirely from their lives.

If bisexual women want to participate in lesbian organizations, or in coalitions, we should be willing to devote at least some of our time to working for lesbian rights, regardless of whether we ourselves live more as lesbians or as heterosexuals. It is not that much to ask.

Working-Class Lesbians

In my experience, bisexual women find more acceptance among working-class lesbians than among other lesbians or feminists. Maybe one reason is that some working-class lesbians are freer from intellectual lesbian-feminist constructs and may not know that according to those constructs they are supposed to be critical of bisexuality.

This "freedom" is a mixed blessing. It deprives under-class lesbians and bisexuals of a certain identity and can keep us from seeing how our struggles are intertwined with those of other oppressed groups. But it can make life easier for under-class bisexuals. Working-class lesbians often must define themselves, so perhaps they are more willing to give bisexuals some latitude in our own identification.

Among the many ways in which lesbians have brought beauty into the world, the contributions of working-class lesbians hold special meaning for me. Working-class lesbians might not call themselves "lesbian" and some may not pay much attention to esoteric political theories, but in my own identification, I have relied heavily on underclass lesbian ways of being. I learned to love dancing in working-class gay bars. I remember goddess rituals I celebrated in the fellowship of self-educated women. I learned something about fear and courage from playing rugby with women strong from physical labor. Working-class ways of living offer a never-ending cultural diversity and do not demand that I adapt myself to the economically privileged point of view of intellectual feminism.

The barrier I now find between myself and working-class lesbians is not that of sexual purity but that of privilege. I cannot erase the fact that I am now educated and more distant from my background. I don't fit in as well with my class of origin, gay or straight. Internalized classism worsens matters, as does the barrier of racism between white women and women of color. I would like to find a place of healing where working-class women can be united.

Where Do We Go From Here?

As I look back into the history of my mother's family in this country, I see ten generations of low-income people, half of them women, and some of those undoubtedly women who loved women as well as men. I reflect on the gifts my people have given me—including unashamed sexuality from my sister—and on the gifts that women of diverse low-income backgrounds bring to coalitions: Strength. Pride. Hard work. An ability to survive. Hope for our families and communities. From all of us, the ability to "make do"with what we have.

"Making do" is a powerful tool to bring to the bargaining table. Working-class women don't wait for change—we make change now as best we can because we can't afford to wait.

Bisexual women bring a special adaptability, too. Some of us live in both the straight and lesbian worlds. Bisexual women can be catalysts for change among heterosexuals, who may find it harder to ignore us than to ignore lesbians. We can harness resources from heterosexual society and use them toward productive ends. As Audre Lorde has written, privilege (even heterosexual privilege) is not inherently wrong as long as we don't waste it.[4]

I believe there is a place for separatism and that oppressed groups will need time to themselves to plan agendas and find solidarity. I believe there is also a time and place for alliances and coalitions, and I hope that bisexual women of all backgrounds will be welcome in them. In this spirit, we move toward a better world for all of us.

Endnotes

1. By "dominant," I mean in relation to still more oppressed working-class communities of color.

2. Jack Lo, Karin Aguilar-San Juan and Jacquelyn Ching Black, "Asian Cultures, Sexuality and Class: Sorting It All Out," in *Gay Community News*, January 21-27, 1990, and Beth Brant, "Recovery and Transformation: The Blue Heron," in *Bridges of Power: Women's Multicultural Alliances*, ed. Lisa Albrecht and Rose M. Brewer (Philadelphia: New Society Publishers, 1990), pp. 118-121.

3. Lisa Albrecht and Rose M. Brewer, "Bridges of Power: Women's Multicultural Alliances for Social Change," in *Bridges of Power*, p. 5.

4. "Unused privilege is a weapon in the hand of our enemies," from Lorde's letter in *Gay Community News*, January 21-27, 1990.

Nina Silver

COMING OUT AS A HETEROSEXUAL

In some ways it was the hardest letter I ever wrote. One of my love poems had just been published in a lesbian anthology, and the editor (whom I shall call Tori) had asked me if I would recite my work at a poetry reading in New York. Tori was traveling to feminist and women's bookstores across the country to promote the book with local authors.

I was thrilled to participate, but Tori's next request glued me to my seat: "Can I stay at your place for one night? It'll be easier for me if I do the long drive to New York the day before the reading."

Ordinarily I would have been delighted to accommodate her; I am very social and enjoy exchanging ideas with interesting people. The only problem was Tori was a dyke—possibly a separatist—and I had recently become lovers with a man. Not only that, he was living with me. Tori might not want to stay at my apartment in that case. After trying to lie my way out of it—with some excuse like, "Gee, I'd love to have you, but I'll be working late that night"—I finally decided to face the music. I would write and let her know.

I met Paul eleven years ago, when I was dating Christine. They were both residing at the Life Center, a collective of land trust houses in Philadelphia whose members lived communally and conducted radical political action together. Though the New York to Philadelphia commute was sometimes draining, my relationship with Chris was nonetheless inspiring and comforting. We would spend hours discussing the link between feminism and spirituality, envisioning a world where people were not afraid to feel and valued others for who they truly were rather than for what stereotypes they embodied.

It was a relief to relate to another bisexual woman for whom being attracted to men was not an issue. Chris understood that when people's masks peel away and they are free to express love toward one another, the possibility for erotic intimacy increases. I felt expanded and wonderful with this sister, friend, lover and spiritual companion.

But my relationship with Christine had its stormy moments, too. She often became possessive and anxious, and worried when I then felt crowded by her. The more I felt crowded, the more she worried and clung; and the more she fussed over me and clung, the more I felt crowded.

Then Chris became lovers with Paul, causing a minor uproar at the Life Center. Paul, who had openly identified himself as gay his whole life, surprised his housemates, the residents of the other communal houses and himself by embarking on this heterosexual affair. Chris, who had been hounded by her lesbian housemates to leave her bedroom door ajar whenever her friend Paul visited so they would be sure nothing was "going on," packed her bags with relief and moved with Paul into a nonaffiliated apartment without a political agenda.

Back in New York, I was only a little jealous. In truth, I felt mostly relieved and happy that Chris had found someone who lived in the same city. Perhaps Paul would be able to give her the attention and stability she needed. Meanwhile, Paul was quite willing to drive Christine to New York on weekends so she could be with me. When Chris and I spent time together and made love, Paul was never jealous. On the contrary, he seemed happy that the bond of intimate friendship between his lover and me had endured.

Eventually, Christine and Paul broke up, she and I broke up, and we all went our separate ways. I grieved the loss of my friendship with Chris, but eventually respected her need not to hear from me and left her alone. I spoke with Paul sporadically in the ensuing years.

Then he surfaced again. He was living in New York now. How had I been, and would I like to have dinner? I trembled during that phone conversation, somehow knowing that Paul would come home with me that night. Over curry, he and I discussed Christine, what we'd been doing with our lives, my staunchly unattached lifestyle and his current live-in situation with a man named Tony. To me, his relationship with Tony seemed like a most superficial and unsatisfying arrangement: they didn't talk to each other about anything substantial and no longer made love, sleeping instead in separate rooms like the courteous but distant roommates they were. I questioned what they were doing together—particularly pondering why Paul considered this a "relationship"—but soon abandoned the issue, figuring it was none of my business.

I also puzzled over what Paul could possibly want from me, though I didn't voice this aloud. I was too busy nursing that fluttery gnawing in my stomach. Did he have any condoms, I found myself wondering. But why on earth would I want to make love with someone who, though nice, seemed so inaccessible?

Paul did come home with me that night, and we indeed made love. (Without fanfare, he bought condoms.) I was surprised at how easily we talked to each other. We also just as easily made love: time stopped, passion streaming high. When we finally went to sleep, I drifted off effortlessly into a sound slumber.

This is called trust, which ordinarily develops over time. That I had no trouble sleeping in the same bed with a relative stranger should have instantly cued me that this was no ordinary friendship. But sometimes humans are dense.

It seemed like a moot point, anyway, had I been alert enough to grasp the implications of Paul's visit. The next morning, he went back to Tony, mumbling about obligation (and hiding his fear); I swallowed my longing and disappointment so fast I never even knew I felt them. The few times I saw Paul after that, even though our lovemaking remained intense, we never considered our association "serious."

About a year later, during 1990's January bleakness, everything changed. Paul, finally deciding that there was more to life than a boring secure job and an equally boring home situation, said goodbye to Tony and moved back to Philadelphia to be caretaker at one of the Life Center houses. That summer, in tears, I telephoned him. Paul had always been a good listener, and I needed help: I had just been propositioned by a married man. "I'm sick of being the object of all these sleazeball men and unavailable women in recovery," I sobbed. "The next time I get involved with someone, I want it to be for keeps." Little did I realize the prescience of my words.

Paul was agreeably understanding, as usual. "You sound like you need a break from New York," he immediately responded. "Why don't you come for a visit? You can sleep with me in my bed." I said nothing. "Or, if you don't feel comfortable doing that, you can stay in one of the other rooms of the house."

That familiar feeling of panic again etched itself in my gut. By now totally frantic, I telephoned Shel, a good friend who used to live in Philadelphia and had known Paul.

"Don't worry," he said, trying his best to reassure me. "Paul won't attempt anything you don't want to do. I know that for a fact, because years ago he propositioned me. I very politely said no thanks, and that was it."

Somehow this wasn't reassuring at all. "I know Paul won't push me. That's not what I'm concerned about." Shel's silence indicated his bewilderment. "I'm not worried that Paul won't take no for an answer. I'm worried that I'll want to say yes."

And I did say yes. The third morning of that sweltering August visit, I rolled over and gasped, "Omigod, we're in a relationship!" This "relationship" had crept up on us in the craftiest way—probably a good thing for a man who had chosen to play it safe and familiar his entire life and a woman whose identity was partly rooted in being (proudly) single. By November, Paul had moved back to New York. Only this time, he relocated right into my apartment, sharing not only the common space but also my bed.

My existence was schizophrenic. By now, one quarter of my writing credits were in gay and lesbian publications, and here I was having a passionately sexual relationship with a gay (?) man, scared to death to tell my lesbian acquaintances and publishers what I was doing. Surely the editors of all those dyke anthologies in which my work had appeared would not be pleased.

I felt exhausted living this double life. I thought of the years I'd spent in college sneaking around with my female lover, hiding our romance from my parents, her parents and our straight homophobic friends, and I realized I couldn't do it anymore. I didn't want to repeat the same scenario, albeit with a different, socially unconventional cast. I was not being true to myself unless I emerged from all my closets, no matter how unacceptable they seemed or who felt betrayed by my choice.

Paul was very sympathetic and supportive, but I realized that only I could extricate myself from this tangle. Making Paul invisible by pretending to numerous lesbians that he didn't exist not only hurt and negated him, it negated me as well. Here I was allowing myself the deepest level of vulnerability and closeness with Paul, only to quickly drop his hand whenever we'd pass by the Lesbian and Gay Community Center. This made a mockery of our relationship; it was like misogyny or homophobia in reverse. My fear of straying from lesbian ethics, I discovered, conveniently cloaked whatever subterranean conflicts I still harbored about loving and being in a committed relationship. It was time for me to let myself love in the best way I knew how—from a place of authenticity, without holding back. Even if the worst-case scenario took place—that every lesbian I knew rejected me, as some had done in the past—I had to be candid about who I was. The only solution was to come out, boldly, yet one more time.

Meanwhile, Paul was busy cleaning some of his own closets. He took me to visit his family, introducing me as his committed partner, and then announced that until recently he'd been living a gay lifestyle. When members of the Life Center who had been unaware of Paul's prior relationship with Christine were informed that he was presently serious about a woman, they proffered more than just amazement and good wishes. Some of Paul's gay and lesbian friends exuded skepticism and criticism, convinced he had defected from their ranks because of a fluke—some misguided, unforeseen set of circumstances beyond his control. It didn't matter (not that they bothered to ask) that his lover was devoted to women and feminist concerns and was dealing with similar (though intensified) hostility in her own circle. It did not seem to make a difference, either, that our relationship was based on mutual respect and shared values, reinforced by our uniquely parallel histories. Nor was it considered important that, simply put, Paul and I were crazy about each other. Clearly, their kind of politics overrode passion.

"This is supposed to be a political change community, but it has a very narrow definition of what it means to be politically correct," Paul reflected ruefully. "When I moved back to the Life Center, a lesbian came up and asked if I was gay. Only after I said yes did she invite me to dinner, with congratulations for my sexual orientation. But when I became involved with you, she challenged my decision in a disapproving tone. She apologized later and wished me luck, but not everyone has been able to extend themselves like that. Where I wouldn't be criticized for being in a gay relationship, there is some dismay about my being in what is perceived as a 'conventional' relationship. I've been demoted because I no longer fill as many categories of political correctness—as according to members of the Life Center, I'm now straight."

Was Paul in fact now straight? I don't know. One could say he was straight when relating to me. But that didn't feel quite right, either. It was true that Paul was passionate and sensual and loving toward me. But he didn't behave like a typical straight man. He didn't behave like a typical gay man, either. In fact, he didn't really behave like a man—or a woman, for that matter. What did it mean to "behave like a man," anyhow?

"Don't you think it's a little risky that Paul has been...gay?" a straight acquaintance inquired. "Aren't you nervous that he might go back to men?"

"No," I sighed. "It's not an issue of men versus women. Paul's with me not because I'm a woman, or because he's grown tired of men, but because he loves me for who I am as an individual."

"That sounds terribly flat and asexual to me. Don't you get turned on to him because of his maleness?"

"Of course," I conceded. "But," I hastily tried to explain, "what you call his 'maleness' is really just sexual energy. He's a sexual being who happens to be male. So even though you might say I love his 'maleness,' I really see that—and 'femaleness'—as simple biological details. I don't love Paul for following the gender persona of 'male' based on what a man's supposed to be, any more than I'd love a woman for behaving like what a woman's supposed to be. I love Paul partly because in some ways he can't be categorized. How can you sincerely love someone as long as they're playing a gender role? What you're relating to is a mask."

This seemed to be such a simple point, but one which a surprising number of people I spoke to had trouble comprehending. The lesbians and gays equated a man-woman couple with automatic, knee-jerk conventionality (read: gender roles), which they objected to; whereas the straights associated homosexual experience in Paul's and my background as dangerously gender-deficient and therefore devoid of any "real" sex.

As I continued to spend time with Paul, this matter of defining ourselves became crazily convoluted. He got: "Come on, Paul, you're really gay. You're just discouraged because you haven't met the right man yet—but you will." Or, "You've really been straight all these years, but were too timid to act like a man. A good woman will fix you up in no time." I got: "Come on, Nina, why don't you admit you're really a dyke. It's written all over your face." Or, "You feminists all hate men, and that's why you can't commit. So stop pretending to be a lesbian. There's nothing about you that a good [heterosexual] fuck won't cure." We were being pigeonholed by gays and straights alike, and didn't feel comfortable with any of the categories that were being offered to us.

Things got worse. Among gays there proved to be enormous latitude as to what exactly constituted gayness. A lesbian, for example, ranged from the heterosexually married woman who abstains from sex with her husband because she secretly hankers for the woman next door to the political activist whose busy pursuits allow room only for celibacy. And somewhere in this kettle was the butch lesbian who wears dildos to bed. Disparate? Yes, but all considered lesbians.

A very different story emerged if you regarded them strictly from the standpoint of sexual activity. The first lesbian was still in the closet and engaged in no sexual activity. Lesbian number two was also sexually inactive. Lesbian number three behaved in distinctly male-defined ways. In two out of three instances, there was no sex in these women's homosexual lives. In the third, the woman-to-woman component might be considered diluted or even nonexistent because one woman was relating to her partner as a surrogate man.

Throw into the pot women who came out as lesbians not primarily because they found themselves attracted to women, but because they needed to make a statement about being women in a male supremacist culture. Now we had the additional classification of "political lesbian."

What exactly did it mean, then, to be lesbian/gay? Was it choice of partner? Lifestyle? Persistence of fantasy? Strength of desire that might or might not be acted out? Categorizing was proving to be confusing, lengthy and complicated. Added to this mess was my recognition that what I had always considered built into homosexual relationships—the blurring and overturning of gender roles, which is one reason why gays are so threatening to the larger culture—was apparently not intrinsic to all of them. Some gays and lesbians were into carefully constructed roles no different from those of heterosexuals: that is, some played at being the "man" and some played at being the "woman" (although this didn't stop them from being politically and socially persecuted).

Nothing made sense to me anymore, as reasons for being in this category or that category swiftly unraveled. Was sexual diversity increasing to the extent that definitions were becoming meaningless? Maybe we should simply call ourselves "bisexual" and be done with all this.

But even "bisexual" had its problems. When Paul and I used it we encountered resistance and homophobia from straights and resistance and heterophobia from gays. I threw up my hands in disgust while Paul, new to this amazing panoply of category choices, continued to mull over the problem of what to call himself. Ultimately, he asked me, what did it matter which chromosomal makeup someone had? Or what their genitalia did or didn't look like? Wasn't the idea that everyone should be liberated? And wasn't liberation about realizing who we are and being nice to each other?

I finally settled on defining bisexuality in a very broad sense. For me, being bisexual strengthened my feminist politics, which included a commitment to egalitarian relationships in which one is free to love whom one chooses. Conversely, being a feminist allowed me to express my bisexuality more easily, as my desire to transcend gender helped me to be more sexual and intimate with both women and men.

But the altercations continue. Where is the tolerance in the lesbian and gay community for those of us who make choices that only appear to link us with the (oppressive) mainstream culture? Does my being in love, and lovers, with a man revoke my right to call myself woman-identified? Does it mean that I now automatically embrace heterosexual tyranny, patriarchy and exclusionary values? In short, have I thrown away a history that helped create who I am and has given me a sense of self? Have I really abandoned who I am and become someone else?

My friend Ruth, a divorced mother of four, thought hard about these issues when she came out as a lesbian well after she was in her sixties. "Never having had a sexual relationship with a woman," she confided to me, "I didn't know if I had a right to be calling myself a lesbian—much less be doing public speaking about it. But the organizers of this one conference said it was okay, that there are heterosexuals who identify themselves as straight but haven't had a sexual relationship with a member of the opposite sex. I feel very identified as a lesbian, and even though I may never actualize those erotic feelings—because after all," she added, laughing, "I'm getting old and this body doesn't work the way it used to—I guess I have the right to proclaim who I am."

Ruth's circumstance underscores the complexity and intricacies of identifying oneself. Outward appearance and behavior are not always reliable—or comprehensive—indicators of inner identity. For those of us who are bisexual, we're often accepted by the gay community only as long as we choose to express the homosexual side of our orientation. But when we don't, it doesn't mean that the erotic attraction toward our own sex is absent; it's just not being expressed at that moment. I would remind those who resent me for my "heterosexual privilege" that when I'm holding hands with a woman on the street, a gay basher isn't going to stop and ask if I also relate to men so he can decide whether or not to beat me up.

On the other hand, I realize the implications and importance of identifying myself as lesbian and aligning myself with other lesbians. I feel more committed than ever to eliminating homophobia and sex-role stereotyping. How can I not be? The patriarchal structures that tyrannize homosexuals also tyrannize heterosexuals, hindering everyone's capacity to relate in open and loving ways. An ally in this struggle is Paul. As a gay male acquaintance said when he suddenly found himself in love with a close female friend, "She's the man I've always wanted."

I should mention that soon after my Philadelphia initiation, Paul and I decided to get married. Our commitment not only shocked our friends, it flabbergasted us—me, because I had always detested what the custom and legal (un)ethic of marriage stood for, and Paul, because as a self-identified gay man, he never envisioned marriage to be an option for him. Nevertheless, we were determined to legally formalize our commitment, only we'd do it our way.

The decision felt right, springing from a place so deep it cannot be described in words. It happened quietly, like water seeping through sand: you don't know afterward how it got there, only that it has. The momentum was spurred by one of Paul's telephone calls during which he said he missed me and—to my speechless amazement—offered to move in. "I wouldn't return to New York for anyone else," he said guilelessly, "but I would for you."

"I don't want to live together," I told him, a week later on my couch. "I've been 'living together' with people since I was in my twenties, and at this point in my life I'm too old for that. It would feel like playing house. Why don't we get married?"

For an excruciating minute Paul silently considered my counteroffer, then smiled enthusiastically. "What a good idea!" he exclaimed. "I'd love to spend my life with you."

Our Celebration of Commitment was held at the local Unitarian Universalist church in the center of hexagonally arranged pews with a high priestess running around our sacred circle of candles and flowers, brandishing the beaded and feathered power-wand Paul and I had made. If our friends were delighted, Paul's relatives were horrified. The ceremony, a cross between a pagan gathering and a radical political caucus, was unlike anything they had ever experienced.

Our celebration text booklets (later handed out to the guests) read:

Under patriarchy, women are an oppressed class and females and males have been assigned exclusive roles that make them caricatures of themselves, fragmented and unable to love in a spontaneous and total way. As long as a woman is considered emotionally, intellectually, and morally inferior, it is difficult for her to love and cherish a male partner who is in a dominant and privileged role. Love and respect cannot exist where alienation and resentment simmer. Likewise, as long as a man is considered weak for being nurturing and vulnerable, it is difficult for him to love and cherish a female partner who is expected to provide the nurturing in the relationship. Love and respect cannot flourish when one is forbidden to connect emotionally to one's partner, self and others.

However, we concluded happily, "our relationship is founded on the openness and respect that stem from relating as equals, for we believe in the power to shape and transform our lives."

Paul and I wore matching silk pants outfits and in lieu of rings swapped the purple, turquoise and green sashes a friend had crocheted for us. As we carefully explained, a material token—by nature static—can get lost, broken or stolen. But for us, exchanging sashes was an act: of taking in and being affected by the other's energy, a gesture whose very fluidity signified the change and growth we felt would continue to be an intrinsic part of our relationship.

The main catalyst for no rings, though, really, was something Paul had said right after I proposed to him. "I don't like jewelry anyway, but do you really want to wear a ring? One look at your hand and everybody will be calling you 'Mrs.'"

Judging from their grim countenances, the women present who called themselves "Mrs." (all of them his relatives) must have been offended, particularly during Paul's surprise announcement of his name change. Because marriage, he stated, regarded the woman as the man's property and robbed her of autonomy, he would combine my name with his to indicate his solidarity, unity and love. On the other hand, I—in a display of self-respect—would keep my name precisely as it was.

"I don't know why they were so grumpy about the change," I complained to Paul later. "After all, Silver-Fox is a great name."

Tori eventually wrote, saying she could no longer have a "working relationship" with me—that although she recognized my difficulty in coming out and losing lesbian friends, the bottom line was she needed to put her energy into lesbians; and since I wasn't a lesbian, I couldn't read my lesbian love poetry at the bookstore. "You mustn't feel that I'm 'trashing' you," she wrote, referring to my letter to her. "Nor must you misconstrue my decision to mean that you are being 'antagonistically invalidated and ostracized.' Don't take this personally...but since you are now either hetero or bi, it's not okay to deny your heterosexual privilege or claim an affinity to lesbian culture and issues." I read her letter with a mixture of despair and outrage. If this wasn't being trashed and invalidated, what was?

Paul didn't escape censure, either. Apparently, my calling him a gay man was a grievous error. "Your male lover cannot be considered to have been 'openly gay.' He is, at the very least, a closet bisexual."

Paul, grimacing, read Tori's letter. "As if I didn't have enough to deal with," he laughed. "First I came out to my friends as straight, then to my family about having been gay; and now, I have to come out as a closet bisexual."

Love always brings us out of closets. My closet was one of attachment and trust as much as it was about sexuality. And by committing myself to another human being—which for me entails being vulnerable, sharing, loving—I can only become more compassionate and inclusive, more politically aware. It is a fallacy to no longer regard me as woman-identified just because I have fallen in love with a man. Paul is not any man; he's Paul. I still don't particularly like men. I detest the machismo and power-over mentality that most men embody and that oppresses everyone: women, lesbians and gays, non-whites, animals, other men. But I don't need to be in love with any man, or most men. I'm in love with Paul. That's just how it turned out.

The pastry chef where Paul works is gay. But, gay or straight, not many people understand our nomenclature.

"I'm going to meet my partner now," Paul declares one day, getting ready to leave work, as the pastry chef prompts, "You mean your boyfriend?"

"No"—then, since the man doesn't get it— "my, lover...uh, wife." The latter is used as a last resort. We hate the term.

The pastry chef's jaw drops. "I thought you were gay—didn't you tell me earlier that you were going to the Gay Pride March?"

"Yes," Paul replies. "I'm meeting Nina there."

I am taking pictures of the parade, enjoying the camaraderie I feel with the strangers I meet and friends I bump into. A lesbian writer acquaintance spots me and runs up to bestow a hug and congratulations: she heard somewhere about my marriage. I start telling her how amazed I am that Paul and I did it, but she detects my note of apology and cuts me off. "The world's not a simple place," she affirms. "What matters is that you're happy. You look radiant. I'm delighted for you."

I am very grateful for her support. But must I hide my partnership status as long as I want to continue publishing my lesbian material in lesbian journals?

I am not the enemy, even though sisters like Tori perceive me as such. In a world that so desperately needs greater cooperation and tolerance of diversity, to be forced into another, newly created closet by a group that itself has been closeted is tragic. Where is the oppression going to stop? And does this mean that on some level the oppressors are winning?

My life is a continual process of coming out. Ultimately, I cannot identify myself even as bisexual. As a human being striving to reach my fullest potential, I can only relate as the lover.

Brenda Marie Blasingame

THE ROOTS OF BIPHOBIA:
RACISM AND INTERNALIZED HETEROSEXISM

When I was a small child, I remember wondering about the world. I would ponder why it is that people cannot just all come together, be happy and treat each other with delightful respect, love and caring.

Coming out as a lesbian was a risk for me: it meant taking my power and the space to do what I needed to do to honor myself. Coming out of the closet as a bisexual in the gay/lesbian community was more than a small risk: it meant possibly losing the one community I felt safe in, the women's/gay community. Yet if it was truly safe there I would not have been terrified to come out as who I am, bisexual, to the lesbian women in my life.

On some level my little kid inside is asking the same question I asked so many years ago about all of us: why can't we come together as one queer community and treat each other with delightful respect, love and caring?

As we move into the nineties, I believe that we will see a rise in hate crimes against our community. As I look around, I notice we are at the same place with the gay rights movement that we were at during the fifties and sixties with the civil rights movement. When I am leading workshops on multicultural issues, I see that people clearly understand the issues of racism and sexism. But when we get to homophobia and heterosexism, the thinking gets cloudy and people find themselves lost in a fog, unable to find their way through to the other side. Many things cause this fog: fear, misinformation, lies, stereotypes and religion. It is my belief that once we conquer heterosexism, we will be able to begin to put our society and world into an order that does reflect "liberty and justice for all." But we will have to come to grips with our internal divisions in order to move against the external forces that will be coming at us.

As a bisexual woman of color in the queer community I am acutely aware of the work that needs to take place in our community on various issues of oppression. That is why I have a commitment to examine the issue of biphobia and what I see as the root causes of the continual exclusion of bisexuals from most parts of the gay/lesbian community.

First and foremost, I do not want to place blame for biphobia on any one group of people. As with any oppression it has grown out of years of inflexible thinking. Though the oppression is not our fault, we do have a responsibility to deal with the eradication of it and all other oppressions because they are linked to each other through a system of structured disequality.

I believe that biphobia partly grows out of internalization of our common oppression, heterosexism. The oppression of queer people, as with any other oppression, places people on one of two sides of a power structure. You are either on the up-side of that structure (the privileged group) or the down-side of it (the group targeted for oppression).

When we choose to stand against heterosexism, the institutionalized oppression of queer people, we are fighting for our lives. Yet we often become shackled to our convictions in a way that replicates the inflexible thinking of those who have oppressed us in the first place. We begin to think in dichotomies. This or that. You are either gay or straight, not in between, not bisexual. This type of thinking excludes anybody who does not fit into one or the other category.[1]

When we experience oppression, we begin to internalize what has been said about us, just as young children who are emotionally abused begin to believe the bad things that are said about them. When this phenomenon takes place, we begin to act out our pain from the external oppression within our own communities. The pain, a result of internalized oppression, leads to horizontal hostility, the lashing out within our own group.

One of the key ways that heterosexism has been internalized is in the monosexual paradigm: either you are gay or you are straight. Within this paradigm bisexuality cannot exist. Biphobia is one of the ways that the queer community has acted out internalized heterosexism/homophobia.

In the same way that heterosexuals have misinformation and

myths about gay people, gay and lesbian people have misinformation and myths about bisexuals. One reason this misinformation about bisexuals exists in the gay/lesbian community is the dichotomy paradigm, the either/or assumption. In the gay community bisexuals have been seen as the other and when a group is labeled "the other" stereotypes and misinformation begin to develop.

Often in our struggle for equality we take on some of the qualities of the ones we are fighting against. We internalize the lies and misinformation that society tells about queers. Every day we struggle to love ourselves in the face of hatred from the world around us. If gays and lesbians are struggling to love themselves and fighting against the daily messages of rejection, it is certainly feasible that they could internalize those messages and use them to reject the bisexuals in their community. Society says that we are wrong for being queer, that it is not "natural" to love someone of the same sex, that if we just get the right kind of help that we could be straight, or that it's just a phase. Similar reasoning can be directed at bisexuals in the lesbian and gay community: how many times have I heard I am wrong for being bisexual, that I am sitting on the fence, that I am experimenting, that I am not really gay but straight, that it is wrong for me to want to be with a man, or that it's just a phase.

The roots of biphobia come from the belief that there is only one way to be with someone of the same sex. Biphobia emerges from the belief in the dichotomy of gay and straight, with no in-between. Therefore bisexuals are not seen as part of the gay community but apart from the community.

The queer community was established on a set of norms of what constituted queer. We need to ask questions when those norms begin to oppress people who are a part of the community. We need to question when we begin to put a box around who a queer is and how a queer should be. If we only replicate the system that has oppressed us, then are we as progressive as we would like to think we are? We must begin to rethink and re-evaluate our community and what it is we are truly fighting for, the freedom for everyone to love who they love and not be oppressed.

As a woman of color, these thoughts generated many memories for me. Part of the internalization of racism in the black community is the belief that some people are not "black enough." There is an artificial box that has been constructed in the African-American community. Inside this box is a description of someone who is "really" black. If you do not fit in this box, then you are seen as not "black enough," a "wanna be," "white-washed," and many other words or phrases that developed out of the dichotomy paradigm of you are either black or white. The thinking is like this: "Black people act this way and do these things, and if you don't then you are not really one of us." This has created infighting within the African-American community, a lashing out at each other that at times appears to be a replication of the external oppression.

This is what heterosexism has done in the queer community. There is a box labeled gay. The box limits you; it is a prescribed way of being with someone of the same sex. If you do not fit in the box, or wear the label gay, then you do not belong. Some people are viewed as being more queer than others. Bisexuals are most often viewed as less queer because they do not identify as exclusively gay or lesbian. When a system that oppresses us now has us fighting over which ones of us are "truly" queer, we must begin to ask ourselves why we are fighting each other and not the system.

We must also begin to look at another root of biphobia: racism. For many years the gay/lesbian community was seen as a white community. Until the last decade, people of color in the gay/lesbian community were not visible. We now see on a national level gay and lesbian people of color uniting and speaking out as a part of the gay/lesbian community. We also see the issue of racism within our community being looked at and worked on more every day. Because the gay/lesbian community was shaped by white gay and lesbian leaders for such a long time, I believe we have to look at how this contributed to the foundation of biphobia and the construction of our current definition of "queer."

To come out as queer in a community of color is still a very complicated and difficult endeavor. I rarely saw people of color visibly out as queer when I was pondering my coming out. The fear of loss of community and more than that, the fact that dealing with racism can be more than enough oppression for any one person. One of the most immediate thoughts I had when I began to think about coming out was about the black community. What was I going to have to give up? I have to struggle with racism on a daily basis; was I going to be able to stand the possible loss of my community, the African-American community? For many people of color coming out can be a choice between family/community and being true to their sexual identity. Coming out could mean a loss of a foundation, a support system. This possibility leads many people of color to choose not to be visibly out.

On the other hand, white people who come out have the privilege of white skin: they do not deal on a daily basis with the effects of racism and in most cases do not have to make a choice between their choice of partners and the loss of their community. All this is not to say that white gay and lesbian individuals have an easier time coming out at all levels, but in relation to this particular issue it may be easier for white individuals to come out. Elaine Pinderhuges states that "using personal identity as a substitute for a strong, integrated sense of ethnicity can be risky. People can and do seek personal meaning in a variety of sources that can be used to substitute for ethnic meaning. Such sources include one's profession, one's talent, a religious group or gay identity."[2] For many white people their community is the gay/lesbian community: it is their family and extended family, the key to their personal identity. This can also be attributed to how racism hurts white people. It takes away their ethnic identity, leaving them to look for this root identity somewhere else. This is not generally the case for people of color, who most often have a sense of identity and community through membership in their ethnic group.

In talking with older people of color who are queer, I've found that they often say that in their community people had relationships with people. Some people chose to be involved with both sexes, whereas others chose to be exclusively involved with same-sex partners. They spoke of how some people were bisexual. That was not what it was called, but that was what was taking place. It was not a subject of conversation: people knew who was in a relationship with whom, that was how it was and life went on. In this community, the community was important. I believe that it was oppressive for people not to be able to come out as who they were. But within this community, there was a certain acceptance that happened between people, a sense of belonging and responsibility for each other. Bisexuality did exist.

I once talked with a Latino male doing AIDS education in the Latino community about his approach to educating the community about safe sex. He said there was no word for bisexual per se, but that bisexuality existed in the community and that this had to be addressed in order to teach safe sex. It was very much like the black community. When they talk about safe sex they have to refer to it as "when you have sex with another man." Bisexuality existed in this community.

In some respects this has been a long path to my key point, but a necessary one to take. The key issue here is that the norms of the queer community have been by and large set by white people who have been the leaders in the community until ten to fifteen years ago. Part of the norms that were established were that bisexuals were not quite queer enough. Now we have as a part of the community gay/lesbian people of color who have chosen to follow the norms established by others. This often happens to us as people of color: we end up following the norms of the mass culture we are a part of. It appears to me as a person of color that our historical past shows bisexuality as part of the way things were, yet people of color in the queer community have often taken on the excluding of their bisexual brothers and sisters. It is as if again the existence of history has been excluded, hidden or wiped away, keeping us from knowing our historical relationship to sexual identity and sexual orientation.

I believe the issues I have been speaking of have to do with unconscious racism, not malicious racism. It has to do with not being aware of privilege and of how power is being used. I do not think anyone meant to overlook our history but it did occur. Often white people do not realize what power they have even after they come out as queer; they don't realize that for many people of color dealing with racism is enough of a load for one lifetime and that our choices around coming out and how we identify cross through many levels of our lives.

We must look historically at how we got where we are today. I think that it is incumbent upon us to question ourselves personally, on a deep level, to understand the roots of biphobia. When there is a continuous message of what you are coming from the outside, then you begin to compare everything to that message. What gets created through this comparative either/or thinking is a narrow vision of who fits in and who does not. It creates a system where everyone is compared to one extreme or the other, black or white, gay or straight. If you do not fit one or the other, you are not included.

This is what bisexuals often face coming out as bi in the gay/lesbian community. To come out as bisexual in the gay community for many means a loss of support in the face of heterosexism. This fear kept me "in the closet" as a bisexual, because I was so fearful of losing my community, the gay community, my support system and grounding.

As we look at how we got here, we may not like what we see on the path behind us, but we cannot erase that path as we fight to move our community forward. I believe exclusion of bisexuals from the gay/lesbian community is based on the internalization of heterosexism. Realization of our common oppression will set a foundation to work on building alliances within our community. From a common foundation we can then begin to look at the issues that are different for bisexuals and gays/lesbians and understand each other in the hope of forming one strong community, a community that is inclusive of all sexual orientations. The only thing between us and that vision is internalized oppression, and we have moved much more than that to get to where we are right now in our struggle.

Endnotes

1. Kathleen E. Bennett, "Feminist Bisexuality: A Both/And Option in an Either/Or World" published in this volume.

2. Elaine Pinderhuges, *Understanding Race, Ethnicity and Power* (New York: The Free Press, 1976).

Dvora Zipkin

WHY BI?

This is a true story: A woman gets on a plane, and a man sits down next to her. They spend the entire flight talking and make an intense connection. It's the relationship everyone dreams about: they see eye to eye on everything and, over the course of the flight, fall in love. The problem is, the woman identifies as a lesbian. So, when they land and the man asks if he may have her telephone number, she says, "No." He is shocked; he asks her, "Why not? It's obvious what's happening here." And she answers, "Because you don't fit into my life. And I don't know where to put you in my life."

In an ideal world, love would be love, and we would love whom we choose; that is, no one would care if we chose to love a woman or if we chose to love a man. But this is far from an ideal world: people do care about whom we choose to love, and those choices put us in boxes called our "sexual identity." The choice we make at one time in our life may not meet our needs and desires at another time. If that happens, we are forced to either walk away from love, as the woman in the story did, or face the fact that our sexual identity may not be so rigid and may, in fact, change.

When I became involved with my first serious woman lover, a lesbian friend said, "I hope you won't let the lesbian community pressure you to discard your identity as a bisexual." I found this somewhat ironic, because she herself had, at least in part, been swayed by the pressures in the lesbian community to move from a bisexual to a lesbian identity. Besides, how did she know I was bisexual when I wasn't even sure myself?

In retrospect, I've probably been bisexual for a long time, but it is only in the past few years that I've named and owned that identity— even if ambivalently. I dislike labels. My past is heterosexual, my present lifestyle is mostly lesbian, and my future is unknown. I have been and will probably continue to be attracted to both women and men (whether or not I choose to act on those attractions). Because I may someday become involved with a man again, because I am unwilling to deny either part of my sexuality; and, further, as a way of owning, acknowledging and validating my past, I *am* bisexual. However, since I am currently involved with a woman, in the "woman-loving-woman" definition of the word, I *am* a lesbian. But neither label feels like a true fit—and that's not just because of my aversion to labels. When others refer to me—or I refer to myself—as a lesbian, I feel a pang of conscience: "I'm not a *real* lesbian." (What *is* a "real" lesbian?) But when I refer to myself as "bisexual," that label also feels less than complete, and in some ways I feel it diminishes the validity of my lesbian relationship. I want to acknowledge and affirm my current choice fully. "Bisexual" just doesn't seem to say enough about who I am (and have been and may be), about what choices I've made (and may yet make) and about what options I see for myself. More fitting for me, I think, would be to call myself a "bisexual lesbian," which is about as close to truth as I can come (and which is sure to put me in some disfavor with both). Even that feels limiting, because I may change. Must I label myself? And, if it's necessary, for one reason or another, does that mean I no longer have the freedom to change?

I was a naive, heterosexual woman in the spring of 1983 when my political interests led me to become involved in local (Albany, New York) organizing efforts for the Women's Peace Encampment for a Future of Peace and Justice in Seneca, New York. I had never felt so comfortable, socially and politically, as I did with the group of women I came to know through those efforts that spring and summer. When it dawned on me one day that I was the only "nonlesbian" among one particular work crew, I wondered if I had somehow crossed some hitherto unknown boundary, over which only lesbians were allowed to pass. I wondered where all the other heterosexual feminists were and why they weren't here with all these wonderfully strong and friendly women? Was it true, as a friend would later tell me, that lesbianism is threatening to heterosexual women? Or that even feminism was? And, if that was the case, why wasn't it threatening to me? Why was I so comfortable here? And why were all my friends lesbians?

As it turned out, there were other "straight"[1] women working on the encampment. Later, back in Albany, I worked with a small group of women—ourselves a diverse mix of lesbians, bisexuals and heterosexuals nicknamed the "Lez-Bi-Hets,"— to plan, organize and facilitate "Facing Our Differences," a workshop with the lofty goal of building bridges between the lesbian, bisexual, and heterosexual women in our community. In one of the exercises designed to explore, understand and affirm our diversity, each woman joined one of four groups: Lesbian, Bisexual, Heterosexual, or Choose Not to Label. I had never slept with a woman, nor did I know if I ever could, yet I no longer felt I really belonged to the heterosexual world from which I had come. I had heard all the prolabelling arguments, how labels can be affirming and empowering, how we have to reclaim them, and so on, but I still didn't like the concept. I chose the Choose Not to Label group. Several women joined the group, some because they just didn't know who they were; others, out of a general philosophical aversion to labels; still others, like myself, because of a combination of those reasons.

A couple of years later, participating in a similar workshop exercise, I again chose the Choose Not to Label group, albeit this time with more hesitancy; I almost chose the Bisexual group (by this time I had begun to acknowledge my attraction to women), but a continuing stubborn aversion to labels won out. This time only two of us were in that group: myself and another woman who had never been involved with anyone, male or female, and just didn't know. Were women becoming more sure of their identities, or were labels becoming more acceptable—or necessary?

Which group would I choose today? Given only those four options, I would have to say Bisexual. It's the closest I can come to who I am. And it's the label with the most flexibility and tolerance for change. After all, I don't want to get boxed in.

In talking with a variety of women about sexual identity, several things have become apparent to me: (1) our sexual identity, although a very personal choice, is at the same time a very public and political statement and may mean very different things to different people; (2) sexual identity can—and does—change over time, as we, ourselves, change; (3) our sexual identity may not necessarily be the same as our sexual behavior; (4) bisexuality itself is fluid—there is no one way to be "bi" (that is, it may mean different things to different people and may include preferences); (5) pressures from and influences of our communities may contribute to changes in our sexual identity; (6) many bisexual women share a general sense of not belonging to either the lesbian or heterosexual world; we may even feel like impostors; (7) support, validation and affirmation for who we are and who we choose to be, whether from writings, groups or individuals, is vital both for maintaining a healthy and self-accepting identity as bisexual women and for promoting a healthy acceptance by others and (8) our stories as bisexual women are as unique and varied as we are.

"Growing up, I always saw myself as bi," says Arlene, who is now lesbian-identified. From age eleven, Arlene had sexual relations with girls. Not until fourteen or fifteen did she finally discover there was a term for being with both girls and boys. "I identified as bisexual because my behavior was bisexual. I never had permission to be attracted to girls, but I was. If I had had permission, I'm not sure if I would have been with boys. There was no option not to be with boys."

"I grew up in the seventies in New York City, you know, David Bowie. . . everyone was bisexual. Being bisexual was not particularly strange or different.

"The women that I knew who were lesbians were butches. So I just assumed that women who were lesbians somehow *knew.* I mean, they had a mark on the bottom of their foot or something, or there was some way that they had this information. And since I didn't have that information, since God never revealed herself and said, 'You are a lesbian,' I didn't know that was an option, that one could just *say,* 'I think I want to be a lesbian.'

"I made a decision to 'become' a lesbian because I realized that I was never going to have the kind of intimate, serious, committed relationships with women that I wanted as long as I kept sleeping with men. That the women I wanted to be involved with were not going to be involved with me. Why? Because it was 1979, that heyday of lesbian separatism, and men were mutants!"

And if it had been a more accepting community, did she think she would have retained her bisexual identity?

"I've thought about that seriously in the last couple of years. My relationship now is the first one I've been in that it's been really safe to talk about that. My partner asked me today, 'Where are you going?' and I said, 'I'm going to be interviewed by Dvora about bisexuality.'

She said, 'Is there something you want to tell me?' I told her I was an expert witness!

"I suppose in some kind of pure sexual sense, I am bisexual. And that's okay with me; I'm comfortable with that. I don't know that I would choose to interact sexually with a man today, so it really does feel like a choice. I know that *choice* is a bad word in queer circles these days, but I think there's a lot of choice involved in our sexual identity.

"I've thought about what would happen if I fell in love with a man. It's a real scary thought to me. Perhaps because it's possible; I could imagine it happening. And then I think about it, and I can't imagine it happening. I just don't know what that would do to my identity or my lifestyle."

That is what happened to Genie. She had identified as a lesbian until she met Ken. Although there was a strong mutual attraction, she denied the sexual feelings. "It just didn't fit in with the lesbian space I'd carved out for myself. The stronger the sexual feelings got, the stronger I denied them. I don't know what would have happened if I hadn't met up with the Boston Bi Group at an anarchist conference I went to. When I learned of the bi support group there, I thought, 'Wow!' I couldn't wait until three o'clock!

"If I hadn't had the bisexual identity option, I might have had to make a choice, between Ken and maintaining my lesbian identity. I could have gotten involved with Ken, you know, 'Okay, I'm heterosexual. They must have been right that lesbianism was a phase.' Or, I could have totally denied him, saying, 'I'm a lesbian,' and missed out on this healthy, loving relationship. If I'd decided hetero, I think I might have always had resentment that I changed my identity for this relationship, gave up loving women. It might have made my desire for a relationship with women stronger, because I was 'ruling it out.'

"I now know I'm bisexual. I'm attracted to other people all the time, and I'm attracted to both women and men. It's a nice feeling."

Shayna disagrees. "Being bisexual is a major conflict in my life. It involves more pain than pleasure. How do you choose? How can I commit? What if? Bi is honest, that's who I am, not because it's fun. I would prefer to be one or the other. I don't care which. I would just like one clear identity. That would be a lot simpler."

Shayna, too, came to identify as bisexual after having come out as a lesbian. She always *felt* bisexual, but in 1975, at the age of twenty, bisexuality was impossible for her in the political environment she was in.

"There was no room for bis. When you were with a woman, you were a dyke." Neither the "straight" nor the lesbian label ever really fit. She came out as a lesbian more out of political identity and anger toward men than because that was who she really was. Some years later, she met and was attracted to a man.

"I knew I was bi, and I acted on it. I didn't label it as such." Today, she identifies as a bisexual. "It's true to who I am. It's a political statement."

Shayna recently ended a six-year monogamous relationship with a man. When she met him, she had been involved with women, and during those six years, even though her lifestyle was predominantly heterosexual, she still identified as bisexual. "It was scary to think I might never be involved with women again," she says.

Like Genie, Jane did not see bisexuality as an option right away. When she first became aware of her sexual attraction to women, she thought, "Shit, I'm not straight anymore, so I must be gay."

"It didn't occur to me that I could be both," she told me. After ten years of ambivalence, "trying desperately to be a lesbian," feeling guilty about her attraction to and involvement with men, "sneaking off" and sleeping with them ("I would only have sex; I wouldn't allow feelings or emotions to come in; and then I would only involve myself with 'unavailable' men"), Jane finally realized she could acknowledge her attraction to both men and women.

Nancy, at thirty-five years old, the mother of two young children, is about to end her seven-year marriage to a man, to be with women. Before she was married, she had pursued several relationships with women that didn't work out and called herself bisexual. Although she had never totally resolved the question of her sexuality, and even though her younger sister has been out as a lesbian for years, it's only recently that Nancy started facing her sexual attraction to women again. She began identifying as a bisexual once more, and now has come to believe she is really a lesbian. Despite two marriages, Nancy says, "I am not attracted to men and never have been." Becoming involved with women again, she says, "has convinced me even more."

Katy grew up very comfortable with and never questioning her heterosexuality. Yet, she recalls an intensely close relationship with a girlfriend in seventh grade.

"We were soul mates. We were never sexual, and I never consciously felt sexual feelings for her. But I remember one time the school paper gossip column said we were gay. I think that people were threatened by our level of intimacy." Katy realized she was attracted to women about four years ago, at age twenty-three.

"I had all these feelings for this lesbian woman who was interested in me, and I remember thinking, why wouldn't this be okay?"

"The longer I was involved with her and the lesbian community, the more I lost my attraction to men, or it was put on hold. I wondered if I was a lesbian, could I ever be attracted to men again?"

Since that time, Katy has been involved with both women and men and identifies strongly as bisexual. "It's something I'm very proud of," she says.

Colette, until six years ago, lived her life in an exclusively heterosexual environment, never exposed to other lifestyles or options. Married at sixteen, in and out of two marriages, she has been a single parent of three sons for the last twelve years. At forty-five, Colette now looks back and puts the pieces of her life together: she finally has a name for her attraction to women and realizes that she's probably been bisexual all along.

"I didn't really want to label myself, because I don't like labels. But it's hard to describe things without them."

Involved with a woman for the past two years, Colette still maintains a bisexual identity. Why?

"Because I'm still very interested in men, and I feel a lot of chemistry when I meet men and talk to certain men, and I know that I still have the feelings I had before, when I considered myself heterosexual. Those feelings are still there, but in addition I'm now admitting my feelings for women." And does she have any preference?

"Not really. I think it would depend on the person. It's *easier* to be in a relationship with a male, because society accepts that. But there are so many things that women can get from other women that you can't get from men."

The experiences of these women show, I believe, that sexual identity is not static, that it changes over time—and may change more than once. These changes may come about because of choice, circumstance, meeting a particular person or persons, or, simply, because of one's most basic sense of self. Many of the bisexual women I have spoken with share a sense of being in two different worlds and of not feeling completely comfortable or fully themselves in either. Those women who have had some kind of support for who they are—whether from friends or lovers, other bisexuals, a formal support group or even a subscription to a bi newsletter—were more easily able to maintain their bisexual identity, even in the face of outside pressures. Most agreed that the support of their partner was especially crucial; in fact, without it, it was likely either the relationship or the identity would have to be given up. Support and acceptance played a determining role in affirming their identity choice and in subsequently owning that identity, whereas, for some women, pressures and assumptions from both the "straight" and gay worlds played a role in making that owning difficult. In those cases, lack of support led to isolation, doubt and/ or confusion and, especially if coupled with ostracism from the surrounding community, abandonment of the bisexual identity.

There's a difference, I think, between identity and behavior. Identity is who I am. This may or may not coincide with what I do.

Unless we are nonmonogamous or celibate, as bisexuals, when we are involved in a relationship, we are in either a lesbian or a heterosexual relationship. And, like it or not, our partner, to some extent, determines our lifestyle. Then bisexuality becomes more theoretical. Even if one is nonmonogamous, unless all relationships are given the same importance and priority in one's life, our lifestyle is still determined somewhat by the sexuality of our primary partner. But if we are identified only by whom we are with at any particular point in time, that excludes us from being recognized as bisexual. It's hard to identify bisexuals; you never know who they are because they are "invisible."

Many lesbian women become involved with men, and yet still identify as lesbians. Their *identity* may be lesbian, but their *behavior* is heterosexual (bisexuality can be classified as behavior, I think, only if one is simultaneously involved with a woman *and* a man). I had long thought that to identify as a lesbian would indicate I would never again be involved with a man. Some women have told me that the definition of lesbian has nothing to do with men, that lesbian means "woman-loving-woman." So, if I am a woman who loves women—but I also love a man—does that mean I'm a lesbian? Why not bi? As one lesbian friend has said, "Lesbian says I am not available to men. Bisexual says I am." I ask, so what if one wants to be "available" to men? For my friend, being identified as lesbian is a political statement, a statement of affirmation and validation for the lesbian lifestyle and a challenge to heterosexism. But, so is bisexuality. Bisexuality says, "Even if I'm involved with a man, don't assume that I'm heterosexual. I, too, live, affirm and validate a lesbian lifestyle. After all, I'm gay too."

Over the years, I have seen self-identified lesbians become involved with men; some of these women subsequently call themselves bisexual, others retain their lesbian identity, still others say nothing at all about it. I don't believe any of them would say that they had "become" heterosexual, even if their lifestyle was such and they didn't identify as bisexual or lesbian (which makes them, if nothing else, appear heterosexual in the eyes of most people).

I have also seen formerly heterosexual women become involved with women, some embracing a lesbian identity, others choosing the bisexual label. I doubt if any of them has retained a heterosexual identity. So whereas I have seen heterosexual women move to lesbian or bisexual identity, bisexual women to lesbian, and lesbians moving to a bisexual identity, in my own experience, at least, I have never seen a lesbian or bisexual-identified woman move to heterosexual identity. If anything, gay women who become involved in long-term heterosexual relationships, if not identifying as bisexual, probably tend to say nothing at all about their sexual identity.

In the fall of 1990 I attended the (nonlegal) marriage of my lover's "ex," to a man. The night before the ceremony, I listened to this woman and one of her best friends talk about their days in the lesbian community and about how they had "done it backward"; that is, gone from a lesbian identity to a bisexual one, rather than the other way around. Each of them had committed herself to a long-term (presumably monogamous) relationship with a man and said nothing about further interests in or involvements with women, and yet considered themselves bisexual and not heterosexual. I think this says something about how bisexuals are really more "gay" than "straight"; that is, once we have experienced a lesbian relationship or identity, no one can ever take away that part of us that is gay.

I believe that sexual preference, in the population as a whole, falls into a bell curve: at one end is a small percentage of people that is totally heterosexual; at the other, a percentage that is totally homosexual. In the middle is a vast majority of the population that is bisexual, to varying degrees, but does not act on that identity for the most part because of societal biases and conditioning. One end of the "bell" is predominantly attracted to the same sex, the other mostly attracted to the opposite sex, moving along with varying proportions of same/opposite attraction, until, in the middle, is that part of the population equally attracted to the same and the opposite sex. I think that you may move around within that "bell" over the course of a lifetime, and without society's intolerance, I believe more people would do so. And I don't think you have to be totally without predilection, not caring whether you're involved with a man or a woman, feeling it's the person and not his or her gender that you're attracted to, to consider yourself bisexual. I think you can certainly have preferences. Perhaps those preferences will last a lifetime. And perhaps they won't.

A friend of mine, Leslie, identifies as a lesbian because she prefers women. "That's called lesbian, so I'm a lesbian. I assumed that to be bisexual, meant you had no preference." But now, she wants a way to feel comfortable owning and acknowledging all her past sexual experiences and emotions with men. "I really *was* attracted to men and enjoyed sex with them." What happened? It's almost a mystery. Her feelings just changed. "Who would have guessed this, so who knows what could happen in the future?" Even though she's not comfortable calling herself bisexual now (it might be misunderstood to mean that her preference is not women, she says), she feels that in the course of her entire life, she is bisexual.

Another woman I know, who has never been involved with a man and believes she probably never will be, does identify herself as bisexual. "It's a philosophical choice," she says; she believes that all people are really bisexual and that it's only society's biases that prevent most of us from acting on or acknowledging it. And, she realizes, it *could* be possible, at some time, that she would become involved with a man. Even if not likely, the possibility exists, and to affirm and acknowledge that, she recognizes herself as a bisexual woman.

When I first met my current lover, a lifelong lesbian, I told her I was bisexual. I was sure she wouldn't be interested in me because of that. It took me a while to believe that she accepts who I am; however, she does prefer to think of me as a lesbian. It often seems as if both communities—heterosexual and lesbian—are trying to get us bisexuals over to their respective "side," consciously or not.

Lesbians like to claim as "one of their own" any woman who has ever been involved with women (whether she herself ever identified as a lesbian or not). The heterosexual world chooses to ignore our woman-loving-woman selves when we are involved with a man. Genie's and Katy's families, for example, have been very supportive of their current relationships with men, even though, for Genie, past non-Jewish male partners were frowned upon. "Why do you bother?" Genie's mother asks her when she brings up the issue of bisexuality, implying that since she's involved with Ken, there's no reason to insist on a bisexual identity anymore. "You're screwing up your life, pursuing this identity."

Katy feels anger at her family, at the whole "straight" community, for now accepting her, "for all the subtle and incredibly nonsubtle messages they give me about how 'okay' this relationship is, compared to my other ones, because this is a man. For instance, my parents have this summer home, and my mother called to make sure I have the first opportunity to pick a week to stay there; what I heard her saying is that, now that you're seeing a man, I want you to be able to spend time together there and have the relationship work. Whereas when I was seeing a woman, we weren't even allowed to use it."

And, of course, bisexual women who are involved with women are perceived and assumed to be lesbians. When I first started questioning my sexual identity, I began to identify more and more with women and hang out in the women's (read: lesbian) community. All of my friends were lesbians. It was often assumed that I was a lesbian, and a friend once overheard the following comment in a bar: "That Dvora is such a dyke; I wish she'd figure it out and come out already!" Maybe I was, and maybe it was meant as a compliment, but I still resented her assumptions.

When I finally became involved in a relationship with a woman, it was almost as if my lover became my ticket "in": Now I was really one of them, now I belonged, now I could be accepted into the club. I resented this assumption as much as any of the others. I resented the fact that now I was more accepted, even though nothing else—my politics, my beliefs, my ideas, how I dressed or looked—had changed. However, though I still don't feel like I'm really a part of the lesbian community I must admit that I do enjoy the tacit sense of acceptance and approval, acceptance I suppose a part of me is afraid to risk losing by saying I'm bisexual. Perhaps more important than this fear is to ask what is to be gained by saying that. In the heterosexual world, saying I'm bisexual challenges a sexist/heterosexist assumption. What do I challenge and what is gained when my upstairs neighbor tells me how nice it is that we're all lesbians in the apartment house I live in, if I correct her and say, "Well, actually I'm bisexual"? It does something to make us more visible, to affirm that we do, in fact, exist, but it is often an uncomfortable step to take.

Imagine. I'm at a party of lesbians, I'm there with my lover, everyone obviously assumes I'm a lesbian. What do I do, announce, "Oh, by the way, I just want you all to know that I'm really bisexual"?! I suppose it's the same dilemma a bisexual woman whose partner is male has at a heterosexual gathering. How do we come out; how do we show pride and openness for who we are? How do we stop feeling like we're only showing part of who we are? How do we stop feeling like impostors, like we don't fit in or belong? How do we stop being invisible?

Even when I saw myself as heterosexual, I resented the role assumptions that sexual identity involved, including marriage, children, and all that goes along with the traditional heterosexual lifestyle. So perhaps some of the anger and resentment at the assumptions has as much to do with being a feminist as it does with being bisexual. Our feminist sensibilities bristle when we are placed in the hetero woman's "role" or when assumptions are made about us based on who we are involved with at the time.

Being a feminist may help in maintaining a bisexual identity. I think feminists may tend to be more openly outspoken and/or political about being bisexual than women who aren't necessarily feminists. Jane, for example, who doesn't really consider herself a feminist, identifies as bisexual because that is who she is, but she's not really into being political or even open about her sexuality. The first time I saw her at a bi support group, in fact, I was surprised; I'd assumed she was a lesbian. For other parts of her life, she lets people assume she's heterosexual.

For feminists, however, the issues of sexual identity take on political significance, and being vocal or at least open about it challenges myths, assumptions and stereotypes. It also may be that, as feminists, we want to be honest about who we really are.

It may also be that a feminist bisexual woman who is involved with a man may be more likely to hold onto and be more vocal about her sexual identity than one who is involved with a woman because it includes a struggle against the patriarchy and sexism.

As Genie says, "People look at me and think, 'Why is she calling herself queer, she's with a man?' But I identify as queer, inside I *feel* queer. As a feminist, it's real important to me to be around women-loving-women. In a way, being bi is a statement that I reject our heterosexist society. I want people to see that they have options, that they can choose. Sexism and heterosexism are so intertwined. By personally not accepting heterosexist ideas and assumptions, I am simultaneously not accepting sexism."

Even some of Genie's lesbian friends have a "why bother?" attitude concerning her holding onto a bi identity after more than three years in a relationship with a man. "Most relationships are not lifelong anyhow," she says, and dropping her bi identity wouldn't acknowledge that nor the possibility of relationships with women in the future.

When speaking with people I'm not that close to, I usually don't use labels at all in describing my personal life. I am more likely to say that "I'm involved with a woman." Let them think what they will (I am sure they think "lesbian"). Sometimes I clarify that I am bisexual (mentioning this essay is one way I do it), but then I sometimes feel obliged to dispel any bisexual myths, whether they arise or not.

Some time ago I had a conversation with an old friend and ex-lover. It had been a long time since we'd spoken, and in the course of the conversation, I realized that I hadn't told him about my current relationship. I had previously discussed with him my feelings toward women, so it wasn't really a surprise to him. He was fine with it (that's one reason we've remained friends for so long), even asking, "Is she Jewish?" (I love it when my heterosexual Jewish friends care about and affirm the relationship enough to ask this!). As our conversation moved on to other things, I sensed that he assumed I was "now" a lesbian. I felt a need to confront this assumption, whether because it feels something less than completely honest or because it denies some other part of me, even if that part lives only in my past (a past that included him). I mentioned to him that I was writing this essay, and he asked, a little surprised, "Is that [bisexual] how you're identifying?" As if he hadn't previously considered this as an option.

I'm not always so ready to challenge the lesbian assumption. When I came out to my mother, I told her I was bisexual, but all she heard was that I was involved with a woman, and that is the issue she has been grappling with. The word "bisexual" does not often come up in conversation, but, then again, neither does the word "lesbian." I sent her a book, *Different Daughters*, a collection of writings by mothers of lesbians, and signed it "your different daughter." Does she realize how "different" I really am?

"I have a friend whose daughter is the same way," she says, meaning (I know) that the daughter is a lesbian, and I want to say, "No, it's not the same, I'm bisexual"; but I don't, partly because it would just confuse the issue even more. (The next time I said the "B-word" to her, it seemed to surprise her—"You're bisexual?" Did she not "hear" me tell her the first time? Or does she not quite understand what it means, or know what to do with the information? To be fair, however, I must say that she has done a great job of coming to terms with her feelings, and in accepting her "different daughter's" choices.) But mostly it has to do with not reinforcing a heterosexist assumption that I'm more "okay" than lesbians because at least I'm "part" straight, that I have the "potential" to be straight. And, I don't want to downplay or delegitimize that part of me that *is* lesbian. I *am* gay, too, after all.

Lesbians have created their own sacred space. Perhaps something violates that sanctity if you sleep with men. Perhaps in maintaining a certain standard of "rules"—how to dress or cut your hair, whether to shave or not, who you can sleep with—a community can better keep track of its members. But I think it works the other way around. If the boundaries are more fluid, more flexible, it's easier to stick around. I grew up Jewish, with a strict set of rules for what it means to be a Jew and how you're supposed to practice that. Those rules sent me running in the opposite direction as soon as I was old enough to rebel. But in further exploring my heritage and learning that I could still "be" Jewish even while making my own rules, I no longer felt trapped in someone else's standards. It was my freeing myself from the Jewish rules that brought me back to being able to proudly identify as a Jew.

Bisexuals are not the enemy. We are no threat to the gay community. As a bisexual, I am far more gay than I am "straight." I experience society's oppression and homophobia, too. Even if I were to spend the rest of my life with a male partner, no one could ever take away that part of me that is, and always will be, gay. It may be true that bisexuals have a "privilege" that many lesbians don't have, but that's true as well for lesbians who "pass." I can be a straight-looking bisexual or a dykey-looking one, just as I can be a dykey-looking dyke or a straight-looking one. And if I have privilege because I can pass, or because I might be able to attend a family wedding with a male partner some day, I also have privilege because I am light-skinned and educated and look "straight." The question is, do I need to give up my identity to affirm another's, to combat the whole privilege question? If I can get a job as a light-skinned woman that you can't get because you're black, and I take the job, is that a bad thing for me to do? Will my not taking the job help you? In the last lines of "Class Poem," poet Aurora Levins Morales writes, "I will not hold back; Yes, I had books and food and shelter and medicine—and I intend to survive."[2] The goal is that everyone should have books and food, not that I should do without them because someone else doesn't have them. How would my denying my bisexuality by identifying as a lesbian instead contribute to working against lesbian oppression? I'm not going to desert my lesbian sisters in the struggle. Is that the fear?

A lesbian friend spoke of two gay male friends, one of whom feels quite comfortable walking down the street holding her hand in public (even though, humorously, they realize that people are assuming they're a heterosexual couple), and the other who will not in any way at all touch her in public. "I think it's a sign that he's much less comfortable with who he really is," she says. "It's so important to him that everyone sees him as *gay*. And to me that's a sign that you're not quite comfortable with who you are."

I think that the people who can accept, support and feel the most comfortable with our identity as bisexuals are those people who feel the most comfortable and secure in their own identity. I know a Jewish woman who worked for a Catholic agency and spent a lot of time with nuns. I told her I thought that would be hard, and she said that she got more support and affirmation for being Jewish from those

Catholic nuns than from anyone else in her life—even other Jews. And it began to make sense. Those nuns knew who they were, were confident in their own faith, and so a person of another faith was no threat to them.

Support and community are not as available to bisexuals as they are to lesbians. But where a supportive and validating community does exist, it has been the vital link enabling many bisexual women to embrace their identity. In lieu of a supportive bisexual community, many bisexual feminists turn to the lesbian community for connections with other women. I would like to be able to find support there, too, whether I was involved with a woman or a man or with nobody as we did in the "Facing Our Differences" workshop. I would like not to have to wonder if it's "okay," if I would be welcome, at lesbian events. And, I would like not to have to worry about the reactions of the lesbian community if I did end up getting involved with a man or "came out" as a bisexual, not to have to worry about being rejected or disappointing people.

Sacred women's space can be maintained, I believe, without excluding and invalidating other minorities. If we can "Face Our Differences" and, as we did in the Women's Peace Encampment in 1983, come to understand, accept and even rejoice in them, then we can work together—gay, bi, and our heterosexual allies—against the heterosexist patriarchy that oppresses us all, and, in the process, supply the support and affirmation to bisexual women to come out, to own our identity and to be proud.

I do think things are changing. Dialogue about the "B-word" is increasing. It's more "acceptable" to be bisexual. There are more groups (social and political) with a mix of "lez-bi-hets" (and even, sometimes, *men*!). "Biphobia" and the myths of bisexuality are being discussed; articles on bisexuality are appearing in gay publications. In 1990 when the City Council in Albany, New York, was considering gay civil rights legislation (it was defeated, unfortunately), bisexuals were affirmed when almost all of the speakers at the support rally included "lesbian/gay/bisexual" in their speeches.

I've recently moved to a new community where there seems to be a certain amount of anti-bisexual feeling, especially among the more separatist lesbians here. The feminist (lesbian) bookstore informed me that *Bi Any Other Name*[3] was not part of their regular stock (but they could order it); while at the alternative collective bookstore, it was on their top ten best-sellers list for several months after release. Bisexual was dropped from the last Pride March title, stirring up quite a bit of controversy, but also leading to a series of Town Meetings and Community Speakouts. In the winter of 1992 there was a community-wide ballot on the issue, and the vote was overwhelminging to call it the Lesbian/Gay/Bisexual Pride March. I feel nervous about being openly bi in this atmosphere, afraid of being ostracized from the lesbian community, but I also feel resentful. Why can't I just be who I am?

Who am I, then? I mentioned that I feel ambivalent about the bisexual identity. The longer I am with women, the less interested I am in men. But since that has changed for me once, it could change again. I don't think I'm about to arbitrarily say, "No more men, ever," even if I may feel that way at times. Sometimes I feel like Shayna, that I would just like one clear identity.

I try to hold on to my friends' advice, not to let the lesbian community pressure me into changing my identity. I can see how that lack of support, that need for "belonging," for being part of a community, especially as a newcomer, keeps me silent about my bisexuality, which wasn't even that loud before. I'm not as vocal about it as women like Genie and Katie are. I feel bad about that sometimes, feel I don't even have the right to be writing this essay.

We live in a society where sexual feelings are not fully acknowledged or embraced, where sexuality is repressed even as it is used to sell mouthwash. Being gay says, I'm sexual, I acknowledge and embrace and rejoice in my sexual feelings. This breaks society's set of rules. As bisexuals, our sexual feelings break *all* the rules, even the gay rules.

Whether we like it or not, whatever the current "politically correct" way of thinking about it may be, sexual identity does change. Women are "straight," and then they're not. Women are lesbian, and then they're not. Women are bisexual, and then they're not. And then maybe they will be again. I think if the limitations of both the gay and straight worlds were not there, there would be far more fluidity in our sexuality. I dream of a day when we will all be accepted for who we are. Meanwhile, I dream of a more fluid, all-encompassing word to describe who we are.

Labels—the ones we name ourselves, not those "given" to us by others—can be limiting, divisive or misunderstood. They can also be liberating, validating and necessary. Jane doesn't often use the word "bisexual" to describe herself. "I'd really rather just say 'I'm sexual,'" she says. Others, like Katy, prefer "bi-affectionate." "Queer" may be gaining popularity on the West Coast to include lesbians, gays and bisexuals, but it hasn't caught on yet here on the East Coast.

It's a shame that we have to have labels that separate us at all, or that it even matters to people whom we choose to have intimate and affectionate relationships with. But, the fact is, it does. As Genie sees it, labels are a necessary step to take before we get to the place where we don't need them any more. "Be out and proud," she says. "That's the only way people will see we're happy with our choices and come to accept us."

Katy is one of those bisexual women who are out and proud. Some of the women I talked with in the course of writing this essay asked that I not use their real names. Katy, along with Genie and Arlene, declined anonymity. "It goes along with my philosophy of bisexuality; I don't want to be anonymous about it," she told me. She wears the label proudly, although she sees it as a paradox. "Often I find labels very rigid and narrow and stifling. Heterosexuality is like that. But, for me, bisexuality does the opposite. It helps define me in a way that can enhance me, so I feel like I need it right now. I think I'll keep it for a while."

I don't necessarily feel like I need the label bisexual; like all labels, it tends towards fixing a limited—and sometimes misunderstood— definition of the wearer. However, it still comes closest to describing who I am, who I have been and who I may become. Might that change? Of course—that's what this essay has been about. Meanwhile, though, I'm not quite ready to give it up.

Endnotes

1. "Straight" is a label I have always been uncomfortable with and hesitant to use, especially in my more "straight" days. As an old hippie, "straight" always connoted "mainstream," "square," "conservative," and I resented being lumped into that category. It felt insulting. I realize that "heterosexual" is a bit cumbersome to use, but, then again, so is "bisexual."

2. In Aurora Levins Morales and Rosário Morales, *Getting Home Alive* (Ithaca, N.Y.: Firebrand Books, 1986), p. 45.

3. *Bi Any Other Name: Bisexual People Speak Out*, eds. Loraine Hutchins and Lani Kaahumanu (Boston: Alyson Publications, 1991).

Stacey Young

Breaking Silence About the "B-Word": Bisexual Identity and Lesbian-Feminist Discourse

I am a feminist and a formerly-lesbian bisexual woman and though my politics have undergone much transformation, I came out as a feminist and as a lesbian in the context of a community that was heavily influenced by radical lesbian-feminist separatism. The fact that I came to identify as bisexual after having been a publicly out lesbian— and one who believed firmly in the moral superiority of lesbians at that—gives me a particular, specific perspective. It's important that I make a point of this because, for me, being bisexual and having been a lesbian are intertwined, but this is by no means true for all bisexuals or all former lesbians. So, what I have to say may not be true for a bi-sexual woman who has never identified as a lesbian; nor may it be true for a former lesbian who considers herself straight, for example.

What follows is a discussion of how bisexuality gets constructed in radical lesbian-feminist discourse, but before I get into that discussion, I want to say a few things about what I am *not* saying here. Though I am critical of lesbians who speak and write about bisexuality from an uninformed position, I do not mean to imply either that all lesbians do so or that only bisexuals can speak about bisexuality. And though I address and critique a certain strand of lesbian-feminist discourse on sexuality—one that has been called radical feminist, or cultural feminist, or separatist—I am well aware that many other lesbians have writ-ten about sexuality in ways that avoid many of the problems for which I fault this particular strain, and I value this other discourse highly.[1] In fact, this discourse has been crucial in developing my current perspec-tive. I am also aware that a lot of people believe that the radical lesbian separatist strand of discourse that I critique here has long since been displaced by a discourse more tolerant of diversity. However, I believe that this is only partially true, in some communities, in some spheres, and with regard to some issues. I address the radical lesbian separatist discourse here because it is within this discourse that most of the discussions about bisexuals and former lesbians have emerged. [2]

In the lesbian community, I see a tendency among some lesbians to talk or write about, define, and often denounce bisexuality on the basis of little or no information about bisexual people. Relatively few women are out as bisexual in the lesbian community—even fewer speak or write about it in any analytic or public way. [3] Lesbians who talk or write publicly about bisexuality often do so from the assumption that bisexuals are a threat to lesbians and are opponents to be fought. This is oppressive of bisexual women.

Some of the fundamental points of debate within the feminist and lesbian communities over the last dozen years have been diversity, difference and the power to define. These debates have been sparked by many different groups of women saying, in effect, "Wait a minute! Your theories about me are based on your experience, not mine. What you say about me silences me, makes me invisible. Listen to what *I* have to say about who I am, what I think, how I got here." Women of color have challenged white women to set aside their assumptions, developed out of a necessarily limited perspective, to hear how women of color construct their realities and define and analyze their own experiences, their relationships to men of their racial and ethnic backgrounds and their positions in feminist and lesbian communities. Jewish women have challenged non-Jewish women to reexamine their generalizations about the oppressiveness of "patriarchal religions" in light of what Jewish women have to say about their relationship to a religion and its cultures that have been under siege for a millennium and more. Starting in the early days of the women's movement (and continuing through the present), lesbians (and bisexual women) have challenged heterosexual women to examine their assumptions about sex, relationships, politics and community; more recently, "sexual minorities" within the lesbian community have challenged other lesbians to rethink the relationship between power and desire, between politics and lust. All of these women have emphasized and reemphasized that the power to define is indeed a potent political tool, and that when people or groups are stripped of that tool because others with the power to do so have appropriated it in their own interest, what has taken place is an oppressive act of silencing. Though the power to define our own experiences is certainly not sufficient for us to be able to change our realities according to our own needs and desires, it *is* absolutely necessary. In the spirit of these debates, we need to examine the assumptions that underlie current discussions about bisexuality as an identity and in terms of politics, and to rethink the relationship of bisexuals to the lesbian and gay community.

An example of the problem of lesbians appropriating bisexual women's right to define ourselves and our experience is an article by Patricia Roth Schwartz from the June, 1989 issue of *off our backs*. Schwartz's impetus to write the article, which appeared in the "commentary" section of the publication, was her learning that a former woman lover of hers was now involved with a man—or, in Schwartz's words, "had gone straight." Schwartz goes on to say that receiving this news led her to "speculate upon why so many lesbians of the seventies...were now going straight." What follow includes Schwartz's public diagnosis of the ex-lover's supposed emotional and political deficiencies in an effort to explain her return to her "college boyfriend" and a list of reasons why some women who have identified as lesbians subsequently choose to be "hasbians."

The article contains a number of problematic assumptions and rhetorical power plays, one of which concerns the word "hasbian," a term I find really offensive. I object to the expression because it defines a person *only* in terms of what she once was. To refer to a woman as a "hasbian" implies that all one need know about her is her relationship to that exalted state, lesbianism. The term "hasbian" also, of course, evokes the word "has-been," which *Webster's* defines as "a person or thing which was formerly popular or effective, but is no longer so." What interests, then, does this term serve? Who has the power to define here, and at whose expense?

Schwartz's analysis has other problems, not the least of which are evident in the following passage:

> This is the greatest fear of all hard-core dykes, out of which separatism has sometimes been born: That a straight woman who is merely dallying will make use of us, then run back and "give her energy to a man." Well, honey, it happens. It happened to me years ago when a lovely creature more or less seduced me (of course I did go willingly), all the while lying about the fact that she wasn't really separating from her husband, as she claimed. The af-

fair was brief and years later I heard she was still married. I also remember a rather lost woman who'd been through a bad divorce discovering *our* women's community (in the city where I used to live) which took her in with open arms. She had a few affairs and got involved in all of the activities; in fact, she even took a job with *our* women's center for a while. Eventually she drifted away, and I ran into her one day with a group of new friends who certainly appeared to be straight. She took from us—but because she gave too I don't begrudge her. Yet that woman is undoubtedly now a "hasbian." Lesbian warmth sustained for a while. Women lovers helped her through a few bad nights, then she moved on. (emphasis added)

I take issue with (1) the paradoxical representation of non-lesbian women as both passive (a "lost" woman "drifts" away from "our" women's community) and deceitful and exploitative; (2) the implicit assumption that a woman who has woman lovers and then has a male lover is straight—not bisexual or even lesbian—and never was a lesbian; (3) the implication that the author only gave, and did not receive, energy from the married woman with whom she had an affair, and that lesbians who have relationships, or even sex, with non-lesbian women lack initiative in that moment and are "made use of"; (4) the assumption that women who explore their sexuality with other women without consistently identifying as lesbian were "merely dallying" and never took their relationships with women seriously; (5) the exclusion of non-lesbians or former lesbians from the women's community implicit in the author's references to "our" women's community and "our" women's center, such that "women's community" equals "lesbian community"; (6) the assumption that lesbians and straight people are distinguishable from each other on the basis of appearance; and (7) the assumption that only lesbians can be political allies of other lesbians, and that they inevitably will be each other's allies, as when Schwartz says later, "Our fragile communities and networks exist under constant siege. We want to know who will stand up with us and be counted, who will be at our sides for the duration...."

Many of the same assumptions and stereotypes surface in a group of letters that appeared in the September-October 1986 issue of *Lesbian Connection* in response to a previous letter about former lesbians. (I didn't see the first letter—only the responses.) The pre-suppositions underpin several models of sexuality that have formed the basis of discussions of bisexuality. One such model could be called, for lack of a better term, the "no autonomous bisexual iden-tity" model or the dichotomous "only two choices" model. (This has also been called "monosexualism"—the assumption that people de-sire only women or only men, but not both.) The following quotes, one from Schwartz's article and the other from one of the letters in *Lesbian Connection*, exemplify this model of sexuality.

Regarding her ex-lover's choices, Schwartz has this to say:

> The loss that accompanies coming out is truly so vast and so deep that I for one could never fault anyone for ultimately failing to go down that road of differentness all the way. Yet what I know in my heart is that to fail to be who we truly are represents a greater loss....I feel sorry for my ex...because she will never be able to fully express her own nature. For her, too much fear gets in the way.

A reader of *Lesbian Connection* from Pineville, Louisiana, articulates the model this way:

> In response to "*EX-LESBIANS?*": I am a True Lesbian....This means I have no fantasies about having sex with men and I am faithful in relationships with women. There seems to be a plague hitting a lot of long-time Lesbians and turning them straight.

A former lesbian or ex-lesbian, then, is a woman who has been hit by a "plague" and "will never be able to fully express her own na-ture." I want to point out the appropriation of experience that's tak-ing place here. Both Schwartz and the lesbian from Louisiana have assigned an identity to former lesbians that we former lesbians have not necessarily chosen for ourselves, and they have perpetuated a sexual dichotomy which makes no room for those of us whose expe-rience cannot be fitted into the two available identities. Schwartz claims lesbianism as the only "road of differentness," categorizing all non-lesbians as "the same," not different, neither challenged by nor a challenge to the heterosexist status quo. I, for one, would call myself neither "hasbian" nor straight. I've already stated my objections to the former; as for the latter, "straight" and "heterosexual" simply do not speak to how I experience desire currently or how I've experienced it throughout my life. Even more important for me is the political effect of these labels that others so readily attach to me and women like me.

One of the political effects of the "monosexual" model has been the definition of lesbianism as the only alternative, antipatriarchal sexuality. This definition ignores the commitment of some bisexual and heterosexual women to challenging the institution of heterosexuality; it also keeps lesbians from recognizing potential political allies. Recall Schwartz's comment that the so-called "hasbian phenomenon" is disturbing to lesbians because lesbians need to know "who will be at our sides for the duration." This conflation of sexual practice and politics seems neither self-evident nor politically expedient. I'll illustrate this point with my own experience.

When I came out as a lesbian, I learned from other lesbians that bisexuality was a "cop-out": it was a label used by women who were really lesbians (that is women who were sleeping with other women) but wanted to maintain "heterosexual privilege" or by women who liked to "experiment" with lesbians but were really straight and, "when push came to shove" (whatever *that* meant), would run back to men and leave their lesbian sisters in the lurch. We said these things, and believed them, and even taught them to our friends and students, even though none of us knew any (out) bisexual women very well. The few who had the courage to claim a bisexual identity in our presence were squelched with charges of treason, because we believed that only lesbians had an antipatriarchal sexuality, which meant that only lesbians were working against sexism; we conflated sexual practice and political action and believed that what one did in bed, and with whom, had direct consequences for supporting or dismantling a patriarchal power structure.

This meant that only lesbians could be trusted, with the exception of a few straight women who learned not to talk about their own sexuality in our presence and whom we claimed as "honorary lesbians," all the while maintaining that they would soon see the light and acknowledge their lesbianism. We were fueled in our convictions, of course, by some bisexual women who subscribed to an earlier countercultural discourse on bisexuality, which we, as feminists, mistrusted. That discourse maintains that we are all bisexual, that all sexual identities other than bisexuality are equally restrictive and that it is possible and necessary to transcend gender. I found that line on bisexuality problematic then and I still do, because I don't believe that gender can be transcended in our current society; because it matters very much to me whether my lover is a man or a woman, even if I don't make gender my primary criterion when choosing to become lovers with someone; and because it matters very much to me that lesbianism and male homosexuality are protected, celebrated, cultivated and promulgated as viable, complicated and rewarding identities.

It also matters very much to me that bisexuality is similarly nurtured as a possible identity, which for me means working against both the discourse that seeks to invalidate bisexuality as being unauthentic and politically incorrect and the humanist discourse that makes bisexuality politically innocuous by claiming that we are all bisexual and that gender can and should be transcended. This resistance is important to me because when, much to my surprise (as someone who had believed I would never again sleep with a man) and against my better judgment (as someone who believed that men were bad for women), I fell in love with a man, and I decided to follow my heart and my desire for this man, I had no way to understand my actions except through the lenses of these discourses. In fact, the humanist discourse never seemed like an option to me, lacking as it is in any very complicated analysis of gender and sexism; so I was left with the discourse that defined bisexuals as colluders with patriarchy, women who get "the best of both worlds" without having to "pay the price," women who were a threat to lesbians.

So I didn't call myself bisexual—not until I had been with the man I'd fallen in love with for three and a half years. For a year or so, I continued to identify as a lesbian, which was possible because my lover lived in another town. I identified as a lesbian partly for political reasons (I had learned that lesbianism was the only effective challenge to the institution of heterosexuality); partly for self-preservation (I was terrified of being cast out by the community that had been so very important to me); and partly because I assumed that this relationship was an anomaly, and that except for this particular man I would only have women lovers. After about a year, though, it became untenable for me to keep identifying publicly as a lesbian. For one thing, I began to sense that this man might not be the sole exception in my lesbian life. Still, I could have continued calling myself a lesbian, but I began to be afraid: I had a new job and was working with a lot of straight people who, for a number of reasons (not the least of which was probably my outspoken feminism and the reputation I had acquired as an out lesbian), assumed I was a lesbian. I was worried that if I referred to myself in conversation as a lesbian they would consider that an invitation to ask me about my sexuality, at which point I would either have to tell them—what? that I was a dupe of the patriarchy? I still didn't know how to explain my situation—or I would have to construct a whole web of lies and risk having them find out that I was really seeing a man and therefore assume that lesbians really did, deep in their hearts, want male lovers.

I was also afraid that if I told the lesbians I was meeting that I was a lesbian, they, too, would find out that I had a male lover and would feel deceived. So I stopped calling myself a lesbian in public, and I began to think that what my friends and I had said about non-lesbians— that they were never political allies of lesbians—was true. It didn't occur to me that as a bisexual I could still be taken seriously as an ally of lesbians or as someone challenging the institution of heterosexuality, and through my silence I—like many other bisexual women—perpetuated the dichotomous "only two choices" model.

My political position vis-a-vis lesbians wasn't my only worry, though. At the time, I was also susceptible to another model of sexuality that was popular among my lesbian friends and which I myself had subscribed to—that is, the "false consciousness" model, as in, "lesbianism is the true sexuality, and non-lesbians simply don't know what's good for them." Our True Lesbian from the letter quoted from *Lesbian Connection*, who fears a plague has hit her lesbian friends, articulates the false consciousness model this way:

> This has happened to a lot of my Lesbian friends recently and has thrown me into a state of shock. These women must be very insecure with themselves and their lifestyle.... Obviously these women who go straight are confused about their sexuality and who they are....When it is your friend who turns straight, then you, too, will feel anger, betrayal, and a wall between you. *She is doing wrong to herself and her lover if she pursues her desire.* (emphasis added)

Well, that's what I thought. For a long time I was dubious about making love with this man with whom I'd fallen in love, and when I finally decided I wanted to, I thought that meant I wanted something that was bad for me and that I couldn't take care of myself. This doubt was coupled with my susceptibility at the time to another model of sexuality, the "sex-as-politics-not-desire" model, which butch-femme and s/m (sadomasochism) defenders have since denounced as a puritanical, anti-sex orientation. This model reduces sexuality to a political tool, positing that sexual practice must be governed by political program and that the only sexual challenge to male power is a practice of disengagement: that is, lesbianism. This argument is implicit in the following quotation from another *Lesbian Connection* reader, Linda Strega from Oakland, California:

> During the past few years, I have become alarmed at how many Lesbians who were once radical have weakened their Lesbian politics and taken on heterosexual values. One of the most upsetting trends is that of *FORMER "LESBIANS"* fucking with men...

Strega sees sex as a direct expression of politics, and lesbian sex as the *only* expression of radical politics; desire can and should be subordinated to a narrowly defined, politically correct version of sex.

Strega and other participants in the *Lesbian Connection* exchange on "ex-lesbians" are not the only ones who hold this view. In the spring of 1990, the lesbian, bisexual and gay community of Northampton, Massachusetts was embroiled in a controversy that centered on the successful efforts of some lesbians to remove "Bisexual" from the title of the local Lesbian, Bisexual and Gay Pride March and to remove bisexuals from the march steering committee. Out-bisexuals had been active on the steering committee for at least five years, and march coordinators had voted the previous year to include the word "bisexual" in the event's title. This change was opposed by a number of lesbians, some of whom had not previously worked on the march but in 1990 attended a steering committee meeting with the goal of getting the word "bisexual" removed from the title of the event. A vote at that meeting came out in favor of removing "bisexual" from the title. Several members of the committee, however, said that they hadn't realized the vote was binding, and it was decided that there would be another, binding vote on the issue at a steering committee meeting one month later. According to a letter to *Gay Community News* from Micki Seigel, a bisexual woman who had been active on the

steering committee,[4] the women who had come with the goal of removing "bisexual" from the title said they would be back the next
month with as many women as they needed to accomplish their goal.
At the next meeting, they brought forty women, and the binding vote
came out in favor of removing "bisexual" from the march's title. Having accomplished that, the group then decided that the steering committee should include only lesbians and gay men, and not bisexuals.

The lesbians who worked to return to the title "Lesbian/Gay Pride
March" and to remove bisexuals from the steering committee claimed
that the appearance of "bisexual" in the event's title made lesbians invisible. In a letter published in the March 11 issue of *Gay Community
News*, Sarah Dreher and Lis Brook of Amherst, Massachusetts, two of
the lesbians who opposed including "bisexual" in the title of the event,
argued that lesbian and gay issues are not identical to bisexual issues
because bisexuals continue to enjoy heterosexual privilege. Referring
to Micki Seigel throughout their letter as "Mrs. Seigel," they concluded
by saying:

> For reasons we cannot comprehend, some bisexual women seem
> to feel they cannot create their own community, but must attach
> themselves to the lesbian community. For many of us, our lesbi-
> anism is a way of life, not just something we do in bed. If Mrs.
> Seigel and her ilk are so concerned with having their sexual minor-
> ity status respected, why don't they march in the Lesbian/Gay
> Pride March as supporters, under their own banner? [5]

Dreher and Brook, like Strega, subordinate sex to politics and see lesbianism (and male homosexuality) as the only potentially politically
progressive sexuality. For them, bisexuality is just something bisexuals do in bed.

This is a view of sex and politics in which I deeply believed at the
time that I fell in love with a man, and it contributed to my fear that I
didn't know how to take care of myself, that I didn't know what was
good for me. I had found this view quite compelling, not the least because, as a prescriptive formula, it promised liberation for those who
followed it. Yet when I found myself in the situation of having been a
lesbian and now having a male lover, my belief in this view of sex and
politics caused me a good deal of grief. According to these models of
sexuality, not only was I betraying lesbians and upholding the patriar-

chy, I was also engaging in deluded, self-destructive behavior. Coming out as a lesbian had been such a healthy, progressive move for me, and I was filled with terror and self-loathing as long as I believed in the identity this discourse constructed for me as a non-lesbian. For quite some time, it didn't occur to me to question, as Carole Vance does in her introduction to *Pleasure and Danger: Exploring Female Sexuality*[6], whether we knew enough about desire and sexuality to be making and following such rigid prescriptions.

Eventually, though, I did begin to question these models of sexuality that I had held to be true. This process of questioning, and reconstructing, my identity, was a long and extremely painful one. As I mention above, I continued to call myself a lesbian for about a year, and it was another two and a half years before I "came out" as bisexual. So, for several years, I was very much in the closet. Those who have been in the closet know what a toll it takes, especially those who came out to themselves long before they knew there were any others like them. I didn't know any other formerly-lesbian bisexuals for a long time. After a couple of years, I met one. There were no books about my experience at the women's bookstore, no cultural events that drew women like me—or so I thought. The isolation was horrible, as was the doubt. I had been absolutely sure of my sexuality and my politics and my community; and because they were all intertwined, they all unraveled for me at the same time. I felt I could no longer trust my mind, and for a while, I lost much of my capacity for critical thinking. I simply didn't know how I felt about any but the most basic feminist issues, and I was resistant to most attempts to engage me in conversation about them. What this meant, among other things, was that during this time I was not outspoken on issues of homophobia and heterosexism. It took several years of my telling myself the story of myself over and over again, working it and reworking it, before I began to trust myself again and to regain my capacity for critical thought. And it wasn't until I trusted myself enough to begin to come out as bisexual that I was able to be as outspoken in support of lesbians and gay men, and against heterosexism and homophobia, as I had been when I was a lesbian.

The moral of the story, as they say, is that discourses which silence bisexuals and define us as enemies of lesbians help to keep us in the closet, away from lesbian community and outside of mutually supportive alliances, so that both bisexuals and lesbians lose out. Our struggles are different, but not so very different; we need to find ways of articulating our differences so that we can work together effectively. And we all benefit when we find ways of being good friends and lovers for each other as well.

I am very fortunate now to have several lesbian and bisexual friends who believe this with me, and who continue to support my struggle to define myself and my experience against the grain of the existing discourses. I've been isolated and afraid, but I have not been totally without allies and intimates, many of them lesbians who recognize our struggles as mutual and entwined and who value me for the things that make me different from them as well as the things we share in common. My hope is that my words here, and those of other bisexuals, will help to make gay and lesbian communities safer for bisexuals, and stronger from our presence and contributions.

Endnotes

This essay was originally a talk titled "Breaking Silence About the 'B-Word': Bisexual Identity and Politics" and was presented at the Perspectives in Lesbian and Gay Studies Conference at Brown University on September 23, 1989. Special thanks to Lisa Moore for encouraging me to write this paper in the first place, Elizabeth Reba Weise for her editorial suggestions, and to Paisley Currah for her love, support and critical engagement with my work.

1. I also value (though in different ways) some of the insights of radical lesbian-feminist separatism, even as I critique it. This strand of feminist thought and feminist politics crystallized certain aspects of women's oppression and offered new ways of living for many women at a crucial moment in the history of the women's movement. It was also responsible for foregrounding issues of sexuality in the emerging "second wave" of feminist politics. No doubt these contributions of lesbian-feminist separatism account for its continued popularity in some sectors of the women's movement.

2. This situation has changed somewhat since I first gave this paper at the Brown University conference, and there is now more writing about bisexuals *by* bisexuals available. For example, Jan Clausen, a former lesbian who currently resists definition, published an article entitled "My Interesting Condition" in the Winter 1990 issue of *Out/Look.* In the spring of 1990, a debate emerged in the pages of *Gay Community News* over the exclusion of bisexuals from the title and steering committee of the Northampton, Massachusetts, Lesbian and Gay Pride March—a debate conducted largely among bisexuals, and which I discuss at length in another paper, given at the National Women's Studies Association Conference at the University of Akron in June

1990 and at the 4th Annual Lesbian, Bisexual and Gay Studies Conference at Harvard in October 1990, titled "Expanding the Bounds of Community: Bisexual Identity and Politics." Greta Christina, a bisexual woman published her article, "Drawing the Line: Bisexual Women in the Lesbian Community" in the May-June 1990 issue of *On Our Backs.* And in the summer and fall of 1990, two bisexual anthologies were published: *Bisexuality: A Reader and Sourcebook,* edited by Thomas Geller, and *Bi Any Other Name: Bisexuals Speak Out,* edited by Loraine Hutchins and Lani Kaahumanu.

3.   Again, this situation is changing, though many bisexual women remain closeted in lesbian company, working politically alongside lesbians but not as out bisexuals. This situation fuels the incorrect assumption that bisexuals are not politically active against homophobia.

4.   Micki Seigel, "Bisexual Invisibility," *Gay Community News*, February 18-24, 1990.

5.   Sarah Dreher and Lis Brook, "Visibility? Whose Visibility?" *Gay Community News,* March 11-17, 1990.

6.   Carole S. Vance, ed., *Pleasure and Danger: Exploring Female Sexuality* (Boston: Routledge, 1984), pp. 1-27.

PRINCIPLES AND PRACTICE

Rebecca Ripley

THE LANGUAGE OF DESIRE:
SEXUALITY, IDENTITY AND LANGUAGE

This paper was originally addressed to women who call themselves "lesbians." There is probably a moral in the fact that it's in a book about women who call themselves "bisexual."

I don't know anyone who talks about "sexual preference" in daily life, which is just as well. It's too weak a phrase to describe dykehood. It conjures up images of "soup or salad?" not of passion—and not of anything worth fighting for. However, I read an interview with a "lesbian" who likes "sleeping with men," and who gives the comparison that she usually prefers chocolate, but once in a while she orders cheesecake. Perhaps for her, sex with women really is no more than a preference.

A self-named lesbian, when she's fighting with her lover, has sex with men because "that isn't cheating." A self-named bisexual has been faithful to one woman for twenty years. A woman who does s/m with women says she is sexually a "pervert"; only incidentally a lesbian. Another says that having sex with women is so "perverse" that s/m is only incidental.

Obviously, more than one kind of sexuality exists among those who share the label "lesbian." At the very least there are two: what I will here call dyke sexuality, which is about women, and bisexuality, which is about both sexes. If these two groups of "lesbians" have anything in common, it's an emotional orientation—falling in love with women—not a sexual orientation.

For a dyke—be she butch, femme, both or neither—men don't have what counts. Sex with women isn't preference; it's sex—the only kind. That describes me as accurately as "chocolate or cheesecake" describes the woman in the interview. Her identity as a lesbian may be based on emotional, cultural and/or political orientation. Mine is based on all the rest plus sexual desire. Each of us bases her practical definition of "lesbian" on herself. This, on a wider scale, leads to a lot of problems.

Neither of us could change to fit the other's definition even if she wanted to. If sexuality and identity could be changed by effort of will, psychiatry would have "cured" our gay and bi forerunners, no one would have started the gay liberation movement and we (as a community) wouldn't be here now. If feelings could be changed at will, straight women could become lesbians out of political conviction. That was tried in the 1970s. It flopped, as will be discussed later in this essay.

Neither of us can change her sexuality, but both are capable of loving a woman, and both have the same social identity: we are part of the lesbian community. To much of the straight world we are the same—both perverts. But there is a difference. A lot of dykes feel betrayed by bis, and a lot of bis feel excluded by dykes. Too many sexualities, too many definitions are competing for the only available word.

The adjective "lesbian" means female sexual desire that is about women. The noun "lesbian" has no single meaning. A quick survey of what self-named lesbians mean by "lesbian" shows what a vague word it is. Definitions include: any woman who calls herself one; a woman who wants or fantasizes about sex with women; a woman who forcefully suppresses sexual fantasies about women; a woman who has women lovers; a woman who had only women lovers; a woman who currently has only women lovers, regardless of what she calls herself; a castrated man who has women lovers.

The categories get blurred in daily life. How about women who go with men but only for money? How about a woman who goes with women in prison and with men on the outside? Or a woman who was straight for forty years and then switched? Or a woman who went with women as a teenager and then got married? One who pays lots of attention to women and little to men? One too freaked out to have any sexuality but who wants to be with women? One who has given up on men because they don't contribute and makes a nonsexual life with her women friends? One who likes men only if they are planning to have a transsexual operation? One who has sex with women and fantasizes hot sex with both sexes but can't find a real man with whom it works out? One who obsesses sexually about both sexes without successfully relating to either? How important is love, rather than sex, in determining who we call a lesbian?   We don't all have the same answers, and straight society has none at all.

English does not provide any word for "woman whose sexual desire is for women only." "Dyke" comes close, but it also means "crossdresser" and "stone butch." English certainly provides no word for a political orientation based on total, including sexual, dedication to women. When a noun is needed, "lesbian" is available.

"Bisexual" means at least as many different things as "lesbian." It can mean having a primary lover of one sex and occasional flings with the other; or falling in love with people of both sexes, serially or at once; or monogamy in practice but feelings that swing both ways; or anything in between. Someone who falls in love only with women but enjoys sex with men too is bi only in the sexual sense. This is hugely different from being bi-emotional. It makes sense that bisexual women who fall in love with women only would want their own particular name. Again, English provides "lesbian."

It makes sense also that women who fall in love with both sexes would want acceptance in some community: a social identity. Even the most liberal heterosexuals seldom accept and support lesbian relationships as much as they do heterosexual relationships. This matter of social acceptance helps make bisexual identity distinct from heterosexual identity.   It leaves bi women feeling that they belong to a non-het community, be it called "gay," "queer" or "lesbian."

In much of the world, as will be discussed, behavior that we would call "bisexual" is not "queer" but normal. In societies where marriage is a stronger economic and social institution, the abnormal thing is not deviant sex but failing to marry. The gay struggle is less about freedom to fuck than about freedom from marriage. This is even more true for women than for men.

The words that people create, and the meanings that they give to adopted words, depend on the realities they're trying to name. Any reading of the international gay press (such as *BLK, Paz y Liberacion, Shamakami-Forum for South Asian Lesbians and Bisexuals,* or *ILIS, the International Lesbian Information Service newsletter*) reveals that the words "lesbian," "gay" and "bisexual" are used and useful around the world, but not always with the same meanings. In our English-speaking culture, some bisexual women claim the social identity "lesbian" because their bisexuality makes them not normal. (I can just about say that in plain, though not graceful, English.) English doesn't properly describe any reality in which people tolerate bisexual behavior but make a gay or lesbian social identity impossible. There are many such "bi-normal" societies, including ones that have little else in common.

For many bi-normal Native American peoples, there was no "gay" or "lesbian" social role. The closest equivalent was the transgendered person: one who, in a society with exactly two sex roles, adopted the dress and social behaviors of the other sex. The hwame or berdache was abnormal but not despised; transgender people were often shamans, healers or witches. Of course transgender people had sex with their own sex, but this didn't determine their social identity. Their lovers, while equally "homosexual," were "normal" people.[1]

In a marriage-based society, "normal" social identity can include lesbian sexual behavior because it's a safe way for girls to keep their virginity or for married women to have fun with no risk of babies unrelated to their legal fathers. An Arabian proverb says: "When a woman lies with a woman, it brings no swelling to her belly and no shame to her father." Young West African women consider it normal to have sex with their girlfriends, as do Chinese boarding-school girls in Taiwan and Hong Kong. The only abnormal thing would be failing to marry.

The same linguistic categories apply to men in bi-normal societies For example, a gay American man in pre-revolutionary Iran had his heart broken by a lover who couldn't imagine living with him; loving a man was "normal," and so was getting heterosexually married. The Iranian man had no need for a word meaning "bisexual." Even where bisexual behavior isn't "normal," the need to conform and marry may make it normal for gay people. A Jewish woman returning to America from a long stay in Jerusalem, where "all the gay people are married," couldn't understand the word "bisexual" at first, even in English.

It's also true for Americans: our cultural limits help create our definitions. For many Americans, especially women, having a forbidden kind of sex means crossing a major border of identity: going from "normal" to "lesbian" or "bisexual." We can speak of "gay liberation" as freedom to have sex with our own sex—a major act of rebellion when many powerful religious sects forbid it. In other parts of the world, the same words may not mean freedom to have gay sex but freedom to live openly gay lives.

This is especially true for women: a married man may be free to ignore his wife in favor of other men, but a woman can't live an openly gay life while working full time as an unpaid wife and mother. "Marriage" means as many things as "lesbian" and "bisexual" do. Without birth control, divorce and well-paid jobs for women, it becomes an unavoidable trap. Lesbian news from India includes many reports of double suicides—those who wouldn't abandon each other under family pressure to marry and saw no choice but death.[2] Two Indian policewomen who married each other for the "nonpolitical" reason that they were in love show what a difference jobs can make in creating a lesbian social identity.[3] Where there is a lesbian social identity, it has to do with living outside of marriage, regardless of sexual behavior. Cantonese silk-workers of the early twentieth century lived in all-female communities and called themselves "marriage resisters." Marriage resisters who formed lifelong partnerships with other women, sometimes close relatives, may or may not have done anything sexual together. Women who "owed" their families one male child sometimes married, had the child, turned it over to the father and returned to their female companions. Some couples killed themselves rather than endure even temporary marriages to men. Were the ones who married "bisexual," or were they dutiful, or merely interested in staying alive?[4]

America has its own, not at all obvious, version of the bisexual norm. To most Americans, homosexuality is a "sin," a "disease" or a "preference." "Sin" and "preference" imply chosen behavior. Those who treat homosexuality as a disease try to create "cures," which means that even though it is a "disease" it is supposed to be changeable. The idea that anybody is essentially, basically, really gay doesn't go down easily with straight Americans. They'd rather think that everybody is bi and therefore "partially straight."

There are arguments for "sexual preference" politics. It's better to represent a choice than a disease. Diseases go with legally required "cures" and quarantines—not to mention "mercy-killings." But the idea of chooseable or changeable sexuality is not useful among women who call themselves lesbians. It only leads to unnecessary distrust and arbitrary demands for change. The lesbian community includes and has always included more than one kind of sexuality. Instead of accepting this, various groups of women insist theirs is the "real" lesbian sexuality and everyone else who calls herself a lesbian is either lying about what she likes or using the name without any right to it. There's always an implication that "she could change if she wanted to"—admit those "repressed desires" or develop spiritually or politically and become a "real lesbian."

This fits with a long tradition of how straight men think about women's sexuality—not in terms of what women want and like (desire) but in terms of what women can be convinced of or forced to do (behavior). Women's sexual behavior always has a political meaning— a meaning in terms of power. Dyke sexual behavior means rebellion against forced heterosexuality. Straight sexual behavior means fitting in with it (although various straight sexual behaviors can be forbidden for other reasons). Bisexual behavior (in our society) means changing sides.

Women in many societies have little recognized authority over anything except their daughters' sexual behavior. Women in many societies have no way to gain respect except through monogamy and bearing sons (that is, via sex). Women's sexual behavior seems to have everything to do with power and nothing to do with desire.

English has plenty of words for virgin, whore, tease and so forth, but no real language of female sexual desire. The language describes what women do and become when they have little if any choice, but not (except accidentally) what women want. It describes how women's sexual behavior affects men, but not (except accidentally) how it feels to women. (Most of the few pre-modern American exceptions are in blues songs written by black women. This could reflect either the resilience of black culture or the stereotypes imposed by white racism, or both.)

English doesn't even have a word for cunt/vulva or masturbating/jacking-off that isn't either clinical or dripping with centuries of male definition. In Isadora Allman's poll of *San Francisco Bay Guardian* readers, "yoni" won as the most positive word for female genitalia - probably because, as an import from another culture and continent, it hasn't had time to become an insult in English.

In most of the world, women's sexual and social identity exists against the background of unavoidable and unequal marriage. In the modern English-speaking world, a lot of people live outside marriage. Economics and pregnancy still trap some women into marriage, but many marry (or hope to marry) for companionship and sexual satisfaction rather than solely for economic security. We can explore what we like and at least imagine refusing what we don't like. We are relatively free. We can discover and try to define our sexuality in terms of what and whom we like. But we have a damned hard time talking about it. The language isn't there, so we fall back on the language of behavior—the language of what women do when they have little if any choice.

We can claim or refuse the label of virgin, whore, tease, but we can only begin to talk about how our sexual desire feels to us. To talk rather than fight about sexuality means being able to talk respectfully about desire, not angrily about behavior. It also means listening respectfully to what other women desire.

In the past ten years or so, some English-speaking women have begun to develop a language of desire—and stirred up a lot of anger as to which desires it's okay to talk about. There are frenzied accusations that almost any writing about sex isn't lesbian enough, but no one can help develop a better language except by keeping up the attempt. On the other side, there are unsubtle innuendos that the accusers just need a good fuck to shut them up. When we talk about sex, we end up playing the boys' game, virgins against whores—girls who do against girls who don't. Behavior, not desire. Those who contribute most to changing the terms we talk in are those who write/draw/photograph/talk about what they like—to do or imagine. Even the clumsiest language can't be worse than what we have now! [5]

A person's sexuality is defined by what (and who) she wants. Most women have few chances to do what they want and aren't always confident enough to try when they have a chance, which makes it hard to talk about "female sexuality." There isn't enough data to define it. But it is possible to speak of an individual's sexuality. This means what she wants, not what she thinks she should want or even what she does. Many women are bisexual only in their thoughts and feelings. Some dykes (most, in much of the world) end up in arranged heterosexual marriages. Some dykes in this society fuck men in an attempt to "prove" they're "normal" or to get back at an ex-lover or simply out of curiosity, but without desire. With heterosexuality enforced in one way or another all over the world, dyke sexuality can be well camouflaged.

Where exclusive heterosexuality is enforced for women, bisexuality will also be camouflaged. This is a matter of self-preservation. At least one bisexual woman in northern California has served time in a civilian prison, and others have been in military prisons or dishonorably discharged, because their affairs with women were discovered. Laws against lesbian sexual behavior don't discriminate on the basis of sexual identity. Neither do husbands who greet the news of any "unfaithfulness" with violence.

For the past few years, bisexual women in the lesbian community have denied or lied about their feelings for men out of a desire to fit in, or because of confused political ideas. Around 1970, some American women started believing, and some still believe, that a sincere understanding of sexism makes it impossible to have sexual feelings for men—period. This is a minority idea, partly because there's so little evidence for it, but a confused version of it is still around: that is, that bisexual women are bisexual only because they're too cowardly to live as dykes.

"Peer pressure," which enforced the idea that lesbian behavior is proof of feminist commitment, was and is pitifully weak compared to entrenched required heterosexuality. Thus the whole business was born and will likely die within a couple of decades, while laws, prisons and death sentences enforce heterosexuality around the world. Nevertheless, some women are so afraid of peer pressure that they lie to their women lovers about ongoing relationships with men lovers—for years at a time.

This late-blooming "political lesbian" conflict serves to mask earlier history. Before the gay liberation movement, in the 1940s, 1950s and 1960s, "homosexuality" was a "mental illness," a "disorder" in someone who "should" have grown from a bisexual potential into a heterosexual maturity. Gay women (and men) called themselves bisexual to get out of calling themselves gay, that is, "incurable." This of course made real bisexuality invisible.

To dykes who didn't want to be "cured," bisexual women must have blended in with the crowd of fakes. Some regarded all bisexual-acting women as lacking character. Some used labels like "ac/dc" without praise or blame, as simple descriptions. Others thought of gays as a third sex and bis as a fourth. Women who left a woman for a man got labeled as backstabbers. However, some married women loved both their husbands and other women and were an accepted part of gay society. The attitudes differed from town to town, from clique to clique.[6]

Plenty of women, dykes and bis who found it too hard being true to themselves under constant attack, gave up and got married, leaving women for men. Married women dumped female lovers rather than let their husbands find out. Losing a woman to a man hurts more than losing her to a woman because he has an unfair advantage—more earning power, more legal respect, and so on. In much of the world, a man can get rid of a female rival merely by calling her a "lesbian," a "feminist" or an "unnatural woman," thus assuring that she ends up in prison or out on the street.[7] Even in more liberal circumstances, where lesbian relationships aren't illegal, lots of external factors affect choices between a woman and a man. It adds insult to injury when one woman rejects another even partly because "my family doesn't like her" or "I want to have children." Rejecting a woman under such circumstances often means rejecting all women—and the life of hiding and danger that usually goes with choosing women. The rejected woman (dyke or bi) knows she was rejected not just as an individual, but at least partly for being a woman. It makes the sexual rejection one more result of sexism, one more loss in a rigged game.

How deeply a particular woman could love; how long she could stay with one person; who actually broke off a given relationship; whether the woman who "went straight" was really bi or just scared and tired—the individual differences got lost in the retelling. The perceived moral remains: "A woman who can leave you for a man probably will."

There is some truth in that moral. It takes courage to live under attack, and not everybody is equally brave. But the truth isn't about bisexuality. It's about sexism. Like any system of oppression, sexism favors those who give in and kills a good proportion of those who rebel. In American-style sexism, women who look or act "like lesbians" count as rebels. The appearance of heterosexuality—even to the point of getting married—has always helped lesbians stay out of psychiatric institutions and prisons. Not every woman is heroic enough to live without camouflage.

Gay liberation and lesbian feminism gave opportunities to many bisexual women who would otherwise have lived totally heterosexual lives. They also rescued many dykes from a life of asexuality or trying desperately to fake heterosexuality. However some truly heterosexual women made a valiant but futile attempt to change. These are the straight women referred to previously, who tried to become lesbians out of political conviction and couldn't. Some of them left trails of broken hearts and stories with the moral that "women who swing both ways can't be trusted." The atmosphere of relative freedom allowed women to discover both their possibilities and their limits. The limits were and are as real as the possibilities. Trying the limits for political reasons increased bitterness and distrust.

Especially to those who found a lesbian community only after years of terror and loneliness, solidarity is important. For bis who call themselves lesbians, solidarity means keeping the label and staying in the community, even if it means living out the "lying bisexual" stereotype. For dykes, solidarity means not trusting anyone who won't stick around. As long as queer women remain a segregated and oppressed community, this isn't likely to change.

Nevertheless, individuals can trust each other as friends, co-workers, political allies—if they're willing to know and accept each other's sexuality rather than try to change or eliminate each other. The only thing we can change is how we think about each other, and thus how we treat each other.

One possible way around the dyke/bi problem is to have a queer political identity. A queer community that includes anyone with non-standard sexuality is inevitable when heterosexual society excludes so many different people. How the queer movement fares politically— how long it lasts and stays unified, what it achieves—remains to be seen. Whether groups like ACT UP (AIDS Coalition to Unleash Power) and Queer Nation can avoid being dominated by articulate young white men also remains to be seen.

The queer movement doesn't appeal to everybody. Its focus on fighting invisibility doesn't amount to an analysis of society, nor does it involve a clear program for change. It can support feminist programs, which are necessary for any women to be sexually independent, but it can't be a movement by and for women. As a movement largely of politically active young people, it doesn't include most older or less politically conscious women who call themselves "lesbians." Queer visibility alone can't dismantle the social structures that created the dyke/bi division.

But though the queer movement won't solve the dyke/bi problem, its chosen name gives some help. The real-life, day-to-day definitions of "queer" and "lesbian" are very similar. "Lesbians," as much as "queers," are a hodgepodge: non-straight women, all forced to the fringe of a straight man's society. We don't have the leisure to sort out either people or labels.

Unlike "queer," "lesbian" also has many more specific meanings. If we asked each women what she means when she calls herself a "lesbian," it would save a lot of heartache—at least if each of us could stand the other's answers. Someday there may be a way to say, quickly and easily, "I only make it with girls but I get the hots for guys," or "I make it with one person at a time, either sex," or "I don't fuck, but I love women," or "I love women but also fuck men," or "I love women and only make love with women," or "I've only loved one person and she's a woman." Some women use labels like "bi-dyke" and "bi-het" to say more about themselves than "bisexual" could. Some use Kinsey numbers. These creative tactics are a start toward needed clarity. Someday women who use the name "lesbian" may face the fact that the lesbian community has always included all of the above. Meanwhile we can only ask.

Those who question whether "bisexuals" should be part of the "gay" or "lesbian" community can't hope for a meaningful answer because the terms are so vague. Bisexual women are and always have been part of the lesbian community. The community of the early 1970s which broke out of invisibility, consisted of dykes, bis, confused straights, coming-out dykes who thought they were bi, and a few hermaphrodites and would-be men. Since then, various groups have had the freedom to begin to define themselves better, but none of the groups have gone away. Different groups need to give each other more space—and share public space. Rather than try to define each other out of existence, we need to accept that we aren't all the same. That won't make any revolutions, but it would save some of the energy we now waste fighting within the community that the straight world will, in any case, call "lesbian."

Endnotes

1. For information on transgender people in various Native American societies, see Will Roscoe, ed., *Living the Spirit: A Gay American Indian Anthology* (New York, St. Martin's Press, 1989).

2. "Bury Us Together," *Connexions* 3 (issue on global lesbianism) Winter 1982. Can be ordered from Peoples Translation Service, 4228 Telegraph Ave., Oakland CA 94609.

3. "The Marriage of Lila and Urmila," *India Currents* 2, No. 3 (1988). PO Box 2965 Santa Clara CA 95055.

4. For information on marriage resisters, see Agnes Smedley, *Portraits of Chinese Women in Revolution* (Old Westbury, NY: The Feminist Press 1976); Judy Grahn, *Another Mother Tongue* (Boston: Beacon Press, 1984).

5. The "sex wars" have been going on since about 1980 in the pages of many publications. Some useful books are the "pro-sex" anthology *Pleasure and Danger* edited by Carole S. Vance (Boston: Routledge and Kegan Paul, 1984), the "anti-sex" anthology *Against Sadomasochism*, edited by Robin Ruth Linden et. al. (Palo Alto, CA: Frog in the Well Press, 1982); and the "neutral" *Anti-Climax*, by Sheila Jeffreys (New York: New York University Press, 1991).

6. For one relevant discussion, see Lillian Faderman, *Odd Girls and Twilight Lovers* (New York: Columbia University Press, 1991). Also, Kay Van Deurs's self-published, out of print autobiography, *The Notebooks that Emma Gave Me* (1978) contains an account of New York lesbians in the 1950s trying desperately to be bisexual.

7. This is true within the U.S. armed forces, where homosexual behavior is illegal; Marine Corporal Barbara Baum was court-martialed and sentenced to imprisonment and dishonorable discharge in 1988, after being accused of "sodomy" by her lover's jealous boyfriend.

Susanna Trnka

"A PRETTY GOOD BISEXUAL KISS THERE..."

Kisses twenty-five cents each, kisses five for a dollar... Sitting between two women on the steps of Sproul Plaza, U.C. Berkeley, watching the bisexual/lesbian/gay kissing booth, some curiosity welling up ... that tall woman, what would it be like kissing that tall woman, really kissing that tall ... applause, cheering as two women's tongues and arms intertwine, testing the strengths of the rickety booth. "Mhmm," says one of the women next to me. More cheering, more applause ... "A pretty good bisexual kiss there," says the other. I look up, startled, to see a man peeling his lips away from the woman in the booth.

A bisexual kiss. Was that a bisexual kiss? Can there be such a thing as a bisexual kiss? Bisexual people, yes, but bisexual kisses? Can there be such a thing as bisexual sex? Bisexual sex—the image the words bring to my mind is crystal clear: two seedy-looking men and two women getting it on, maybe one of them wondering if she should have bothered to learn these other peoples' names before jumping into bed with them. Where that image comes from is clear enough, but why it's still in my head, I don't know. Perhaps because I have nothing to replace it with. If that is not necessarily bisexual sex, than what is?

When I make love with a man, can that be bisexual sex? When I make love with a woman, is that bisexual sex? Or would they have to be in the same bed, at the same time, with me? I don't usually go for the third, it seems too impersonal for my taste, too disrespectful for all those involved. So assuming we each stay in our separate beds, bathtubs and wooded groves, is our sex any different because of who I am, because I identify myself as capable of loving both men and women?

What about my steady relationship with my male lover, housemate and friend. Is it radically different since I came out as a bisexual? Maybe not to the neighbors who nod hello when John and I walk out of our apartment arm in arm, maybe not to the hotel receptionists when we book a room on those frantic, widely spaced forays into vacationing, maybe not to all the people in the restaurants and dance clubs and movie theaters we hang out in together. But beneath the surface, I think my intimate relationship with my male partner is different from the heterosexual couplings we see depicted all around us.

My bisexuality has brought into our relationship a sense of greater space between us. I don't mean this in a negative sense but in a very positive way, as a very positive break from all the illusions of love that have been fed to us. Both of us grew up on television and movie depictions of true love as an all-encompassing experience, especially for women. When I was in high school, I went so far as to believe I could stop studying science because my (male) lover was better at it; one humanities specialist and one science fanatic in a family would make a good balance, I thought. I guess I always thought of the whole in terms of the two united: man and woman, husband and wife, functioning as one. I once heard some preacher on the radio explaining his concept of God creating one male-female being, splitting it in two and putting both of them on earth. Only once they find each other and fall in love (and marry and have two kids and a house in the suburbs) will they be complete. I thought it was amazingly beautiful. I felt incomplete, but after hearing that I thought all I had to do was find my other (male) half and I'd be fixed for life.

I fell in love for the first time when I was fifteen. It wasn't with my other half but with a woman. Laila was an exchange student from the Middle East, and we shared a sense of not fitting into the Virginia suburbs way of life. We talked a lot about Marx and Morrisey and what their ideas meant to us. We covered a lot of questions that we both needed to ask, like "is homosexuality sick, or is it just unnatural?" We got continually stuck in the "are people basically good or bad?" trap. "How can we change the world?" was another popular one. I don't think that together we ever satisfactorily answered any of these questions, but we grew to a better understanding of ourselves and each other. Though we never acted on it, we developed a sense of our sexual feelings toward each other and a trust in our physical and emotional closeness. And we learned how to be honest, both painfully and exhilaratingly honest.

I have a vague memory of trying to come out to my parents. I told them I was thinking about lesbianism, but they retorted that there was no such thing. They said that Laila and I were good friends, and just that: good friends. I dropped the subject, and I haven't mentioned it to them since. But my silence has not been without a price. Although the memory of my relationship with Laila never faded, my understanding of it slowly withered away. I don't know how it happened, but somehow the relationship slipped into simple friendship, into nothing more than passing memories of innocent, unimportant girlhood.

It wasn't until I dramatically came out as bisexual to another high school friend and heard her response—"Yeah I know that, you told me a long time ago that you were in love with Laila"—that I realized that I had actually lost this sense of myself as a woman-loving woman, only to reclaim it four years later. Why? That is a question I still can't fully answer.

Six months into what is today a three-year relationship with my present partner, I finally figured out how all my mysterious sexual feelings fit into my life. I came out as bisexual, to him and to the woman I was in love with at the time. I thought the consequences would be difficult to deal with, but I discovered that the confusion and pain were greater when my feelings raced through me unnamed and unspoken than when I let them out to myself and to those who love me.

A year later I took my first women's studies course at school. Again, I felt like a lot of misunderstood emotions and reactions were finally being pulled together into some kind of meaningful whole. Feminism has taught me how to explain the unexplainable fears and frights that I thought plagued only me. It has led me to question why I am the way I am; it is no longer acceptable to me to assume I am naturally shy; now I wonder where that shyness came from and how it can be changed. It is no longer acceptable to me to mutter, "I like it that way;" instead I explore how my desires and my understanding of what is right for me have been shaped and formed. How many times have I caught myself saying something or thinking something that I know is unfair toward myself as a woman? How many times do I fall comfortably into the pattern society has prescribed for me, only to recognize this with shock?

Feminism has not only taught me to recognize those patterns but has also given me language with which to go beyond them and to discover who I really am. There is something immensely empowering in being able to name and conceptualize feelings and ideas. As feminist scholar Dale Spender notes, it is a big step to go from saying to a man, "I didn't like that," or "you hurt me," to saying, "that was sexual harassment."[1] In my life it has been liberating to go from, "I think this, and this is unfair," to "I believe in feminism," from "I think I might like both of you," to "I am bisexual."

Though I came to them at different times in my life, with different needs and reactions, my feminism and bisexuality are united. Like the tongues of the kissers on Sproul Plaza, they curl around one another into indistinguishable elements of the same kiss, the same bisexual feminist kiss. And united, they have changed the ways I live my life, the ways I relate to both men and women and the way I love.

Our kissing, mine and John's, has not changed. But our ways of relating to one another have shifted since I began to explore my sexuality and feminism in what, for me, is a truly holistic way. The key for us is space. Space is ever present between us; my feminist bisexuality has shaped an explicit understanding that our relationship can never be the be-all, end-all of our existences. There is an understanding between us that much of my life will be devoted to women and women's issues; that my body does not belong to anyone, nor does anyone (other than me) have any kind of right to it; that assumptions cannot be made about whom I will love tomorrow, or whom I will make love with tomorrow.

Nonmonogamous bisexuality adds fluidity. It wipes out fantasies of running away together to some desert island and completely fulfilling each other's dreams and replaces them with an honest trust in one another. Trust not as in, "I will love you forever" or "I will never love anyone but you"—promises that can very easily fall apart—but trust as in, "I will be honest with you," "I will not deny you the right to be, to explore, to change who you are." We live with the possibility that we might be together for the next fifty years, the possibility that this might not exist next month . . . the certainty that this will be something very different a year from now.

It's not that being bisexual automatically makes a person nonmonogamous (one of the stereotypes we constantly have to face), but that bisexuality often brings nonmonogamy up as an issue. The knowledge that there isn't one person out there who is perfect for you, that for some of us there isn't even one type of person (male or female) you're looking for, makes the search for a partner all the more difficult. After all, the possibility that "Mr. Right" may be a woman shows how ludicrous the entire idea of a "Mr. Right" is. If, when you sit down and try to imagine your perfect partner, you can't even say whether that person will be a he or a she—gender being perhaps the fundamental division of people in our society—you aren't going to get very far with your description. And once you've thrown out the illusion of finding a perfect match, your present match becomes a little more tenuous. Again, I'm not trying to say that a bisexual person can't be monogamous, but that perhaps she or he is a little more aware of the fact that no one person can fulfill one's every desire.

Realizing all this isn't easy, and I am not going to pretend that it is. There are times, especially since my lover came home saying he thinks he should rethink this "heterosexuality thing," when I am scared out of my mind. There are times when I want to crawl into a tight, narrow space of promises and true love forever, with signatures on the dotted line. But somehow that image always conjures up scenes of dirty diapers, dinner parties and beatings.

I don't think I can ever again make a man promises of devotion. Maybe a woman, but not a man, because I see promises as a trap of need that I never want to fall into again. There were times, especially when John and I first met, that I wanted to bury myself in our relationship, to embrace the illusion that nothing mattered except the two us us, that nothing existed except the two of us. This relationship became the defining force in my life, and my life became this relationship.

Our summer together ended, I left for college and the rest of the world slowly came back into focus, and along with it my sexual and emotional attraction to other people, particularly women. After a year away at college—a year of exploring lesbianism, feminism and radical politics—the pendulum swung the opposite way, and I wanted nothing more than to pronounce men the Enemy and separatism my liberation. I was torn—do I celebrate my (re)discovery of myself as a woman-loving woman by leaving John, or do I throw myself into my relationship with him and forget about the possibility of ever going out with anybody else? Those choices may seem extreme and simplistic, but in my search for a sense of identity, for an anchorage, it seemed that nothing other than total commitment, one way or the other, could do it.

I still want security in my life; I want the knowledge that I have a home to come to, food on the table and warmth at night, but I don't want to be a "secure" person, a person who doesn't change and grow, or a person who does all her changing on the inside, and is terrified of letting it seep out because it might cause some kind of turmoil. So I find my strength not in an identity that doesn't belong to me, and would only be a straitjacket rather than the liberation it is for others, but in myself and in a community of lesbian, gay, bisexual and a few straight folk who accept me as the feminist bisexual I really am.

The greatest drawback I've encountered so far is time. I still have trouble figuring out how to balance focusing on myself, exploring my connections with other people and developing my relationship with John. I worry about whether I should spend more time with the person I already love or discovering somebody new. And what about the time I need for myself? Perhaps this all stems from watching my mother devote so much of her time and energy to her husband and children, ending up with so little space for herself, let alone for her friends. I worry that I'm following her example and turning a blind eye to the rest of the world, only to focus on what is already close at hand.

But one thing that I don't seem capable of ignoring anymore is my desire and my sexuality. I explore it whenever I have the chance to taste something new. I feel no guilt because I am honest. I have learned to say: this is who I am, and if this relationship isn't for you I understand. I renege, I renege on my promise to love you forever, I take back my promise to be yours. I am finding myself, and you are a part of my exploration, and through honesty and with trust in that honesty our love will be stronger than any movie lines can ever make it.

I am twenty years old. I live and love with a man and I am a "practicing" nonmonogamous feminist bisexual. But these words aren't always enough. In fact, some people find them incongruous. A bisexual feminist? A feminist who still sleeps with men? After all, they say, "feminism is the theory, lesbianism is the practice."[2] But lesbianism is only one of the ways to live an antipatriarchal lifestyle. And it is true that feminism is an integral part of my life. Not only because I wash only half the dishes or because I drive the car most of the time when we go out, even though these are things I think about, things that I am learning as I unlearn all the images of being a good woman that I have been taught, but also because feminism, and in particular bisexual feminism, is a part of the way I relate to people.

I am, to be honest, wary of men. Their flattery no longer thrills me but instead makes me cautious. I guess that, over time, I have grown further away from being the kind of woman who desires to interact sexually with men. I know that if my male lover and I broke up, my attraction toward men would continue, but I probably wouldn't act on it. I am not likely to become newly involved with a man because, along with the differences in power that society grants (forces?) upon us, there are so many issues in my life a man and I would be unable to connect across.

Some bisexual women claim that being bi makes a person more aware of the "cultural" and communication differences between women and men, and that being aware of these differences makes a bisexual woman more able to bridge them. But personally I don't find that an awareness of the barriers in communicating with men makes me all that enthusiastic about putting in the work it takes to knock them down. As one of my bisexual friends says, "I don't want to put in the energy to educate them." I've heard some of my few "straight" friends echo that sentiment. Sometimes they say, "if I broke up with Bob, I'd never go out with a man again! I'd be a lesbian." These women are probably just as aware as bisexual women about how much harder it often is to communicate with men than with other women, but they choose to replace the Bob with a Rick or a James instead of with a woman.

To me gender is a very important consideration in choosing those I love. As a feminist, I recognize the power imbalances society has set up between men and women and the ways in which these imbalances are played out in both our political and personal interactions. So I personally disagree with bisexuals who assert that, for them, it doesn't matter if their lover is a man or a woman, it is the person inside who they love. As a bisexual feminist, I see the person inside as having been shaped in various ways (in accordance with or against) by the gender stereotypes promoted by our society.

I also tend to find myself more physically and emotionally attracted to women. I guess I am one of the women Alice Walker describes when she writes "[a womanist is] a woman who loves other women sexually and/or nonsexually. Appreciates and prefers women's culture, women's emotional flexibility (values tears as a natural counterbalance of laughter), and women's strength. Sometimes loves individual men, sexually and/or nonsexually."[3]

So, you might ask, why am I in a committed relationship with a man? I am with a man about whom I can honestly say that we grow with each other. We educate one another; we understand each other; we have dived into a lot of new areas of our lives together. We help each other see around corners, and we help move each other forward. And yet, with all our closeness, we still sometimes see things in very different ways, which is a source of great growth, surprise and, sometimes, true annoyance.

Feminism is real in both our lives, real in the small details, real in a sense of still growing, of discovering and unfolding aspects about ourselves we never knew, strengths we have, and oppressive behaviors we "unconsciously" act out—unconscious only because we never bothered to give them a second glance.

Our relationship is necessarily fluid and changing. We do not set up boundaries that must be adhered to; we have no rules to live by, except for honesty and the push toward exploration, be it sometimes exhilarating, sometimes exhausting. Politically and emotionally we have both journeyed far since we met. Feminism, bisexuality, Berkeley and the Persian Gulf War have changed our senses of who we are and how the world is. Our ways of relating and our ways of understanding ourselves and one another have altered and will hopefully continue to change.

Although much of my personal life is spent with a (heterosexual?) man, support and encouragement for the exploration of my sexuality comes not only from him and my bisexual friends, but also from the lesbian and gay communities on campus. I can hardly compare coming out as a bisexual in the nineties with coming out in the seventies since I wasn't born until 1971, but from talking to older lesbian and bi women, it strikes me that queer women's communities are probably a lot more responsive to bisexuality now than when the movement was still young.

I came out in a very receptive queer environment. By the time I came to the University of California at Berkeley, the university's equivalent of a gay student union was already called the Multicultural

Bisexual Lesbian Gay Association. Last year the M.B.L.G.A. gave out the "Queerest Couple" award to a bisexual woman and her straight boyfriend. Obviously I didn't have to create a space for bisexuality (at least not in Berkeley); I just had to claim my place in it.

I probably haven't come across as much biphobia from queer-identified people as older bisexual folks have, but when I have felt it, it has stung worse than anything a straight person could have ever said to me. But although I think it is important to confront biphobia wherever it arises, it bothers me how much of our attention has been focused on going off on tirades against the lesbian and gay communities. I think the pain we feel from biphobia from our lesbian sisters and gay brothers is justified, but we should not forget the great gains that the lesbian and gay movement has achieved for all of us. Many of us, I think, would have had a much more difficult time coming to terms with the "gay or lesbian side" of ourselves had it not been for the courage, stereotype-smashing and outreach of the lesbian and gay communities.

From bisexual accounts you might think that we were less welcome in these communities than in "straight" society. But, as ludicrous as this reminder might sound, we must remember that it is not our gay brothers and lesbian sisters who fire us from work when they find out we have a lover of the same sex; it is not they who "fag bash" us as we walk out of gay clubs. It's the Supreme Court that rules that sodomy is illegal; it's our local courts that take children away from lesbian or bisexual women, whom they deem "unfit" to be mothers.

It is the heterosexual mainstream that embraces such oppression, and it is the heterosexual mainstream that I fear the most, and against whom I feel the most anger. Thus, in contrast to the suggestions of many bisexual activists, I do not see myself as some kind of "bridge" between the heterosexual community and the gay and lesbian communities. Certainly I have friends "on both sides," but so do a lot of gay men and lesbians I know. "Educating" straight friends is something I rarely do because most of the straight people I choose to be with are already gay-positive. The suggestion that I am somehow better equipped or more adept at sensitizing prejudiced heterosexuals is an idea I find offensive; I am not some kind of evolutionary link, some kind of natural mediator, between the oppressors and those they want to victimize.

I am queer, and I am in alliance with all queer people, all people whose sexual expression and ways of loving are considered "unnatural" by the mainstream and who have suffered (economically, spiritually, psychologically, and so on) because of it. Within this group of queers I feel a particular affinity with other women because the political and economic repressions we have been placed under unite us in another kind of struggle; not only our sexuality but our entire selves have been deemed not good enough or bad. It's not just what we do, but who we were born to be that makes us unacceptable.

As queer women we are unified in our struggle against oppression of us as women and as sexual minorities. But this unity should not be used as an excuse for overlooking the fundamental differences that exist among us. Two lesbians in a long-term relationship who are raising children together are in a very different social, economic and legal situation than a bisexual woman who lives with a man. The point is not to attempt to calculate which one of these women should be understood as "more oppressed," whose troubles should weigh heavier on the golden scale of justice, but to remember that we as non-heterosexual women are separated not only by class, race and age but by the choices and necessities of how we live our lives as well.

We as queers are a multitude of different people, not one side in a "them" versus "us" struggle for survival. Homophobia is not as simple as two factions at war, and the solution to it cannot be as simple as somehow building a "bridge" of common understanding between them. I certainly am not that bridge, nor am I the water flowing underneath it. I am not somebody caught between two opposing extremes, but a member of a wide and diverse community of subjugated and rebellious people, all of whom I believe should band together to fight the oppression they each face. Only if we can accept our differences and unite on those issues that affect all of us within our own diverging ways of being and living, can we form a more viable union of queer politics and an even stronger movement toward overcoming sexual oppression.

Endnotes

1. Dale Spender, *Man Made Language* (Boston: Routledge and Kegan Paul, 1985), p. 185.

2. According to Loraine Hutchins and Lani Kaahumanu's "Bicoastal Introduction" to *Bi Any Other Name: Bisexual People Speak Out* (Boston: Alyson Publications, 1991), Ti Grace Atkinson coined the phrase "Feminism is *a* theory, lesbianism is *a* practice. As the [lesbian] movement developed, it was translated into "Feminism is *the* theory, lesbianism is *the* practice." (p. xxiv) Hutchins and Kaahumanu attribute Atkinson's quote to her 1970 speech at Columbia University, New York City, as quoted in Sidney Abbott and Barbara Love's *Sappho was a Right On Woman: A Liberated View Of Lesbianism* (New York: Stein and Day, 1972), pp. 119-121.

3. Alice Walker, "Definition of Womanist," in *In Search of Our Mothers' Gardens* (San Diego: Harcourt Brace Jovanovich, 1984), pp. xi-xii.

Sharon Gonsalves

WHERE HEALING BECOMES POSSIBLE

I began my process of healing from rape and incest in 1979, about a year and a half after being raped by a man with whom I had been sexually involved. Like many women I did not identify this experience as rape until months after it happened. What precipitated my healing was a second similar incident; this time I was sexually assaulted by a man I was out on a date with. I promptly went into "crisis" and sought help at a mental health clinic. A few weeks later, back at college, I joined the Women's Union and began searching for other rape survivors to talk to. I soon became a politically active feminist, channeling my anger at the atrocities of patriarchy into marches and demonstrations, discussion/consciousness-raising groups, writing, women's studies and academic discourse. Through feminism I discovered a love for myself and other women. Connecting with other women emotionally and sexually has been very healing for me.

I love making love with women for many reasons. Their soft, smooth bodies are like mine. I love their breasts, smooth faces, round hips, shoulders, necks, ears. I love sharing power with a woman. We don't arrive knowing that one of us is assigned to give, the other receive. And with women there are no penises. There is no intercourse, there may not be any orgasms. When I first came out as a lesbian, to me that meant safety. I was afraid of the penis as weapon. I needed there to be no weapons in my bed.

So a significant act of my healing was to reject men as sexual partners. This was the first time I stopped having intercourse. I remember having a very difficult time recognizing which men I could or could not trust. The men who raped and sexually assaulted me seemed like nice enough people. How could I have known they would become abusive? I decided that because men are basically socialized to become perpetrators I wasn't going to let them get close to me. This way I wouldn't have to figure out who was or wasn't "safe." I also recognized I had been socialized to link my self-esteem to my sexual activity with men. If a man wanted me sexually, then I must be worthwhile. Before becoming a lesbian, I participated in a lot of self-destructive sexual behavior with men in an effort to find my self-worth—a tragic result of growing up female.

I identified as a lesbian for four years and during that time a great deal of psychic healing took place. Being in women-only space was very freeing. I was not a sex object. I was valued for my thinking and my organizing skills, for my humor and my dedication. I thrived on being part of a community. I began creating an alternative family—a family of friends among whom I felt safe. I started acknowledging the sexual abuse in my biological family, although not to any of my blood relatives.

As a lesbian I also became aware of the ways sexual abuse was interfering with my ability to be sexual with a partner. Because lesbian relationships were free of penises, semen, and so on, I expected sex with women to be easy, comfortable, blissful. After about six months in my first long-term relationship with a woman, I began experiencing flashbacks to my rape during sex. My partner and I tried as a couple to work through my trauma, but lesbian bed-death[1] prevailed. We shared a bed most nights and did lots of cuddling for the next year and a half until my lover left me for, among other reasons, lack of sex. I decided to start working on my sexual abuse history as it related to my ability to remain present during chosen sexual encounters. Although I had been expressing a lot of my fear, anger and sadness regarding rape in re-evaluation counseling sessions,[2] I decided to enter individual and group therapy focusing on incest. It was 1983. I broke silence about the incest with several family members and confronted my perpetrator in the presence of my therapist. All were significant events in my healing process.

Becoming Bisexual

My interest in men was again sparked after I made a career decision to work in electronics. I had always liked fixing things and the idea of having a nontraditional job really appealed to me as a feminist and a dyke. I wanted to prove that a women could do anything as well as a man and be tough, working class and blue-collar. My first job as a technician, though only temporary, was quite a thrill. I wore a hard hat, uniform and steel-toed work boots and was the only woman on the job. I then took a job repairing cable TV boxes. It was hard for me as a feminist to step into a work environment that was so blatantly sexist. Most of the women did quality control or cleaning. The technicians and supervisors were, for the most part, men. I was one of the few women technicians. I liked the work and I wanted the experience, but some of the guys gave me a pretty hard time.

I got broken in at this job and learned about "the secret language of men."[3] This language included jostling, making fun of each other and teasing as ways of showing acceptance or even affection. I scoffed at this "typical male" behavior, but soon learned that what felt to me like put-downs and nastiness were to them camaraderie. I had a hard time adjusting to this way of interacting. Among women, I was used to much more open and direct communication. It was important for me not to take their "razzing" personally if I was going to make it in electronics. I worked in this shop for two years and could see real differences among the men who were my co-workers: they ranged from being pure assholes to decent human beings and everything in between.

Recognizing these differences was another part of my healing. I needed to learn that men are not all the same. They may get a lot of the same information growing up, but they do different things with it, just as women do. Some women try hard to conform to society's expectations, where others reject those messages to varying degrees. The same is true of men. They don't all become perpetrators. Some reject traditional roles and become nurturing, gentle individuals.

Although now I wholeheartedly believe that men are not all the same, it was difficult for me to accept at the time. From 1980 through 1984, I lived in a world where men didn't matter. The belief system adhered to in my lesbian-feminist community included seeing all men as oppressors. I had put a lot of energy into stripping men of their power in order to stay alive. I believed that women who had sex with men were giving away their power to people who would necessarily oppress them by virtue of their being male. My friends believed this, too, and we openly put down the two women in our community who identified as bisexual. The heterosexual feminists who were political activists in town got the message as well and made few attempts to connect with us.

It was clear to me that sleeping with men was unacceptable among my friends. Although I was considering doing it, I did not discuss that with other lesbians. I knew I spent more time interacting with men than they did because of my job, but I didn't even begin to try and defend men as individuals because I knew I'd only be wasting my time.

The first man I became interested in during this period was someone I had met at the college radio station where we broadcast our weekly women's music program. I had been doing the radio show for three years and had trained as a broadcast engineer with the students who ran the station. I had always been attracted to John, but considered it out of the question to act on that because I was a lesbian. When I started doing paid work in electronics, John mentored me and we did some projects together around the station. It was fun. I really enjoyed it. I felt very safe around him and eventually very horny. I knew I wanted to become sexually involved with him, but I spent about four months weighing the pros and cons of actually doing it. I knew the cost would be high in my community. Eventually I decided it was more important to be true to myself and do what felt right for me than to be a good lesbian.

Word traveled fast about my relationship with John. I did not try to keep it a secret. My lesbian friends who also worked on the radio show knew him. Some of them lived with me, so if I stayed out all night I would have had to lie about where I'd slept and on principle I wasn't willing to do that. Besides, I wasn't doing anything wrong, so there was no reason to act "guilty."

I remember a few incidents from around this time that are indicative of my friends' reactions. One day, early in my relationship with John, he and I were helping a heterosexual friend of mine move to a new apartment. A lesbian friend was there also, and when John was out of the room I told her that he and I were lovers. She thought I was joking and laughed hysterically. One evening I was at a potluck, and women started asking me about my relationship with John. They seemed to assume that now I was a straight woman and had forgotten the values I had learned as a lesbian. They thought I wouldn't want to be in women-only space anymore since my lover couldn't be there with me. I clearly had become a completely different person now that I was involved with a man. This shocked me since I had known these women as more than acquaintances. They were good friends. I had seen them every week for years. I'd organized women-only events with them and been an activist right alongside them. How could they think my values had changed so completely overnight?

Lesbian friends would sometimes confess to me their attractions to men. At times I felt good about providing a place to speak the unspeakable. Other times I felt angry that our culture was so unforgiving and intolerant that we were afraid to be ourselves. I was glad I wasn't hiding like they were. I couldn't have survived.

It was clear to me that women were talking about me, wondering how I could have done such a thing and why. My ex-lover was very confused by the whole thing. Strangely enough I did not align myself with the other two "out" bisexual women in the community. Instead I basically dropped out of sight. I became less and less comfortable at lesbian events. I stopped organizing. I didn't feel welcome anymore. I continued to spend time with lesbian friends individually. Eventually, I moved into a household of straight feminists. I felt lonely and isolated. The community as an entity could not understand my choosing to be with a man. One of the last events I helped organize was a workshop for lesbian, bisexual and heterosexual women to begin building bridges among ourselves and strengthen the women's community as a whole. It was an effort to help my friends understand.

John turned out to be an excellent partner for working on my sexual abuse issues. He discouraged me from even trying to have intercourse when my fear prevented me from lubricating, and eventually he told me about his own history of sexual abuse. Although we stayed together for only six months, the relationship was a good re-entry into heterosex for me.

From the time I started having intercourse willingly at age sixteen, I've always gotten vaginal infections. They seemed to be directly related to my sexual activity. Whenever I would go to the gynecologist to have my vaginal infections treated, I'd be instructed to wear clean white cotton underwear and loose-fitting jeans and to drink cranberry juice. No one ever suggested that I stop having intercourse. Trying to enjoy it came from outside voices telling me that sex with men had to include intercourse. Choosing to be sexual with men again, being open to men again, made me feel as if I had to at least try to engage in activities that were pleasurable for my male partners, particularly intercourse.

My discovery that impending vaginal penetration caused my vagina to dry up and my muscles to tighten was very important. Understanding this I could tell my partner (male or female) to ignore my crotch unless I asked to be touched there. I instantly gained control over the demons of the past by simply stating what I liked or did not like before we ever took off our clothes. Then I learned to talk during sex. To say, "I need to stop. Would you please just hold me?" Before I learned to do this, I had felt like a victim all over again and that I had to endure the sex until it was over, until my partner came, whether my partner was a man or a woman. The biggest part of my sexual healing was to reclaim sex for myself. I realized that if I wasn't having fun, then I shouldn't be there.

As a rape and incest survivor, I have a difficult time relaxing during vaginal penetration. With my muscles constricting, my mind fighting the intruder, it is hard to enjoy having anything bigger than a finger inside me. Pelvic exams are hell in that I must endure a speculum holding my vaginal walls apart for several minutes. Needless to say, if I'm going to choose intercourse, the smaller the penis the better. Fortunately for me, my first male partner after coming out as bisexual had a very small penis. When we finally did have intercourse, I truly enjoyed it and would have orgasms. The myth that all women want to be fucked by a huge dick is just that—a myth. Why men believe this is beyond me. Like women, many men feel that their self-worth is connected to their sexual activity—the size of their penis, how long they can keep an erection, and so forth. It is unfortunate that men are socialized to believe that bigger is better and anything less than huge is inadequate. I have met several women (lesbian, heterosexual and bi) who do not enjoy vaginal penetration or who prefer penetration only with small dildos, penises, fingers, zucchinis, whatever. Men need to know this, and women need to feel just fine about it.

For the past four years, I have chosen not to have intercourse with my male partners. This decision has allowed me to enjoy sex with men more consistently. This is the second time I have stopped having intercourse, and getting here has been a lengthy but rewarding process. I've found several men who understand that no means no. Some even prefer the absence of "pressure to perform." In all cases it makes practicing safer sex with men easier.

Relationships and Self-Love

My first two years as a bisexual were pretty rocky. Exploring relationships with men again was fraught with mystery and uncertainty because of the differences between how women relate to other women and how they relate to men (or how men expect women to relate to them). This was especially difficult when it came to expressing feelings. I had little patience with men's inability to communicate verbally about emotion. Crying was totally misunderstood and seen as something I would do in order to get my way rather than as a release of tension and emotion.

I can remember having to deal with body issues again after a long absence of comments like "why don't you shave your legs," "you're getting fat" and "how about dressing up once in a while." Give me a break. Finding a male partner with a feminist consciousness wasn't easy. Finding a female partner seemed nearly impossible. I was a pariah now that I was sleeping with the enemy and publicly acknowledging it. I decided to leave town and moved to Boston where a large bisexual women's network already existed. This was another step in my healing.

Having a women's community was of primary importance to me. I spent most of my social time with the bi women's network as an organizer. I also had enrolled in the electronics program at the Women's Technical Institute in order to further my career goals in a supportive environment. I went to events at the women's center including an incest survivor group. I also checked out a neighborhood gay and lesbian organization, where I met a bisexual woman who became my friend and casual sex partner during that first year in Boston. At school I fell in love with my lab partner, a straight woman, which turned into an emotional disaster (not surprisingly).

The best thing for me about moving to Boston was that I felt accepted as a bisexual and as a feminist. There was life after lesbianism. I felt very hesitant about being around lesbians because I'd found so little acceptance upon coming out as bi. I attended many "lesbian events," but didn't really meet or talk with anyone unless I knew them from the network or from school. I went dancing at the women's bars with my friends, but for the most part I knew very few lesbians. It was safer that way.

Eventually I became involved with a bisexual man I met through the network. We had a four-year relationship during which I did most of my sexual healing. His feminist consciousness and willingness to learn from me were wonderful. I taught him about lesbian sex, about arousal and pleasure. I told him that traditional sex was too goal-oriented, the goal being orgasm, and in heterosex the goal being vaginal intercourse leading up to male orgasm. Between women it's so much easier to focus on foreplay. There are shoulders and ears and necks and breasts and thighs and fingers and toes to focus on as well as clits and labia and vaginas and anuses. Bringing my lesbian sexual self into a relationship with a man was very healing. We took the focus off intercourse, put it onto pleasure and built a trusting safe place for me to heal.

It was during this relationship that I learned to say no to heterosexual intercourse. Realizing that I could be sexual with a man without having intercourse and then finding a man I could do that with in an ongoing relationship were remarkable steps for me. It was where lesbian feminism met bisexuality and where my own sexual healing became possible.

About a year into our relationship, I became involved with a lesbian I met through my roommate. During this time I was able to participate in a lesbian community again, but the biphobia of some of her friends made that unappealing. I was accepted there only because I was involved with her and assumed to be a lesbian. When we broke up a year and a half later, those other friendships did not endure.

The most important thing to me in any relationship is that my partner and I communicate well with each other. I have found that in my relationships with women I work on different issues than I do with men. With women I have to pay more attention to maintaining my sense of self, my separate identity. I'm also much more willing to be the caretaker in relationships with women and postpone having my own needs met. Sexual trauma does come up for me with women, but not as much as it does with men.

Being a feminist bisexual with a background in the lesbian community gave me the strength and understanding to be able to make demands on male partners that as a heterosexual woman I didn't have. Knowing there were other options and learning the ways two people could be together from being with women allowed me to demand that same kind of interaction with men, a kind of interaction that doesn't come easily with men in American culture.

My feminism has allowed me to find different ways of relating to men than I knew before my enlightenment. Healing from abuse has allowed me to apply that knowledge to all my relationships. Having self-esteem, recognizing my self-worth as connected to myself only, not as dependent on someone else's interest in me—sexual or otherwise—has really made a difference. It's unfortunate that I couldn't or didn't learn these things growing up or have them modeled by women in my family. Low self-esteem is what makes women victims, targets of abuse. We need to love ourselves enough to defend ourselves, to put ourselves first always and stop taking care of everyone else before taking care of ourselves.

I finally learned this important lesson at age twenty-six. I concretized it on July 27, 1986, by marrying myself in a very private ceremony in Provincetown, Massachusetts. I bought a gold wedding band at a women's crafts store in this wonderfully gay vacation spot. The ring is a reminder that I come first and that I must love and care for myself above all others. I have often said that I would rather be in no relationship than in a bad one because my primary relationship is with myself. I wear the ring on my right hand, since many gay couples wear wedding rings there. I've gotten some interesting questions about this ring. Many people assume that it's connected to a long-term lover of mine. Others think I'm heterosexually married. When I tell them I'm married to myself, they snicker and make jokes about masturbation as if the only reason to get married were for sex. Many women and especially child sexual abuse survivors understand the significance right away. Learning to love oneself and take care of oneself is a hard lesson when you grow up feeling worthless. We need constant reminders to avoid slipping back into self-hate.

Through being sexually abused I learned that there is a real difference between sex and love. The two don't always go hand in hand, and in some ways that's really sad. I'd much rather be sexual with someone who cares about me than with someone who doesn't, but sex isn't something sacred that I only do with a person I feel committed to "forever and ever amen." Sexual release is a human need just like food or shelter. The human body has an instinct for arousal and release. If I'm not involved in a relationship I might fantasize or read erotic stories for arousal and then masturbate for release. Or I might have sex with a friend I trust and feel comfortable being sexual with. Similarly, I might choose to be sexual with someone I'm attracted to even if I'm in a relationship with someone else. Why? Because it's fun, because it feels good, because my lover is far away and I'm horny now. Sex is one thing, love is something else, and it's great when both happen at the same time, but they don't always, and they don't have to for me.

Although bisexuality does not imply nonmonogamy, as a bisexual I have been nonmonogamous in my relationships. So often, monogamy feels like ownership to me in the same way that marriage feels like ownership—laying claim to my partner based solely on our sexual relationship. Love, affection, emotion and trust are so much more important to me than sex. I'd rather have these things any day, but for me it doesn't all come as one package. I think we tend to put a lot of expectations on the person who is our partner when we're in a relationship. We rely on that one person for companionship, emotional support, sex, friendship, financial stability, social support, nurturing, affection and so forth. We expect to get all our needs met in this one place, and it's a big mistake. If you should lose that relationship, then there goes your entire support system. It makes more sense to me to get my needs met by a variety of people and to have strong support systems in my life. Another issue regarding nonmonogamy for me is that if my sexual partner is a man who enjoys having intercourse then he's not going to get all of his sexual needs met if I'm his only partner—especially if his penis is bigger than a pencil.

A Note on Surviving Sexual Abuse

I'm sure there are many lesbians with sexual abuse histories, just as there are many heterosexual and bisexual women with sexual abuse histories. If all women who had been sexually abused became lesbians, there'd be a lot more lesbians in this world. Although I know my coming out was precipitated by incidents of abuse, I believe that if the abuse had never happened I still would have found my way to loving women. It just would have taken longer.

In this essay I am describing my own journey of healing from incest and rape. I am not advocating sex with men as a method of healing for other survivors. Each survivor, female or male, has her or his own story to tell. Each of us has our own healing to do and must do it in our own way and in our own time. I am told that I am one of the fortunate ones. I have found in myself the strength and perseverance to move through the muck and come out the other side in one piece.

My healing process is far from complete, and my sexuality continues to evolve. In the fall of 1990, I began recovering memories of sexual abuse from my early childhood. My memories have surprised and frightened me. They have also made my relationship with my body very difficult. After months of struggling to put my life and my body back together, I am proud to say that I feel whole, at least for now.

Endnotes

1. An end to or lack of sexual activity, which occurs in many lesbian relationships. This phenomenon is described in *Lesbian Passion: Loving Ourselves and Each Other* by Joanne Loulan (San Francisco: Spinsters/Aunt Lute, 1987), pp. 65-66, 103-117.

2. Re-evaluation counseling, also know as co-counseling, is an alternative to traditional therapy. The peer relationship is crucial in R.C. Co-counselors take turns in the roles of client and counselor. A goal of the co-counseling session is discharge (tears, trembling, perspiration, laughter, angry shouting, yawning) of feelings from old hurts leading to recovery from distress and re-evaluation of behavior patterns. For more information see *The Human Situation* by Harvey Jackins (Seattle, Rational Island Publishers: 1973).

3. This term comes from an unpublished manuscript by Chris Austill, 1991.

Robyn Ochs

BISEXUALITY, FEMINISM, MEN AND ME

Where does feminist consciousness come from? Why do some women begin to question what has been presented to us as given and, as a result of that questioning, come to understand the ways in which women have been systemically limited? Each of us takes a different road to feminism. Many of our journeys begin with a pivotal event or transition that forces us to question our assumed reality.

My own route to feminism was long, convoluted and closely connected with my developing bisexual consciousness. In my early twenties I realized that my emotional and sexual attractions toward women as well as men were not going to go away, and I began to address those feelings. Forced off-balance by the turbulence of these emotions and their implications for my future, I began for the first time to consciously question the assumptions I had made about my life. I began to understand that many of my choices had not been freely made, but rather had been made within the context of a system that Adrienne Rich calls "compulsory heterosexuality," a system that posits heterosexuality as the only way to be.[1] In this essay I describe my own journey: what I learned and what I unlearned, and how these changes in my thinking have fundamentally changed my relationships with men.

I grew up believing that women deserved equal pay for equal work and that we had the right not to be raped or battered and the right to control our own reproduction. These beliefs were firmly held by my mother and my grandmothers. In the kitchen of the house I grew up in, a cartoon showing two toddlers looking into their diapers was tacked to the bulletin board next to the telephone. One of the toddlers was saying to the other, "So *that* explains the difference in our salaries." Had I been asked as a young person whether I was a feminist I would have answered in the affirmative. To me, these issues were the essence of feminism.

But despite adopting the feminist label for external causes, I did not escape female socialization. I learned some "basic truths": that as a woman my value was in my body, and that mine was not "good enough": that sooner or later every woman needs a man; and that I would have to behave in certain ways in order to get myself one. These truths, which very much shaped my behavior for many years, I'll describe in greater detail below.

My Body and Me

Like many women, I grew up hating my body. I remember wearing shorts over my bathing suit as a preteen to hide my "ugly" fat thighs. As a teenager, I spent a lot of time worrying whether I was attractive enough. Of course, I was never quite up to standard. I wanted very much to have the kind of exterior that would cause scouting agents from pinup magazines or from modeling agencies to approach me on the street to recruit me. Needless to say, this never happened, reinforcing my belief that physically I was a total failure as a woman. I fantasized about being a dancer but knew I did not have the requisite "dancer's body." I thought my size 7 1/2 feet were enormous. For the record, I have always been more or less average in weight. But average was not good enough. As long as I didn't look like one of those women in *Playboy*, I wasn't pretty enough.

Too big too short too stocky too busty too round too many zits blackheads disgusting pinch an inch fail the pencil test cellulite don't go out without makeup don't let them see what you really look like they'll run away in terror but if you are really lucky and have a few beers and do it in the dark he might not notice so make sure to turn off the light before...

I never questioned my standards of measurement, never realized that these standards are determined by a male-dominated culture and reinforced by a multibillion-dollar "femininity" industry that sells women cosmetics, diet aids, plastic surgery, fashion magazines, liposuction, creams and girdles. I took my inability to live up to these standards as personal failure and never drew any connections between my experience and that of other women.

Men and Me

Men, you can't live without 'em. Sooner or later I would end up with one. My grandfather used to tell me that it was good that I was short, as that way I would have the option of marrying either a tall man or a short one. There aren't enough men to go around and it gets harder and harder to find one as you get older. Men aren't comfortable with women who are more educated/smarter/earn more than they. My fifty-year-old aunt never married. She waited *too long,* and by then it was *too late* because she was *too old, poor dear.* It's just as easy to fall in love with a rich man as a poor man. Men lead.

I always had a boyfriend. From age thirteen until after college, I don't remember going for more than a month without being in a relationship or at least having a crush. Having a boyfriend was a measure of my worth. I would select the boy and flirt with him until he asked me out. Most times, like the Mounties, I got my man. In dance, this is called backleading, directing the action from the follower's position. It allows the man to look like he is in control.

I learned that there's a man shortage. There are more women than men. And "good men" are extremely rare. Therefore, if you manage to get hold of a good one, you'd better hang on to him. This message got louder as I moved into my twenties. I saw older women in their thirties and beyond searching frantically for a suitable partner with whom to reproduce the human species and make their lives meaningful. I learned that you'd better pay attention to your "biological clock."

The Unlearning

These messages had a powerful grip on me. How did I begin to unlearn them? The women's studies class I took in college helped a bit. However, I continued to consider feminism only in terms of situations outside of myself. I looked at my environment and catalogued the injustices, but did not look inside.

It wasn't until I was considering a relationship with a woman that I began to see the relevance of the feminist theory I had read as a first-year college student to my own life. My perspective changed dramatically. For example, in my first relationship with a woman, it became quickly apparent that in many ways I fit quite neatly into the passive "femme" role of the butch/femme stereotype. I was behaving as I had always behaved in relationships, but for the first time, now that my lover was a woman, my "normal" behavior appeared to me (and probably to her as well) strange and unbalanced. Why were my lover and I behaving so differently? Suddenly our roles appeared constructed rather than natural. I won't pretend that I woke up one day and found myself suddenly freed of my conditioning. Rather, I spent several years unfolding and unraveling the layers of misinformation I had internalized, learning more with each subsequent relationship or incident.

My body image began to change. Through the firsthand experience of my own attractions, I learned that women, and their bodies, are beautiful, though I did not immediately apply this knowledge to my opinion of my own body. There was one woman friend on whom I had a crush for more than two years. I thought she was beautiful, with her solid, powerful angles and healthy fullness. One day, with a sense of shock, I realized that her body was not so very different from mine and that I had been holding myself to a different, unattainable standard than I had been holding her and other women to. It was this experience of seeing my image reflected in another woman that finally allowed me to begin developing a positive relationship with my own body.

I learned from firsthand experience about the privilege differential that results when the gender of your partner changes. Before I had experienced some of society's disapproval and disregard, I had no sense of the privileges I had experienced in heterosexual relationships. In subsequent years, each time I changed partners I was painfully aware of this absurd double standard and began to strategize ways to live in such a way that I could challenge rather than collaborate with these injustices. I have made a personal commitment to be "out" as bisexual at every possible opportunity and to avoid taking privileges with a male lover that I would not have with my female lover. For these reasons, I have chosen not to marry, though I hope someday to establish a "domestic partnership" and have a "commitment ceremony." If I feel someone would be unwilling to hear me talk about a same-sex lover, I disclose nothing about *any* of my relationships, even if my current partner is of the opposite sex. This is not very easy, and occasionally I backslide, but I am rewarded with the knowledge that I am not contributing to the oppression of lesbian, gay and bisexual people when I am in an opposite-sex relationship.

It was empowering to realize that men as romantic partners were optional, not required. I no longer felt pressured to lower my relationship standards in light of the shortage of good men. Yes, I might get involved with and spend the rest of my life with one, but then again I might choose to spend my life with a woman. Or perhaps simply with myself. This was to be my choice.

I realized how I had been performing my designated gender role. It's amazing how being in a same-sex relationship can make you realize just how much of most heterosexual relationships is scripted from the first date to the bedroom to the dishes. In relationships with women, I learned how to lead and learned that I like to lead sometimes. As sometimes I like to follow. And as sometimes I prefer to negotiate every step with my partner, or to dance alone.

Finally, I made a personal commitment to hold men and women to the same standards in relationships. I realized that in our society women are grateful when a man behaves in a sensitive manner, but expect sensitivity of a woman as a matter of course. I decided that I would not settle for less from men, realizing that it means that I may be categorically eliminating most men as potential partners. So be it.

My experience with being in relationships with women has been in a way like a trip abroad. I learned that many of the things I had accepted as natural truths were socially constructed, and the first time I returned to a heterosexual relationship things felt different. I hadn't yet learned how to construct a relationship on my own terms, but I was aware that things were not quite right. As time passed, my self-awareness and self-confidence increased. I gathered more experience in lesbian relationships and began to apply my knowledge to subsequent heterosexual relationships.

It is not possible to know who or where I would be today had I remained heterosexual in my attractions and in my self-identity. Perhaps other events in my life would have triggered a feminist consciousness. At any rate, it is entirely clear to me that it was loving a woman that made me realize I had fallen outside my "script," which in turn forced me to realize there *was* a script. From there, I moved toward a critical self-awareness and the realization that I could shape and write my own life.

Endnotes

Thanks to Marti Hohmann, Rebecca Kaplan and Annie Senghas for their feedback and support while I was writing this essay.

1. Adrienne Rich, "Compulsory Heterosexuality and Lesbian Existence," *Signs: Journal of Women in Culture and Society* 5, no. 4 (1980), pp. 631-60.

Vashti Zabatinsky

Some Thoughts on Power, Gender, Body Image and Sex in the Life of One Bisexual Lesbian Feminist

The issues of power, gender, body image and sex have been enigmatically intertwined in my life for as long as I can remember. Like a twisting, inconsistent braid, these strands inform the way I feel about myself, the way I relate to women and to men, and which of my secret attractions and desires I allow to surface and speak.

From childhood, I had sensed that my attractions were not "normal"—I had had crushes on other little girls since early grade school—and I consciously, fearfully monitored my sexuality as it developed. I remember trying to force myself to become heterosexual, to develop sexual attractions to men because I was terrified of my budding, unnamed lesbianism. The first time I ever heard the word "lesbian" was when one of my older cousins hurled it at her sister as an insult. Not knowing the meaning of the word, I could only imagine that "lesbian" was some horrible monster or other undesirable thing.

I remember being twelve years old and dancing a slow dance with an older man at a party, gauging how much I wanted to be in his arms. Seventy-five percent, I registered on my own heterosexuality scale. I was well on my way, I assured myself, to "normalcy."

I grew up without a mother. Lacking any real female role models, I looked to my father and other men in my life for mentorship. I would experience extreme jealousy, competitiveness and frustration around these men. I simply didn't get that they literally and figuratively had something that I didn't. I didn't get sexism, and I didn't get how I could be powerful as a woman and as myself. To this day, when I imagine myself doing something powerful or public, an image of a man in a suit, a man in charge, comes to mind.

It wasn't until I attended a workshop on gender presentation at the 1990 National Conference on Bisexuality that I found a model that described my experience. That model was presented by Tom/Thalia, a biological male in very convincing drag, such that he appeared to be a gorgeous, if femme, woman. S/he pointed out the vast number of elements that make up gender identity, one of which is internal identity, which can contradict outer presentation. In other words, s/he introduced the idea that it is possible for a person to feel like one sex on the inside while being comfortable presenting an image of the other sex to the world (as opposed to "complete" transsexualism, in which a person wants to change his or her outer presentation and/or body to conform to inner feelings). That expanded definition of gender identity struck a chord for me. Those images of men that filled my head when I tried to imagine a powerful me always confused me. When I was younger, I thought that those images meant that I wanted to be a boy, that I should have been born a boy. I felt like a boy. I also felt like a girl. I had liked "girl things" until my best friend, who was very tomboyish and butch and very "out" about thinking that being a boy was better than being a girl, convinced me that girl things (like Barbies, lace and liking Donny Osmond) were sissy stuff, to be disdained and rejected outright.

Until Tom/Thalia's workshop, I was puzzled by my own gender identity permutations. Now, I understand my inner "male" identity as an ultimately ungendered expression of my strong and powerful personality. I am still, and probably always will be, angry about sexism and the limitations of the prescribed female gender role, and I have found particular, limited arenas of transgression that suit me: I love being physically strong. I love that I can do sets of pushups. I love my strength of will, my assertiveness, my power to be articulate and to present convincing arguments.

As a teenager I played both ends against the middle. On the one hand, I exploited my ability to fit society's stereotype of the femme fatale. I mastered the elaborate cosmetic routines that allowed me to emerge from my bathroom coiffed, blow-dried, powdered, blushed, mascaraed, high-heeled, tightly cinched at the quasi-anorexic waist, perfumed, bejeweled and accessorized with a studied flair I knew few teenaged girls could match. The resulting image, which has caused current friends to shriek and drop photo albums in horror, graced the pages of fashion publications more than once.

One the other hand, I was very intelligent and articulate, and I delighted in knowing the answers in class, being skilled at debate and cutting through my male peers' bullshit. I attracted the lust of many young men because of my looks, would reel them toward me knowing they couldn't possibly get the point of who I was (not that I did at the time...), knowing that who I was had nothing to do with what I looked like.

I made up for the socially accorded power I lacked for my sex by maximizing the kind of sexual power I was encouraged to exercise as a socially defined attractive female, and by raising my aggressive, insistent, articulate, confident and persuasive voice when and wherever I damned pleased. In other words, if I couldn't command the easy respect accorded my male counterparts, I would equalize the skewed arrangement by both bringing men to their weak knees with my sexual charisma and being intellectually aggressive. The combination was offputting to most boys my age. (I read in a recent survey that ninety-five percent of men were intimidated by the combination of competence and sexuality in a woman; this statistic corroborates my experience.)

I remember a young man in high school who was a hard-working, well-respected student leader, bright in a dull sort of way. He could "talk back" and still be respected. He got lots of attention from teachers and advisors. Unlike most of the other seniors, who were bound for one of two state schools, *he* was going to Dartmouth. He, too, was intimidated by the combination of competence and sexuality I put forth. I reveled in this, but would have traded it in a second for the kind of respect he could command just by being male.

Though I could not articulate it at the time, I felt painfully aware that playing both ends against the middle, although it was the best I could do to cope with sexism, was selling myself short. My contrived beauty attracted the wrong people, and my veneer of bravado precluded emotional honesty. But, at that time, it was my best attempt to cope with sexist limitations on my personal power.

I went through a period of preferring men. I enjoyed and enjoy the aggressive pursuit of ideas and passionate debate. I majored in philosophy in college and men, with their rocky egos, would spar with me. I had difficulty doing this with women. I could find women to engage with intellectually, but I was too concerned with their approval and their feelings to do the kind of mental "sparring" that came so easily with some men. In some ways, men were safer—there was a buffer between me and them in which I could hide from feeling my feelings. Men could be buffeted about without breaking and appeared to enjoy the tumble.

An important part of my personal growth has been unlearning the emotional numbness that characterized this period. Somewhere along the line, I got permission to begin feeling my feelings and later to get support for this. I began to learn to be vulnerable, to cry on people's shoulders, to ask for help. In so doing, I became more nurturing, effusive, open—characteristics traditionally associated with femininity. To do this, I had to overcome a lot of internalized oppression, specifically the message that the way women are, that is, nurturance, effusive, open, is undesirable. As I reclaimed these characteristics as desirable for me, I gained more affection and respect for other women and became more open to closeness with women and more ready to realize and accept the lesbian part of my bisexuality.

To value and reclaim the "feminine" parts of myself, I had to face a great deal of shame. In this respect, I identify with men who are unlearning socialized male conditioning to repress feelings. I am acutely aware that, although acknowledging and expressing one's feelings increases personal power, it can remove social power. Society still sees "control" over one's feelings as a sign of "strength," as was evidenced by the hoopla over Congresswoman Patricia Schroeder's tears during her 1984 campaign for the presidency. Tears are still seen as a sign of weakness, associated with femininity. I rejected the "weaker" parts of femininity, along with my own feelings, while reaping the benefits of my socially defined sexiness. With feminine men, I felt safe in reclaiming some of my vulnerability. As long as I was slightly more macho, that is, more stoic, more "in control" emotionally than the man, I could allow myself some leeway to feel my feelings.

During the summer of 1984 I met an androgynous man; Ryan was Catholic, spiritual and an aspiring actor (we met at a casting call—I was a theater major). His nurturing, emotional attributes complemented my rational machismo in a neat reversal of traditional gender roles. (I remember telling friends in amazement, "He cried three times in the first week I knew him!") I got off on this transgressive arrangement. Our spirituality (I was Christian then), love of dark chocolate, common interest in acting and joy in each other's company made for a rich and challenging summer. At the time, I remember feeling that this relationship was queer (before I defined the word the way I do now), and that I liked its queerness. With this man and others like him, I felt safe from my vulnerability being used against me in a sexist fashion, as in, "You women are always so emotional." I think that is the reason I have, for the most part, chosen male lovers who have qualities more traditionally associated with women—effusiveness, nurturance, compassion.

In general, I am attracted to women and men who transgress their gender roles. Although I value and love audacity and strength of will as general personality characteristics, it is easier for me to appreciate those qualities in other women, because in men, those qualities are often blended, or at least tinged, with sexism.

In my last relationship with a man, I felt I was the more powerful in terms of strength of will, command of the language and confidence in my words and actions. I was more "masculine" than he was. A budding activist, David was often intimidated by me, both in groups and alone. I unconsciously de-emphasized my intellect and passion for ideas to accommodate his fragile ego. I focused more on my interpersonal skills, my nurturance, my sensuality. I was loving and loved, but the truth of my whole self was being only partially expressed. I realized this fully only after we broke up, and then I was sad and horrified. How could I, a strong feminist woman, have given up core parts of myself to preserve a man's ego?

The answer, of course, is that I loved David and I wanted the relationship to succeed. Like water, I sought a level; automatically and unknowingly, I adjusted myself so that the *relationship* would flourish optimally. I did this at my own expense. (I have done this with women, as well.)

Puzzled, I began to wonder if I would end up a lesbian by default, since the only men I seemed to feel safe enough around to be attracted to were those whose powerlessness patterns dominated their personalities too much for them to be truly my peers. Since this equation seemed relatively watertight (I had yet to meet a male counterexample, that is, a man with personal power equal to my own who wasn't unbearably sexist), I saw nothing wrong with letting go of the possibility of being with men. In other words, I have long recognized that sexism is a powerful enough force to keep me away from most men, and that

I cannot live with extreme powerlessness, no matter what the gender of the person. But my attractions to men remained.

My challenge in relating to men has been to find a way to honor and act on those attractions outside of socialized gender patterns. I bring certain of those patterns to relationships, and so do men. I bring varying degrees of willingness to give up, suppress or deny parts of myself to accommodate a man's desires or fears. I know that I do this with women, too, and I haven't figured out if the dynamic is the same or different with each sex. I know that with certain men I am able to recognize a "danger zone," that is, a manner of behaving in which I give up things that are important to me. I normally catch this pattern in the early stages and either work to correct it or stop spending time with the particular man. A good example of such a "warning" sign is missing scheduled time with women friends or relatives. When this happens, I ask myself, "what's going on here?"

Something I now invariably look for is whether a man has strong emotional connections with other men in which gender issues are examined in a supportive way. While in college, I became friends with a few men who were very eager to talk to me about feminism and were especially interested in my bisexuality. I would engage with them for hours, and they would drain me of energy. Ironically, I felt objectified for my intellect. One man in particular, an intellectual "sparring partner," was always eager to bounce his latest idea off me, and often his opening sentence was, "What do you think about 'X'?" Before too long, I realized that he never asked me questions like, "How are you?" Indeed, he was interested in my thoughts, but not so much in me as a whole person.

Then I realized that "feminist" men who sought out women and engaged them in in-depth, challenging conversations about feminism were recreating an old, sexist pattern of casting women in the role of moral guardian. Feminism was the new morality, and these modern men looked to the women in their lives to articulate the new social order and, implicitly, to confer moral legitimacy on them. Meanwhile, we women read the books, attended the events, did the work and were then expected to do more work by educating the curious men! Not only that, we were expected to be grateful that these men were interested enough to listen to us.

I was uncomfortable with this for many reasons. One, it felt again like women were doing the shitwork for men: oh, honey, don't bother reading all those books; I'll read them for you (iron your socks, cook your dinner, and so on). Two, I felt it was unfair to feminism itself for me to be someone's sole source of information. Three, it was very draining to be putting out energy on a topic so important to me to men who rarely gave much back, and who ultimately had the power to dismiss what I said if they disagreed. I began to encourage these young men to get together with one another and discuss what was difficult and challenging about being men. I told them if they were interested in being really radical, they should try making honest emotional connections with other men. Glomming onto women was easy and fun; now it was time for them to do their part. They didn't get it, couldn't handle it. I begged off.

Now, when I meet a man, I specifically look for conscious, committed connections with other men. If the man is white, I also look for anti-racist work, commitment or at least consciousness. As an active anti-racist, I feel I need to have other white people support me in this work. In general, I find it very difficult to discuss race issues and anti-Semitism issues with white Gentiles. People shut down very quickly! Since coming out as bi and having regular contact with a bi community, I have found many antiracist, feminist, Jewish and Jewish ally bisexual men and women.

In my first major lesbian relationship, I had my guard way down. That is to say, knowing that I wouldn't have to contend with sexism in this relationship, I sort of assumed there would be no power dynamics whatsoever, and I lay back to enjoy the ride, so to speak. I was dead wrong. Though I felt Bianca's love strongly, I never felt the same kind of respect she accorded her older, degreed professional friends. From a status-conscious upper-middle-class family, she would gleefully admit to being elitist, to my confusion and disappointment. I gave away big parts of myself. I was so excited to be with her that I assumed the role of wife-companion-armpiece in many subtle and insidious ways. The example that sticks out most clearly is a conversation we had about having children. She described a process by which an egg from her ovaries could be fertilized and implanted in my womb. Who would care for the child, I asked suspiciously. Of course, she answered without missing a beat, the partner who earned more money would continue to work while the other stayed home to care for the child. So her scenario was that I, being less socially and economically powerful, would bear and care for her genetic child. I was appalled.

Throughout our relationship, I had a gnawing feeling that she was missing the point of who I was. My activism is a big part of that core, and I always felt she viewed it with a sort of detached, almost condescending amusement. Even though she never came right out and said as much, I felt she thought it was "cute."

Also, in this relationship, as in all my relationships to that point, I was the one in charge of emotional process. That is, I would bring up issues, state how I felt about them, ask her how she felt, encourage her to express herself more, work to create "safe space," and so on. Again, I had this expectation that, being with a woman, there would be more give and take in this department.

Instead, I got a bit of an education about loving men and women. For one thing, I realized that, in general (and in particular with me, given my propensity for gender transgressors), in relating to men and women as lovers there are at least as many similarities as differences. Another thing I realized is that sexism is not the only, and often not the most important power dynamic in a relationship, even with a man.

My recent relationship with David was a good example of one in which sexism was not the main power struggle, at least not directly. This relationship was also the first in which I did not feel forced into the role of Process Queen. David was also a Process Queen and often gently pushed me to be more expressive in areas in which I was "stuck." Again, this was a role reversal: the man drawing the feelings out of the woman.

Body Image

Sexism comes in many forms: every male lover I have had, even the most "feminine," has, in one way or another, invoked his socially accorded power to judge my body, whether positively or negatively. One male lover several years ago (by far the most traditionally masculine man I have ever been involved with) observed that I had a "classic" figure, as he put it, that my body resembled certain early Greek statues, or some such thing. Classic figure? I was furious. Who was he to tell me which historical archetypes I did or did not conform to? Who appointed him? Clearly, I was bringing my own baggage to the interaction, my own internalized body image distress, the other half of the dynamic so easily reproduced.

I love having my body appreciated by a lover or close friend, male or female, and I even love having parts of my body appreciated separately from the rest of me. But certain kinds of appreciation feel different from others. It is much easier for me to take in appreciation in the form of owned feelings, "I am really turned on by your body," "I love your touch, your mouth, breasts, skin," or whatever, as opposed to, "You've got a great ass." But, as I get older and more comfortable with my sexuality, the latter kind of compliment turns me on more and more.

When I was younger, I easily relinquished to men the power to judge my body. Like most teenaged girls, I was preoccupied with my weight and shared this preoccupation with my male lovers (I was heterosexual then), constantly seeking their approval for my perpetually imperfect body.

My friends and I were preoccupied with body fat. We would zero in on a dimple or dollop of flesh on our otherwise lithe bodies and obsess, obsess, obsess. Now I wonder. To what or whom were we comparing ourselves? Certainly not each other, for we were much more alike than different. We all (or most of us) had a fold of skin between our waist and our abdomen that we called "fat," and we all had flesh on our hips, thighs, buttocks that grew rounder and more prominent as puberty progressed. No, none of us stood out particularly from the rest. To fashion models? Perhaps. And, implicitly, to *men*. Men are naturally endowed with far less body fat than we are. So no matter what we do, this fact of biology (along with chromosomally and hormonally induced physical characteristics) differentiates our body shape and texture. Were we using men as the norm by which to judge our soft bodies substandard? Part of me believes so, at least for myself.

Maybe it was becoming women that we were so ambivalent about, and we focused that ambivalence around something we felt we could judge and control: our swelling flesh. Men's hardness was tantamount with power, our softness to our weakness and vulnerability.

Interestingly enough, most of the women I have been involved with are large, whether tall and muscular or round and voluptuous. Not that thin women don't attract me as well, but I seem to gravitate more toward fleshier women. I am fairly thin myself, which is unusual in my biological family. Women in my family are mostly shorter than I am, with round, full breasts and hips. So, there is some sense in which fleshiness feels like home.

When I came out as bisexual, I went through a physical transformation that resembled that of other women in their coming-out process. I cut my long, permed hair. I stopped shaving my legs. I gained some weight. I got rid of my makeup. I was coming out as bisexual and feminist and lesbian, all at the same time. More accurately, I was coming into myself as feminist, out to the world as bisexual, and joining a lesbian-identified women's community centered around the college I was attending.

As a bisexual person, I was very isolated; there was no bisexual community in my community, and only one bisexual activist, who wasn't very helpful to me. Slowly, with the help of a very supportive lesbian activist friend of mine named Robin, as well as other out lesbians on the university campus, I began to speak up.

My bisexuality was still largely theoretical at that stage. Once I noticed that I was attracted to women, it took me a good three years to get used to the idea that I might actually have sex with a woman, or women. In retrospect, given the massive amounts of internalized homophobia I had to contend with, that makes sense. Once I decided I was ready to get into a relationship with a woman, it took another couple of years of hits and misses before I found one. The prospect of finding a woman to approach and flirt with, let alone date, left me stymied. I began to form a new sympathy for teenaged boys.

My first full-blown relationship with a woman nearly knocked me over. Bold, brazen and twelve years older than I was, Bianca loved women, loved women's bodies, loved being a lesbian with a capital "L" (nearly a six on the Kinsey scale), loved her body and loved my body, both in theory and practice. This was a new thing, indeed! For the first time, I felt wholly affirmed in my female body. For the first time, I felt sure that my female textures, shapes, smells and sounds were fully welcomed and loved. For the first time I felt that loving another's body had everything to do with loving myself.

These days, I never fail to be amazed at how affirming making love with a woman is. No matter how different our body types. I invariably have the sense that we are interesting variations on a theme. One lover I was involved with briefly, a stunning Danish woman with waves and waves of long blonde hair and a beautiful Rubenesque figure, upon seeing my naked, comparatively lean body, smiled with delight and said, "Different!" As we embraced and brought our bodies together, there was a certain symmetry reflected from my body to hers and back again: the curve of our bellies, the dip of our breasts, the swell of our hips. As we feasted our eyes on each other, she giggled and said, "Well, not so terribly different!" Indeed. As I lavished attention on her soft, delicious curved flesh, I appreciated my own body even more. The gnawing sense I had always felt to some degree with men, of wanting to trim off the "excess" was completely absent. If it had been safe enough to realize my bisexuality and my feminism at an earlier age, I am sure my feelings about my body would have developed very differently!

Sex

I didn't particularly enjoy sex with the first ten men I slept with. I certainly didn't come, though I was physically able, having masturbated since before being able to say the word. Convinced that orgasm through intercourse was the *sine qua non* of feminine sexuality, I taught myself this Freudian trick (no pun intended) by essentially masturbating on the body of a man who was half asleep as he was fucking me. For a long time, I needed to be on top in order to come. My first college boyfriend found, or awakened, my G-spot, upon which I came and came for what must have been ten full minutes. I loved this man dearly and felt comfortable with him, at least initially, so this may have contributed to the orgasmic sex.

I discovered that I loved fucking (intercourse with men), or trained myself to love it, perhaps. Having been blessed with an extremely sensitive clit, intercourse actually provided exactly the right kind of indirect stimulation I craved. This became an issue when having sex with women: I had to coach my female lovers to avoid direct clitoral stimulation. They would look at me in amazement. Then they would ask me to give them more direct clitoral stimulation. I learned that it's very difficult, as a woman, to remember that genitals so similar to one's own could possibly enjoy such different kinds of stimulation. We tend to touch each other the way we ourselves liked to be touched.

Duplicating intercourse with women was more of a challenge. My lover would gladly give me "fiveplay" with me on top, but I wanted to do it "no hands." I couldn't afford the wonderful leather harnesses with pastel-colored, non-penis-replica silicone dildos I saw advertised in women-oriented sex catalogs, so Bianca and I went shopping at a local sex store.

This particular store was quite male-oriented; upon entering, one saw on the right a glass case of multiracial penis facsimiles, arranged in order of ascending size (from pinky dimension to what must have been modeled after an Indian elephant), pointing outward like a twenty-one gun salute. From the other wall of the store hung plastic blow-up dolls. Not exactly a dyke haven! We asked for dildos that didn't look like penises. We got a sympathetic smile and an apology from the woman behind the counter.

We took a deep breath and bought a springy, caucasian flesh-colored dildo complete with two "glans," one on either end. It was more than a foot long. When we got home, Bianca insisted we mutilate the dildo so that it was no longer anatomically identifiable. We cut away the ridge of the "glans" with a knife until she was satisfied. I was amazed at how much she enjoyed this. We even tried to dye it, but the rubbery material was nonporous and wouldn't hold pigment.

After all this, we took our new toy for a spin. It was sensational— for about two minutes (long enough to get one or both of us extremely aroused), and then the goddamned thing would *slip out.* I learned a basic rule of thumb, or rather, of appendage: the person fucking must have her apparatus securely anchored, so as to control stimulation to the person being fucked. Otherwise, the whole thing gets really fucked up.

An interesting sexual/political irony occurred about a year later when I met first David. He was in the middle of reading *Intercourse* by Andrea Dworkin,[1] a scathing critique of heterosexual intercourse, whose basic premise is that intercourse has been a metaphor for the oppression of women and is thus politically incorrect. I had to convince him to leave his politics at the bedroom door; I wanted to fuck! He eventually came around, so to speak.

Afterthoughts

I have struggled with hard questions about relationships, particularly the male-female variety since lesbianism makes so much more sense to me as a feminist. For example, how *can* two people—one male, one female—hope for any semblance of equality in a relationship when one gets infinitely more social power than the other? And, given the powerful influence of compulsory heterosexuality, how can a woman be said to be making a truly free choice of a male partner? And, of course, given the power of love, that is, how identified women become with their lovers, why would I as a feminist give this kind of loyalty to a man when I could give it to a woman? And given how much more affirmed I feel sexually with a woman, how could I, knowing that I have an equal capacity to be intimate with a woman, consciously choose a man as a lover?

I have only fragments of answers. In a compelling essay, "Do You Have To Be a Lesbian To Be a Feminist?" Marilyn Frye introduces the concept of *virgin* as one who is free of the socialized patterns of gender roles.[2] Outside of these patterned ways of relating, she argues, is the possibility of feminist relationships between men and women. However, as I learned with David, a transgressive, gender-bending man does not automatically guarantee an equal relationship. I unconsciously *oppressed myself* for him! And, as I learned with Bianca, inequality and oppression are possible even between two women. I have learned that, although certain ways I give up power are easily recognizable, it is the more subtle, insidious ones I need to be wary of. Whether with men or with women, I want to make conscious choices about what I will and will not sacrifice.

It can still be argued that, no matter how much work is done inside a heterosexual relationship, the outside world still reinforces gender inequality. I agree, but one can challenge this. I have worked with male lovers on feminist projects, attended women's rallies together and truly been partners in eradicating gender inequality. I can't imagine being involved with a man with whom there wasn't at least some degree of participation in gender-role-challenging activity. I have done such day-to-day consciousness-raising activities as grabbing checks back when they are handed to a man, pointing out people's heterosexism when they ask whether I have a boyfriend or husband, and putting gay, lesbian and bisexual buttons, cartoons and stickers up in my office. Vigorously challenging heterosexual privilege in this way feels very good!

I noted above that sexism is not the only, and often not the most, important form of power struggle in a relationship. My challenge in relating to men now is grappling not only with sexism, but also with the rest of the voices in my head, the chorus of oughts and shoulds that, along with generic intimacy issues, can drown out my true feelings.

As I have come to reaffirm my "feminine" characteristics, I realize that personal power, for me, has little to do with the kinds of attributes valued by the society at large. I feel powerful when I can be vulnerable. I feel powerful when I am making clear, conscious, loving choices. Connections with others, whether men or women, are most powerful for me when I and the other person have access to and permission to express our deepest feelings, our most profound joys and sadnesses.

Finally, the outside world reinforces lots of inequalities other than gender; I don't want the outside world's values to determine whom I do and do not get to love.

I recently heard a woman in a sexual diversity workshop say that since she has come to think of gender roles as sex toys, she has been much less afraid of men. I like the idea of thinking of gender roles as sex toys. It invokes the notion of choice. Once one has really struggled with a prescribed way of being and no longer feels forced into it, she may then choose that behavior from a much freer, clearer, more comfortable place. And for those of us who do not wish to use our lives as political statements first and foremost, arriving at that place is both an important end and a lifelong process. I want to make choices from my heart, or whatever other organ I may choose, not because of outside forces, whether heinous or noble, that beckon me.

Endnotes

1. Andrea Dworkin, *Intercourse* (New York: Free Press, 1988).

2. Marilyn Frye, "Do You Have to Be a Lesbian to Be a Feminist," *off our backs*, June 1989.

Rebecca Shuster

BISEXUALITY AND THE QUEST FOR
PRINCIPLED LOVING

I came home to a bisexual identity in 1979. Yes, this was me, really me: a woman who had loved women, a woman who had loved men, a woman determined to base her relationships on individual passion, not societal dictates. From the night I adopted the identity, I felt wider, surer, more secure in the knowledge of who I was willing and unwilling to be.

Deep down, everyone was bisexual, I thought. Everyone would admit it eventually. All we had to do was end lesbian/gay oppression and sexism, and all the earth's people would join together in a glorious bell-shaped curve along a Kinsey scale of love and sexual preference with no one at the beginning and no one at the end.

It was an exciting time in my life, and I was figuring out important things about myself and the world. Yet, I remained unknowingly limited by what I had been taught to expect and what I had been injured into accepting. The truth, as it so slowly becomes evident to me, has more breadth, dimension and color than the furthest ideal I could imagine then.

Distinguishing Sexual Behavior From Sexual Identity

Recently, four women friends and I gathered to talk about bisexuality. Three of us considered ourselves bisexuals: one was in a monogamous relationship with a man, one was in a monogamous relationship with a woman and one was currently involved with a woman and a man. The fourth woman said that although she had recently married a man, in her heart she thought of herself as a lesbian. The fifth woman was seeing a woman and said she considered herself a lesbian, too, though she couldn't rule out a future sexual relationship with a man.

I asked myself whether the self-identification of the latter two women as lesbians could be true. Were they simply afraid of taking on a bisexual identity and the oppression that comes with it? As we each spoke about our lives, I knew the answer could not be cowardice or denial. Alice and Toni were two of the gutsiest women I knew.[1] Alice, for example, had continued to co-lead a lesbian/gay/bisexual organization throughout her long-term relationship with her partner, Zack. With courage and integrity she handled a range of responses to her heterosexual relationship, including tentative acceptance, confusion and outright hostility. She had frequently spoken up for the inclusion of bisexuals in the organization and had initiated an evening forum to discuss the issue.

Fortunately, the five of us had known each other a long time. In an atmosphere of respect and caring, we tried to piece together how and why we had arrived at identities that did not always have an apparent correlation with our sexual histories or present activities.

Finally, we arrived at a surprising and exciting conclusion: sexual activity was not equivalent to sexual identity. No matter whom we were making love with or might someday make love with, some of us had a bisexual identity, some had a lesbian identity, and, had we invited other women, some would have had a heterosexual identity.

Our society forces every woman consciously or unconsciously to buy a sexual identity package-deal somewhere along the way, often as teenagers or young adults.[2,3] We take on a label, and with it, a whole collection of beliefs about ourselves and our world. The overwhelming majority of women assume a heterosexual identity and internalize a package that includes traditional rules about how to relate to women and men, tremendous pressure to conform, the necessity of marriage and a fear of resisting and of those who do resist that can manifest itself as prejudice and violence.

If we choose a lesbian identity, we are subject to systematic oppression and internalize that oppression in a package that includes marginality; invisibility; isolation from heterosexuals and bisexuals that can manifest itself as prejudice, superiority or resentment; and countercultural rules about how to relate to women and men. If we choose a bisexual identity, we are subject to systematic oppression and internalize that oppression in a package that includes a feeling of not belonging or having a home; defensiveness; isolation from heterosexuals and lesbians that can manifest itself as prejudice, superiority or resentment; and countercultural rules about how to relate to women and men.[4] Precisely because bisexuality represents freedom of choice, society ensures that the identity comes with its own package of mistreatment and constraints.

When women who have identified as heterosexual have sexual contact with a woman, when lesbians have contact with a man, and when bisexuals make a long-term monogamous commitment, they may take on a new identity or retain their original identity. Two women with identical life stories can honestly hold two different sexual identities.

Identity as a Tool of Oppression and Liberation

The societal oppression of lesbians and bisexual women attempts to coerce all women to participate in heterosexuality without question. It is the complex whole of who we are as individuals that seems to determine whether we cooperate and what identity (or identities) we adopt throughout our lifetimes. Some of us feel comfortable with the set of permissions and restrictions within a bisexual identity and cannot imagine tolerating the lesbian or heterosexual set, whereas other women cannot imagine tolerating the bisexual set. Our individual strengths and difficulties lead us to become a feminist-heterosexual woman, a lesbian-identified bisexual woman, a lesbian with a husband and so on and to cope with the package deal that accompanies our choice.

Identity is a set of beliefs, not the immutable contents of a person's soul. Personal and social transformation requires us to claim our identities fully and proudly and to cast off piece by piece any ways the identities have limited what we believe to be possible for ourselves and other women. As this transformation occurs, we will eventually discard the identities, replacing them with our ability to make individual, creative decisions unique to each person and situation we encounter.

If our goal is to rid ourselves of every rigid construct of gender and sexuality, our vision for the future will be without any Kinsey scales, bell curves or identity packages. "Bisexual" will hold no meaning. Instead, we will simply be ourselves: people with stories to tell about whom we have known, whom we know and whom we dream of knowing.

What is to be preserved of bisexuality is a single kernel of truth: a quest for principled loving, a vision for what is possible among human beings, and a commitment to pursue that vision. Underlying a bisexual identity is a decision to seek to love without gender as a constraint, a basic goal for all people. The remaining components of the identity as it is currently constructed (such as sexual desires, sexual history, internalized restrictions and permissions) will cease to exist or lose their significance.

Part of gradually destroying the machinery of sexual and gender oppression is facing that we as bisexuals do not alone hold that kernel of truth, that heterosexual women and lesbians seek the same principled love and that struggling inside those identities are women who (just like bisexuals) are fighting to be close to other people despite societal definitions for and limitations on their lives. To transform we must reach through the identities and our mutual fears to respect every woman as she works toward liberation.

As bisexual women, we can be proud of each step we take—personal, political, private, public—to free ourselves and others from oppression and internalized oppression. We can take stands against sexual and gender oppression and all oppression, not because we are uniquely capable of doing so as bisexuals, but because it is the right thing to do. All ages, classes, dis/abilities, ethnicities, genders, races, religions and sexual identities bring an essential perspective to strategizing social change. Bisexuals belong as partners with each of these constituencies, each equally and fully welcome. Sweeping and lasting change relies on that broad partnership.

Taking Principled Stands in Our Personal Lives

As feminist-bisexual women (or women with any identity), we can take principled stands in both our personal and political lives. In political organizations and movements, we can help set policies, organize people behind those policies, and back other policy-makers and organizers. Here, I focus on taking stands in our personal relationships.[5]

In the same way we formulate political policies (for example, the inclusion of sexual identity in nondiscrimination clauses), we can formulate personal policies (for example, taking the initiative to build friendships with gay men). We need to formulate and apply the most humanitarian policies we can envision about how to treat our lovers, friends, co-workers, co-activists, families and all people with whom we come into contact.

These policies need to be continually re-evaluated and modified. We cannot wait, for example, until there is no sexism to select a man to join a household of women. Instead, we must proceed by acting on the furthest vision we have, making mistakes, welcoming correction and trying again. When we slip up, when we are "unprincipled," we are simply exposing what the society has programmed us to do. We do not deserve to be blamed for our mistakes or the ways in which we fall back on our conditioning. Our responsibility is not to hide our wounds and confusions but to do our best to name, heal and transcend them. The oppression of lesbians, for example, is like polluted air all children in our society are forced to breathe. Showing our fear of lesbians and our ignorance of their issues is not the problem; the problem is refusing to face our fear, acknowledge our ignorance and begin to learn.

To be principled in relationships between members of the same group (age, class, dis/ability and so on) requires us to expose and dismantle internalized oppression. Two women friends, for instance, might agree to spend time together weekly (whether both are single or not) and thus challenge how we were trained to undervalue our friendships. Two older women who work together might arrange to play basketball together during their lunch break each day and thus defy societal prescriptions about age and gender.

To be principled in relationships between people who are members of different groups requires us to expose and dismantle how we act out oppressor and victim roles. In a friendship between a heterosexual woman and a bisexual woman, for instance, the heterosexual woman can ask the bisexual woman to speak at length about what has been good and hard throughout her life as a bisexual, and the bisexual woman can resolve to tell her without withholding or editing any details because she feels distrustful. The heterosexual woman can vow to interrupt any anti-bisexual, anti-lesbian or anti-gay comments or jokes she hears; the bisexual woman can welcome the heterosexual woman to walk with her at a pride march.

Every relationship, whether between people of similar or different backgrounds, is equally vital to human liberation. As bisexual feminists, choosing a relationship with a woman is not inherently better than a relationship with a man (or vice versa). A relationship between members of an oppressed group (such as women) or members of an oppressor and oppressed group (such as a man and a woman) creates distinct opportunities, difficulties and responsibilities. Feminist separatism asserts that participation in the second kind of relationship is destructive. The feminism I propose asserts that every relationship presents a chance either to simply reproduce ancient patterns of domination and collusion or to forge a potential pathway to liberation.

Our lovers and other close alliances, then, would include a variety of both kinds of relationships, each offering us particular possibilities. There is no single best option for everyone, or any one person. What matters is our commitment to heal the injuries of oppression, to grieve together, to proceed through shame and fear to reach into one another's deepest selves, stretching to show the whole of who we really are, daring to love, to tell the truth, to change.

Within these relationships, myriad decisions will propel us forward as individuals, as women and as human beings: whether a woman or her male partner does the dishes, whether she helps devise a household policy about who does the dishes and what she does when that agreement is broken; whether two women lovers choose to come out—individually or jointly—to their families, friends and co-workers, whether they sue their respective employers for spousal benefits and how they treat each other throughout the infinite process of making each of those decisions. Those decisions, those steps are the substance of transformation, the daily grit and sweat that move us along.

Our personal integrity and our resolve to end all forms of oppression require us to constantly distinguish the ways we are breaking free of our training from the ways we are playing it out. This is particularly difficult in the area of sex, where we have been so massively hurt and confused by childhood sexual abuse, misinformation and manipulation by the media. In our sexual relationships, we can commit ourselves to sex based on closeness and caring. We can remember not to blame ourselves or others for internalized oppression around sex or for conditioning to oppress through sex. Instead, we can devote our energy to healing and assisting others to heal; recognizing fantasies, attractions and repulsions that result from these wounds; and striving not to act on them. For example, choosing never again to enact a sexual fantasy that contains elements of an abusive incident one recalls from childhood is a powerful act toward true "sexual liberation."

Conclusion

Individually and collectively, we can explore what decisions and situations allow us to peel away the layers of our training as members of oppressor and oppressed groups. Reflecting on that gathering of friends where I was able to learn so much about sexual identity, I can see some of the ingredients that permitted that kind of realization and transformation. We had built long-term relationships with one another, sticking with each other through hard times in our lives and through disagreements among us. Our conversation rested on a base of mutual respect that enabled us to take risks, to cry and tremble and laugh our way to speaking and then to listen to all that was said. As bisexual women, we can seek and forge these kinds of opportunities, constantly experimenting with ways to make them more effective.

As bisexuals, we hold a position similar to that of the middle class, making it appear as if someone can "make it" in a system where no one truly can. We are victimized by the overall system of lesbian/gay oppression and forced into the role of preserving that system by representing a freedom of choice that cannot fully exist as long as the oppression exists. Therefore, it is vital that we take responsibility as bisexuals for the ways we benefit from the privileges of heterosexuality and simultaneously demand that no one, including bisexuals, is targeted for being non-heterosexual.

Our future as bisexual feminists, then, offers an exciting opportunity to improvise our lives, making complex choices, taking falls and getting up again, becoming more and more ourselves, creating increasing numbers of meaningful relationships that continually grow deeper, uprooting oppression based on gender and sex more slowly than we have sometimes hoped, but far more quickly than we often fear. We can find true security, pride and joy in each layer of internalized oppression we shed, each step we take outside of our training for oppressor roles, each relationship and alliance we build that transcends societal divisions, each decision we make and stand we take based on principle.

Endnotes

Thanks to Josephine Dombrowski, Maggie Gladstone, David Jernigan, Aliza Maggid and Clare Thompson for their contributions to and assistance with this article, and to Elizabeth Reba Weise for her invitation to write it. My thanks, too, to the many friends and colleagues who have welcomed my love and generously allowed me to apply my evolving principles, however flawed, to our relationships.

1. The names used here are fictitious.

2. The term "society" is intended here to refer to the United States, though some statements may accurately describe other cultures as well.

3. This article focuses on the issues and experiences of lesbian, bisexual and heterosexual women. Many of the conclusions may also be applied to an understanding of gay, bisexual and heterosexual men.

4. For a longer description of bisexual oppression and internalized oppression, see Rebecca Shuster, "Beyond Defense: Considering Next Steps for Bisexual Liberation," in *Bi Any Other Name: Bisexuals Speak Out*, eds. Loraine Hutchins and Lani Kaahumanu (Boston: Alyson Publications, 1991), pp. 266-274.

5. See my article in *Bi Any Other Name* for proposals for taking principled stands in our political lives as bisexuals.

Amanda Yoshizaki

Breaking the Rules:
Constructing a Bisexual Feminist Marriage

August 10, 1987. Yosemite Valley was hot, the air tinted with the smoke of fires that had ravaged the park's woodlands. We didn't notice the heat or the smoke however; we could see only the glint in each other's eyes. We clattered across the wooden bridge, Paul in his black tux and top hat, me in my ivory satin dress and matching heels. We were, after years of discussion, getting married.

The traditional aspects of our wedding stopped there. We wore the "appropriate" costumes and smiles, but what we said to each other was original. I was not going to vow to obey and honor, and he was not going to accept such promises. Instead our vows consisted of promises to communicate, to understand and to support. I kept my name, and he kept his. For the most part, being with great-aunts the exception, we refer to each other as "my partner" not as "my husband" or "my wife," for if we use traditional terms, people assume we have a traditional arrangement. We are determined to construct our partnership from the start.

The obvious question then emerges: why marry at all? The importance of ritual bonding ceremonies can be explained by anthropologists; however, I think we can agree that they bear importance in many cultures. In this day and age the significance goes beyond a legal one, since, for the most part, women are no longer considered pieces of property and many states' laws no longer reflect this attitude.[1] We had been in a relationship for five years before we decided to marry. Despite anthropological or financial reasons,[2] we finally married because it was psychologically important to us. Perhaps this is our personal shortcoming, but we felt that marriage was the next step in our development as a couple. Although the kind of commitment engendered by a bonding ceremony or marriage will differ from couple to couple—some heterosexual people change husbands or wives as they do seasonal coats, whereas some same-gender couples will bond for life—for us, "official" marriage felt important. It felt more powerful than a bonding ceremony, perhaps because it had the columns of tradition and society holding it up. At the same time that we felt compelled to marry, we felt the necessity to tear down some of those same columns that made the event seem so monumental. We wanted to leave in place the scaffolding of commitment, communication and love that should make up a healthy partnership, while working at tearing down the assumptions of sex roles.

Yet the decision to marry was not one I took lightly. My quandary about marriage sprung not only from my feminist ideology, but also from my connections to the gay and lesbian communities. I am a bisexual woman who has had relationships with men and women, and who was lucky enough to find a person (a bisexual person to boot) with whom I can share my life. However, when I come out in the lesbian community as having married a man, I am often viewed as a traitor at best and leper at worst.

The "heterosexual privilege" I gained by marrying makes me suspect. I realize that the lesbian community might wonder where I will be in the fight for queer rights. They may assume wrongly that I won't be in the front lines with them. To believe that is to buy into the stereotypes and myths that bi women are really straight voyeurs. I did not choose to marry because of the heterosexual privilege it bestowed. On one hand, my political life would be easier if I were with a woman—but I am not. On the other hand, I could choose to leave my political life as a feminist bisexual activist and easily live hidden in the shadows of heterosexuality. However, to retain my integrity and my values, I can do neither. When I married, I realized that to continue as a bisexual activist in the lesbian community I would have to explain and defend myself often.

People in committed same-gender relationships often struggle for legitimacy. They work to help others understand the nature of human bonding and their relationships. They have few models to follow; they have to make up a new set of rules. Heterosexual marriage or relationships, however, have a history of rigid rules that plague them. Traditional sex roles as exemplified by the Cleaver family still exist. If I say I am married, people immediately have a preconceived idea of the dynamic of my relationship. People assume that I do the cooking and cleaning. People assume that Paul's needs and desires come first. People assume that I subjugate my ideas and wants to his. People assume far too much.

In the 1970s straight feminists spoke of the need to equalize the work in heterosexual relationships. They urged women to make choices beyond the realm of the house. They spoke of equal work for equal pay and for the valuing of traditional "women's work." These feminists began tearing down the preconceptions of rigid sex roles. For example, Jill Johnson claims that:

> [e]very woman who remains in sexual relation to a man is defeated every time she does it with the man because each single experience for every woman is a reenactment of the primal one in which she was invaded and separated and fashioned into a receptacle for the passage of the invader.[3]

Joyce Trebilcot continues this logic with the argument that women should choose lesbianism regardless of whom they are attracted to. She states, "Sexuality is socially constructed, in reconstructing it we need not assume either that erotic feeling should lead to love making or that love making ought to occur where there are erotic feelings."[4] Admittedly, sex between men and women can reflect the power dynamic when men consider themselves superior to women. However, this does not make the sexuality itself intrinsically wrong. In fact, I have spoken to many bisexual women, as well as to a few self-defined lesbians, who enjoy or have enjoyed intercourse with men. I don't believe sexuality is socially constructed, it is more innate. (From my experience sex and bonding are much more satisfying with someone I am attracted to.) Although we may not have control over who attracts us, we do have control over how we relate to them. Relationships are socially constructed. Relationships between men and women need to be developed with an acknowledgment of the sexism and heterosexism in society and a commitment to work toward equality. As a bisexual woman I have difficulty with lesbians who claim that heterosexuality is the root of patriarchal evil and that to be a true feminist a woman must not be involved with a man and most certainly should not have intercourse with him. Heterosexuality—love and attraction to a man—is not the problem. The problem rests in the power dynamic of sexism and the assumptions of heterosexism.[5]

When I was small I was taught that girls learn to cook, clean and iron whereas boys take out the trash and mow the lawn. I was told that when I stood with my legs apart I was standing "like a boy" and that girls shouldn't call boys on the phone. I was also taught by the television that women do the housework with Ajax or Comet or Mr. Clean and take care of the children with Pampers and Gerber Foods. Men go to the office and make money. Men buy cars and take business trips. Although later I gained a feminist consciousness that made me independent and assertive, I still retain some of those original messages. We live in a sexist society and we must constantly battle sexism from external sources such as the media, our co-workers and our bosses. We must also battle our internalized sexism. Recently my partner and I discussed our future. We both had applied to graduate schools and were accepted at a number of fine institutions. However, during our discussions I felt that my options were less important than his, that we should go to the best place for him. My own reaction made me angry. I cannot escape my internalized sexism. I can be aware of its existence and confront my own responses. To resolve this, we discussed my feelings and desires and eventually agreed on a compromise that met both of our needs.

In revised heterosexual relationships, sexism and internalized sexism are a dynamic that must be confronted constantly. I confront it daily in my own frustrations about the disparity between Paul's and my earning power. I am a teacher and he is a computer analyst. If we both work full time, he makes twice as much as I do. I have a master's degree and he just finished his bachelor's. Since he has been working part time, our take-home pay has been about the same. I have the knowledge that although our jobs are equally skilled, I am less valued by our society. Perhaps disparities in income are struggles for many couples regardless of sexual orientation; however, when the situation so clearly reflects the sexism in our society, the disparity takes on a larger import. My partner and I share our funds and talk at length about the social and psychological ramifications of the inequality of our paychecks. He listens to my anger that "women's work," such as teaching and child care, are poorly paid. In a traditional situation, he might expect me to forgo my profession and spend my time or part of my time caring for the house and his needs: after all he makes more money. However, it is short-sighted to think that the actual paycheck is the entire issue. The issue is more about needs and expectations. My profession is important to me and to him because it fulfills my need for intellectual stimulus and challenge. I have no desire to become a computer programmer. He, in the same spirit, did not go into computers because it makes money. He enjoys his work. So despite my frustration about inequity, we value our professions more for the intangible self-worth and satisfaction they give us. This is not to say that the inequity doesn't ever cause friction. It does. Yet we realize that because of our patriarchal sexist culture, our relationship starts off imbalanced and it takes effort to be aware of that imbalance and to work toward equitable compromise.

As I was taught traditional gender roles, I was also taught that monogamous heterosexual relationships are the only ones to be considered. In high school I fell in love with my best friend, Sharon. In our junior and senior years, we were lovers. Although I didn't actively hide my feelings, I told very few people. We didn't talk about our relationship with close friends and we didn't share it with our parents. I felt isolated. I loved Sharon, and still do, if the truth be told. The message that our relationship was not normal was clear. Similarly, the message that nonmonogamy is sick and perverse was also clear. Currently, my partner and I have a nonmonogamous relationship. We both have had lovers over the nine years we have been together. For us, these relationships are separate from ours and they meet different needs. I am not into the "swinging" in which some bisexual people participate. In my relationships outside my partner, I am honest from the start. I do not believe in lying to anyone. My partner and I have an agreement to complete honesty before we have sex with anyone else and to participate only in safer sex. We have found that the relationships with others are not the threat to our bond, the threat is the betrayal that dishonesty breeds. We have an unconventional relationship, one in which we have had to define its parameters.

With few models of healthy heterosexual relationships to follow, it seems to me we need to turn to women. My relationships with women, including intimate relationships as well as close friendships, have given me a perspective on the dynamics of relationships in general. They can serve as a model of relationships with men. I think of a greeting card I recently saw. On it was a cartoon sketch of a woman who was crying. The bubble above her head said, "My boyfriend ran off with my best friend. Boy am I going to miss her." I contend that our partners should be our best friends.

My relationships with women have been grounded in dialogue. We talk. We talk about our pain, our joy and our feelings. We share the common experience of being women in a sexist society. We share the fear of walking alone at night and the wonder of small babies. We share common conditioning. From these commonalities we develop a shared understanding. This type of understanding is what women and men need to strive to build.

Revised marriage no longer means that he does the dishes half of the time. It no longer means that she works in an office. A revised marriage goes beyond the realm of the division of labor and into the realm of interpersonal dynamics. Men and women need to learn to talk and listen to each other, and it isn't easy. In my relationship, we have spent hours upon hours chipping away at our social conditioning. He's learned to express his feelings and I've learned to explain my needs. A few years ago, when I decided I needed to go back to school, he agreed to continue working full time to support us, despite his desire to go back to college as well. When he feels frustrated at my busy schedule, he has learned to say something and not wait for me to guess there is something bothering him. We are committed to the work of dialogue. By re-visioning marriage and starting from scratch, we are radical. As reformers and queers we struggle not only within the confines of heterosexual constructs, but also in the fight for queer rights.

As a man and a woman in a heterosexual relationship, our struggles are different from same-gender couples. It is more accepted to be in a "different" heterosexual relationship than in a same-gender one. Although I could easily hide behind my relationship and deny my bisexuality, I don't, because then I would be denying an important part of myself. It would be analogous to denying my Japanese ancestry. I am mixed heritage, not white, not Japanese-American—both. I am also bisexual. I am also in love with a man. As a bisexual woman in a heterosexual relationship, I have a responsibility to speak loudly against homophobia. My marriage shields me from much of the targeting that gay and lesbian people often receive. I have the privilege of stating radical ideas without the same fear of persecution and I have a responsibility to do so. Radical straight people also have the responsibility to do so. If people are concerned with human rights, we must do all we can, large and small, to combat racism, sexism, classism, homophobia, biphobia and heterosexism.

Yet, as part of the queer struggle, I need to feel part of the queer community. I need to feel accepted for who I am—a married bisexual feminist. I need not to feel forced to closet my "straight side" in the lesbian/gay community. My marriage doesn't make me any less bisexual. In some ways, my marriage to a bisexual man has broadened my interaction with the gay community. My partner brought with him gay friends whom I have come to love and many of whom we have lost to AIDS. His bisexuality means that he starts with an understanding of oppression that most straight white men do not have. Because he has experiences from which to draw parallels, the work of communication is easier.

Although the needs of lesbians, gay men, bisexual women and bisexual men are not always the same, thus making the need for single-issue groups important, there is a strong need for coalition. Queers cannot win acceptance and rights if we are isolated from each other and wasting energy on political infighting. We must examine when it is appropriate and necessary to be with our specific group (be it with bi-women, bi-men, gay men or lesbians) and when we must bridge our differences and work together.

August 10, 1987, didn't change my or my partner's identity. We are part of the struggle for queer freedom and refuse to be silenced.

Endnotes

1. This is not to say that upon divorce the situations between men and women are at parity. Because of inequalities in economics and child-raising responsibilities, to name a few, single women with children are the new poor. Even in our relationship, he has the capacity to earn more than I do.

2. Actually, because we are two working people making similar amounts of money, marriage was a disadvantage for us financially. We are taxed at a higher rate than if we were single. As I discuss later in the essay, he has greater earning power than I do; however, for the past few years he has worked part time to finish his degree.

3. In Carol Anne Douglas, *Love & Politics: Radical Feminist & Lesbian Theories*, (San Francisco: Ism Press, 1990), pp. 165-66.

4. Ibid.

5. Heterosexism is the belief that heterosexuality is the norm, a belief that results in the systematic structured inequality that targets queer people. This results in discrimination and denial to access that heterosexual people are allowed to have. (Thank you to Brenda Blasingame for working with me on this definition.)

Diane Anderson

LIVING WITH CONTRADICTIONS

When I was eight years old, I would gleefully run to my cousin Judy's house at the drop of a hat. At those times when our parents hosted dinner parties or barbecues Judy and I would be ushered into Judy's bedroom to "play." There, unbeknown to our parents, in the safety of her French-provincial bedroom—complete with pink canopy bed and baby doll curtains—we took off our shirts and began exploring each other's budding breasts, acting out a scene from Wonder Woman, where she is captured and taken to a secluded Greek island to become the ruler's love slave. Nine-year-old Judy was full of quiet curiosity and I was a teacher most willing to oblige.

My ten-year-old cousin Eddie, however, was not a quiet and patient learner. Just entering puberty, his sexual prowess was alarming. Encounters with Eddie at family reunions and holiday get-togethers were intense sessions of visual stimulation and aural gratification, where we would remove all our clothes and discuss our gender differences in a frenzied rush. With both Eddie and Judy though (when all three of us were together), we would hug and kiss, massage each other, remove our swimsuits in the pool, and rest our heads in each other's laps while we swung back and forth on the front porch swing.

After Judy, there was Pam and Beth and Michelle. After Eddie there was Tom and Dan and Greg. A childhood full of explorative, touching moments with members of both sexes. Then I entered my teen years, where girls' interests turned to boys and vice versa. Like most of my friends, I began dating guys in high school. Even though I was having intimate sexual relationships only with guys, I told everyone I knew that I was bisexual. No one ever reprimanded or insulted me. No one ever looked askance when I made this proclamation. Most people, in fact, rarely even acknowledged it.

At that time, however, I thought bisexuality was very much based in its root word—sex. I'd have sex with guys, and my attraction to women would fuel my relationship with the guys, propelling our erotic fantasies to a level of almost complete camaraderie. I bought them *Playboy* magazine, which I read; rented explicit movies, which I watched; and even hired a stripper for one male friend's birthday party that I attended. (I even tipped the stripper pretty heavily for a less-than-average performance.) But I was very attracted to men. A woman had to be drop-dead gorgeous to get my attention.

I had learned—through the media, my friends and family, my community—what was attractive in a woman. I was attracted to the type of woman I wanted to become: sexy, smart, feminine, but by most standards, straight.

Although my girlfriends seemed to find wicked delight in my "eccentricities," no one else admitted to having erotic feelings about other women. I was very secure in my attraction to men, so any feelings of arousal I had for women didn't exactly keep me awake at night. In fact, I considered my "flexibility" an augmentation of a normal sex drive. It was the early eighties, and many teen idols were said to have "swung both ways"—Janis Joplin, David Bowie, Elton John, Rod Stewart. Billie Jean King was sued by a former female lover; Erica Jong wrote best-selling novels that promoted uninhibited sexual experiences with men and women. The radio played "Johnny, Are You Queer," "Gimme Gimme" and "Valerie"—all homopositive songs—and at the box office movies like *Making Love* and *Personal Best* featured bisexual characters. Every erotic magazine or pornographic movie I saw had two attractive women together—sexually—at some point. To me, bisexuality was chic, sexy and trendy; it meant I was liberal, open-minded and uninhibited about sex. I viewed lesbians as being as close-minded as straight women. They were, in my mind, butch and strong and single-faceted, never once intersecting with my sense of myself as bisexual.

So, imagine my surprise when I began falling in love with another woman. I was nineteen and had just returned home from college. I spent many hours with a friend from high school discussing ideals, equality, liberation and love. Tina and I shared every waking moment together—taking long walks, watching the sunset on the river, picnicking at the beach—falling in love. Before I had seen her only as a female friend and as a sex object. I had often imagined sleeping with her, but never imagined myself falling in love with her.

I discussed my feelings about Tina with my boyfriend of three years. I was—and still am—a stickler about monogamy, both emotional and sexual, so these feelings of emotional infidelity disturbed me. My boyfriend interpreted my feelings to be purely sexual in nature. So, I'll take her to bed, I decided, and I'll be satisfied and better from the experience.

After a four-month-long chase, I did take her to bed, and although I was better from the experience, I still wasn't satisfied. I left my boyfriend, and Tina and I moved away to attend a college in the South.

Neither of us had been exposed to any sort of lesbian community. We didn't even realize there was such a thing. We both had stereotypical images of lesbians as women with masculine qualities that just *met* places—like playing basketball or something. In our tiny town of four thousand, we had never seen any positive models of lesbians.

Lesbians were something totally different from what we were. They had little or nothing to do with my sexuality. Bisexual women, we thought, were the sexy, eat-your-heart-out types that all the men wanted to date. So instead of seeking support from the gay community, we remained closeted for three years. We tried to convince ourselves we had gotten together for sex, so neither of us could understand why we only wanted to be with each other in and out of bed. We tried in vain to accept our relationship as a passing thing, rationalizing away our commitment well into our third year together. We told each other that we were just really close friends who, perhaps, had spent too much time together. And so we waited for the time when the right man would come along and all the feelings between us would just disappear. I think I worried most that the right man would come along for her first and I'd be left flailing, alone, hopelessly in love with this forbidden woman. I felt that sex wasn't enough to hold two people together, especially two women. From all I had learned, two women just couldn't live a "normal" life together—marriage, dual careers, parenting. We never realized the true nature of our relationship because we never saw validation or role models—we never imagined that it was "okay."

All our friends were straight, and none of them knew about our relationship. We coached each other on dating etiquette, and on rare double dates, I would always end up leaving the restaurant in a huff if Tina seemed to be having a good time. Sex with another woman was enviable, but somehow I thought to myself that "loving" another woman was not. In 1988, we transferred to Xavier University, a predominantly black Catholic university. We attended Xavier not just for the experience, but also, ironically, for a certain type of anonymity. As the only white students in campus we were so different from the other students that we hoped they couldn't possibly pinpoint exactly what *was* different. While we were there, we never told a soul we were sleeping together. We never touched or whispered or winked in public. We wouldn't even wear the same color lipstick for fear someone would think we had kissed earlier. They knew, but we didn't know they knew. It was the worst time of my life.

A year and two colleges later, with the help of a supportive professor, we came out into a wonderfully supportive lesbian and gay community in Los Angeles. We immersed ourselves in the community, soaking up the special richness—the heritage and herstory—that came with a new cultural identification. Our now almost six-year relationship began anew then, and we pledged our undying love and commitment for each other.

During my time in L.A. I read every book by Andrea Dworkin and Kate Millett. I attended bisexuality workshops at college campuses and gay and lesbian community centers. I found few bisexual role models and even fewer that I could relate to. Some were in heterosexual relationships; many others were swingers. It wasn't until I moved back to New Orleans to edit a weekly lesbian/gay newspaper that I started to see the importance of a bisexual identity. Not only in Louisiana, but all over the country, I saw few, if any, books on bisexuality in bookstores and libraries, I saw queer groups where "open" bisexuals weren't welcome and I heard those cutting remarks and name-calling that separate lesbians and gay men from bisexuals. What was even worse, was that through all this soul-searching and debate, I found myself suddenly the most biphobic individual I knew. Tina, who strongly identifies as a lesbian, would constantly say to me "what about bisexuals" or "maybe she's bi" or "you're not like that, and you're bisexual." I'd find myself constantly saying, "that's different" or "she's not really bi—she's just closeted" or "I'm different from most bisexuals."

It took me those months to realize bisexual women and men are as diversified as any other group of women and men. There is more than one way to be bi, and I am no more and no less bisexual than the next bisexual. Just like pregnancy—you can't be sort of bisexual; you either are or you aren't.

As a bisexual lesbian, I constantly face contradictions in theory and reality. In theory, I enjoy men and women, but in reality, I share my life and my bed with only one woman. In theory, I want to maintain that bisexual identity even in the face of an assimilated lesbian community, but in reality, I'm afraid to lessen the strength of the lesbian community by "diluting" it. I'm afraid, even now, that if I say I'm bisexual, some lone bigot will stand up and proclaim, "I knew it. You do *need* men. Two women can't be happy together," but more unsettling than these theory-reality contradictions are other people's misconception that bisexuals can't be trusted because they want one thing today and another thing tomorrow.

Never in my life have I woken up and said, "Gee, I feel like sleeping with a man today. I'm not even attracted to this woman I was with last night!" And I really doubt that many other bisexuals experience such turn-about.

I did, at one time, think relationships with men were more real, more credible. That is what kept me from acknowledging the primary nature of my relationship with Tina. Now that I've spent so much time in the women's community, I tend to see relationships with men as *less* real. I'm not sure if this is because I'm in love or because I don't want to exploit the heterosexist privilege bisexuals can have or because I've finally seen women as being totally equal with men.

Alfred Kinsey acknowledges in his sexuality report that on a six-point scale, some people may change three or four points during the course of their adult lives. (See appendix, "The Kinsey Scale".) He notes, however, that this switch usually occurs over a long period of time, rarely overnight. This theory has been true for me in terms of sexual attraction. I have never felt a 50-50 ratio in my attraction to men and women. I used to be very attracted to men—physically and sexually. That attraction is learned at a very early age through books, music, movies. Women are not taught to find other women attractive. When girls hit puberty, they rarely pass around secret copies of *The Joy of Lesbian Sex*, as we did with *The Joy of Sex*.

Even though I was in love with Tina already, I felt like I didn't know how to be attracted to women. But after six years with a woman, I feel very attracted to women and less attracted to men. I can't even describe this process. I dropped out of the mainstream (media, norms) to unlearn those attractions and started to be attracted sexually to people on a more than one-dimensional scale. I am sexually attracted to women and men whom I don't find physically attractive. I see the whole, not the piece. I don't know how. I think, perhaps, if I were to go back to having intimate relationships with men, my attraction, over time, would evolve again.

If I weren't monogamous now, I would be a sequential bisexual—a person who has sexual relationships with only one gender at any given time. People fall into this category for many reasons.

The main reason I have tended toward sequential bisexuality is that the focus of my sexual attraction has changed over time. When I spent summers with Judy, I was interested in little girls. When I spent summers with Eddie, I was interested in little boys. When I was involved with men, women were my visual stimulation because they were taboo. Now I'm a lesbian and men are taboo, so they provide me with some visual stimulation. I crossed the line from men to women because I fell in love. And that relationship helped me break free of the power imbalances in opposite-sex relationships. I won't cross the line back to men for the same reasons. The longer I've been out of a male-female relationship, the harder it is to imagine having a serious relationship with a man. Sexually, I can still imagine desiring a man, but otherwise, I don't think a man can match the depth and intimacy that you can find with a woman. But still that is inherently a societal choice—not a sexual one. I could choose relationships with men or women out of sexual desire, but, politically and emotionally, I choose women.

One of the experiences that has changed the focus of my sexual attraction is spending a lot of time in the lesbian community. Face it, if you're around lesbians you'll fall in love with lesbians, not just because of the enlightened, kindred souls that they are, but because there is incredible power that comes from the strength of a strong gay and lesbian community. That sense of belonging to something very special is intoxicating in itself, and after having been an integral part of the queer movement, I don't know how anyone can go back to living an average heterosexual lifestyle. I've joined hands with lesbian Republicans to march for gay pride. I've talked "girl talk" with sixty-year-old drag queens. I've sat with several African-American men to watch a film on black gay life. I cried along with many, as I listened to Karen Thompson talk of her lover who was paralyzed in an auto accident. In a hall full of queers—Jews, Catholics, Wiccans, Unitarians, Buddhists—I debated the impact of the Persian Gulf war on spirituality. What in an average heterosexual existence can compare to this? You can't unlearn experiences; you can't stop shouting or fighting back; you can't forget pink triangles and rainbows and lavender anything. The gay/lesbian community is like a separate world, with its own rules, customs and cultures, yet with more diversity than you can usually find in one community.

Once a woman had to be amazing—like Tina—to grab my attention, and yet I found something attractive in almost every man I met. That remained the case until I had been in a lesbian relationship almost five years. It wasn't until I was very secure in my relationship and my bisexuality that the axis revolved and my attraction became more women-centered. I finally felt comfortable with women. I had been asking "what do I do" only to be told "you'll figure it out." Suddenly, I knew! In lesbian bars or coffee houses, I would always see a new woman whom I was attracted to. It was as though I bloomed—graduated from lesbian puberty. Suddenly men who used to attract me no longer did, while women that I used to complain did nothing for me now aroused me. Tina would constantly say, "I thought you didn't like that haircut on women." And it was true. All the things that had threatened me before—like butch/femme clothes—now turned me on.

What distinguishes me from many other lesbians and makes me retain a bisexual identity is that I'm not attracted to people on a gender-specific basis; I am still attracted to both sexes. While growing up, I never felt stifled or different because of my sexual identity. For me, choosing to spend the rest of my life with a woman was a very conscious decision. For me it was a choice. I made that choice because I was in love with a woman, but after we had been "out" for a year I decided that it wasn't just *this* woman. If we broke up or chose to be non-monogamous, I would still choose to focus on women. My relationships with women—in all aspects—have been more fulfilling than my relationships with men.

Just months after Tina and I began coming out, I watched an interview with a lesbian author. She was explaining how the women's movement propelled her to choose lesbianism as a lifestyle. I fell in love with these ideas—these radical feminist ideas—and I sought out all the information on feminism, lesbianism and the women's movement I could find. A lot of women were led to lesbianism through feminism. Well, my bisexual lesbianism led me to feminism. Now that I'm a feminist, I expect a lot more from men, in any kind of relationship. Before I started studying feminism, I would tolerate a large degree of misogyny and sexism because they were seemingly acceptable in society.

Wendy Wonderful's proclamation in support of Kate Millett, at a 1970 conference, is a case in point. Wonderful, an outspoken lesbian activist from the Northeast, said, "I'm a bisexual, but I've realized something. I can tell my friends I'm bisexual, and they say how groovy, as long as I'm having a relationship with a man. If I say the same thing and introduce them to a woman I'm having a relationship with, they are very cool about it. I'm bisexual, but it is for my homosexuality that I'm oppressed. Therefore, I say I am a lesbian as a political statement."

I couldn't have said it better. Only I recognize that despite a growing bisexual movement, bisexuals are still oppressed in the gay and lesbian community. So I retain my identification as a bisexual lesbian, even though I've lived as a lesbian for many years. When my first relationship with a woman began, bisexuality was a sexual preference and lesbianism was an emotional preference.

My relationship has greatly changed my self-definition, changes I may not have made had I not been with Tina. I haven't been sexual with a man for six years. I have little desire to be with a man—sexually—ever again.

So why do I insist on the bisexual label? Because I recognize that I am inherently bisexual and that my sexual preferences are experiential in nature. Because I am evolving, moving up or down that Kinsey scale, does not mean I forgot where I began and how my choices have affected that evolution. And to keep open the possibility of an opposite-sex relationship, whether or not I choose to act on it, is indeed an political statement.

Anna Freud had a theory that, in essence, concluded that masturbatory fantasies are the ultimate criteria in sexual preference.[1] I believe that dreams and fantasies are a part of that criteria and that they are proof that sexuality is experiential and programmable. Your mind and your senses can be trained or regulated—programmed—to perform in a certain way. With sexuality, I think, we tend to program ourselves against the backdrop of influences around us. One night a few months ago, I listened to k.d. lang crooning "Big, Big Love" as I fell asleep. I had an incredibly erotic dream with lang as the star—and I awoke with a sudden yet incurable attraction to short-haired, brunette, androgynous women and country music. For weeks after that, at every nightclub we went to, I'd pester Tina with comments like, "Did you see her? She has eyes just like k.d. lang!" or "She's so attractive. She looks just like my k.d.!" Just that one dream opened me up to a new titillating attraction. I had never been particularly attracted to that androgynous look before, but now I'm most attracted to a person whose sex is not known at first glance, regardless of that person's sex.

My sexuality is ever-changing. Things I never thought I'd like, I now love. Things I used to love, I no longer need or desire. One thing that has stayed constant for me is a desire for a committed monogamous relationship. In planning for our wedding ceremony, Tina and I had to discuss her misconceptions about bisexuality and monogamy. She felt that choosing a bisexual identity meant that I was declaring my sexual ambiguity—my need to have my cake and eat it too. Tina felt that I was giving up my dreams of a traditional family, so the hardest part was convincing her that I would not choose the so-called easy life (read: heterosexual) at the first chance; that I did not need a man and a woman in my life to be bi; that one person could fulfill me because I am fulfilled in myself.

The great part about bisexuality is that it's just one of the roads that can lead women to other women. Bisexuality for me was a bridge to the sometimes unwelcoming women's community. Although some lesbians believe bisexual women have no place in their community, I've found many to be curious and kind. And I've learned more about my bisexuality from a fifty-year-old dyke than I have from any bisexual person. Women have a lot of strength and connection with life that they sometimes don't express because they see themselves through the eyes of men. But expressing my sexual attraction to women has led me to discover the latent power inherent in what is female.

Because of where I grew up and when and where I came out, I didn't experience the women's movement, consciousness-raising or a personal feminist awakening, but they seemed to be about choices, equality, acceptance and the reconsideration of gender roles. This call for reconsideration is what pulled me out of the lesbian closet and made me say to everyone that although I may not have had sex with a man in many years and probably never will again, I am still unequivocally, inherently bisexual. I recognize that I am attracted to men and to women. I have the capacity to love a person of either sex. My sexuality is continually developing and maturing.

Ti-Grace Atkinson said, "Feminism is a theory; lesbianism is a practice."[2] I am bisexual by nature, feminist by choice and a lesbian by practice. But, I am bisexual—no matter how I choose to live my life. Although for me bisexual has become an adjective rather than a noun, it is still my basic orientation.

Bisexuality is my sexual orientation. Lesbianism is my sexual preference. Feminism is my religion. If that still leaves me with contradictions, then I'll live with it.

Endnotes

1. Anna Freud, *Before the Best Interests of the Child* (New York: The Free Press, 1979), p. 121.

2. Ti-Grace Atkinson, quoted in Lani Kaahumanu and Loraine Hutchins's introduction to *Bi Any Other Name: Bisexual People Speak Out* (Boston: Alyson Publications 1990), p. xxiv.

Eridani

IS SEXUAL ORIENTATION A SECONDARY SEX CHARACTERISTIC?

I think that part of the explanation for some of the conflicts that have arisen in the communities of lesbian, bisexual and feminist activists since their revival in the late 1960s—conservative gay male versus radical lesbian, "political lesbian" versus bar dyke, or anti-porn activist versus leather dyke—is that women, compared to men, tend not to have sexual orientations.

That is, if to some degree women have a choice about whom they relate to sexually, that is a basis for arguing about the ethical implications of various styles of sexual expression. As a bisexual feminist, my original thinking on this was as a possible explanation for biphobia in the lesbian/gay community, which is an almost exclusively female phenomenon.

In 1990, the organizers for the annual gay pride celebration in Northampton, Massachusetts, added the word "bisexual" to the event title. A group of lesbians packed subsequent meetings and voted to remove it. A similar fight against adding "bisexual" to the New England Association of Gay and Lesbian Psychologists was led by women. In San Francisco, when the *Bay Times* added "bisexual" to its masthead, all the letters objecting to the new title were from women. Why is it that women, and not men, think that the gay community is being contaminated by the presence of bisexuals? I have known gay men to get angry at individual bisexuals for keeping them on hold or otherwise denying recognition and significance to gay relationships, but never have I heard of a gay man who thought that bisexuality per se was a threat to the gay community as a whole.

Why? I think the reason is that most women have some degree of choice about their sexual orientation and most men don't. Researchers using the Kinsey scale (see Appendix, "The Kinsey Scale") have long been aware that women tend to be distributed more evenly between the scale poles of 0 and 6 and that the corresponding distribution for men is more bipolar, that is, two populations tending to be clustered around 0 and 6. I understand that the Kinsey scale is an attempt to put sexual behavior into some kind of analytical framework, but I have never really been comfortable with it. The entire notion of sexual orientation is based on male experience. It certainly doesn't correspond to my experience. It fits me like the old-fashioned "women's" athletic shoes which were actually only small men's shoes. I have the same problem with bicycles. "Normal" bike riders are supposed to be male, so most bikes have top bars that are too long for me and seat stems that are too short, which requires an extensive amount of fiddling on top of a basic design that is inherently uncongenial.

In my opinion, having a sexual orientation is a male secondary sex characteristic, like greater muscle mass, height and facial hair. Of course, just as there are many women who are taller or stronger than the average man, there are a lot of women who have sexual orientations. Comparing any typical "male" or "female" characteristic yields a large area of overlap where perhaps a majority of us dwell. I would therefore suspect that many women have sexual orientations, and some men don't.

I should at this point define my terms. By "sexual orientation" I mean a deeply rooted sense, dating from earliest memories, that serious relationships are possible only with persons of the opposite sex or the same sex, as the case may be. Whether biological, conditioned by early experience or both, a sexual orientation can be suppressed or ignored, but not readily changed. People without sexual orientations can form serious, emotional/sexual relationships with members of either sex, though they may value same-sex and and opposite-sex relationships differently.

I have often used "bisexual" as shorthand for "not having a sexual orientation," although "bisexual" implies having two sexual orientations rather than none. It has the virtue of being a single, commonly understood word. "Bisexual" is often used to refer to the fact that, for most people, erogenous tissue responds to rubbing by other people, regardless of sex or sexual orientation, but that is a trivial meaning not germane to this essay. Although I have suggested a biological basis for having a sexual orientation, I think that the factual observations about what is actually occurring in the lesbian/gay community still hold even if one assumes that this particular sex difference is purely a social construct.

Some characteristics that are for the most part exclusive to the gay male community can be explained by the hypothesis that sexual orientation is mainly a male characteristic. There is a large, highly conservative male group of gay people who are pretty happy with society just as it is, except for the homophobia that denies them their full due as privileged white men. They attempt to look as straight as possible, and many would be straight if they could be. People voluntarily seeking counseling to change their sexual orientations are almost exclusively male. Just as a biphobic letter to the editor is almost certain to be signed by a woman, a letter castigating socialistic notions like national health insurance and asking what this has to do with AIDS organizing is sure to be signed by a man. Though the majority of lesbians and gay men understand the connections between homophobia and other forms of oppression, specific denial of them is almost entirely a male phenomenon.

In our society men's patterns of sexual expression are far more narrowly channeled than those of women. This may be biological, or it may reflect the heavy suppression of women's sexual expression by men. To have a sexual orientation at all seems to me to be similar to being a tit man, a leg man, a fat admirer or, in the case of gay men, being a size queen, preferring cut to uncut, shaven versus hairy, and so on. Personal ads specifying only well-defined types are almost always submitted by men. Although the majority of men's ads are like women's, that is, I want a friend who shares some of my interests, and maybe we can get it on if things click—there seems to be a significant statistical difference between male and female populations when it comes to being picky about "types."

Although the population of women having sexual orientation is smaller, there are plenty of them around. When Cherríe Moraga says, "How could I say that I wanted women so bad, I was gonna die if I didn't get me one, soon!" she is certainly talking about a sexual orientation.[1] There are also a lot of women who feel that way about men sexually, even when they have trouble getting along with men the rest of the time. Any of Marilyn French's fictional female lead characters can serve as an example here. For instance, Dolores in *The Bleeding*

Heart and her women friends have the sort of tight social bonding that is typical of the lesbian-feminist community, but adding sex to those social arrangements is out of the question for her despite her acceptance of her daughter's lesbianism.

I can't honestly say that I have ever felt that way about either sex, although I have certainly been sexually besotted with individual women or men. I used to think that I was heterosexual, but in retrospect what was really happening was that I gave the only cultural meaning available to me at the time to generalized adolescent horniness. Joanna Russ's essay in *The Coming Out Stories* has a particularly sharp dissection of the obliteration of potential lesbian identity by the dominant culture's control of the naming of sexual experience.[2] Sexual experimentation with her girlfriends had a powerful intensity for her. When she experienced a similar but far less intense feeling for a boy, the feeling for her special friend was banished to the realm of things that didn't exist because there was a name for her experience with the boy—"love."

If one assumes that large numbers of women are like me, then there is an obvious reason why gay men have until recently outnumbered lesbians. There is a strong tendency on the part of people without sexual orientations to accept the available heterosexist cultural context because alternative images have not until comparatively recently been available, and because there is no strong internal force pushing the other way.

1970: Sisterhood Is Powerful

Now we get to the question of who is a "real lesbian." In the early seventies the visible lesbian community increased exponentially in size, fueled by the rising feminist tide. Large numbers of women discovered that sexual and emotional relationships with women worked beautifully. The sociologist Jessie Bernard quantified what women (regardless of sexual orientation) have known for a long time—men's well-being improves with marriage and that of women declines.[3] Many of the women who preferred the solidarity and support of the new women's communities did not have sexual orientations. A few even had heterosexual orientations, which they suppressed. A clear sex difference in the prevalence of sexual orientations is apparent here. Who ever heard of a heterosexual male who decided to become gay on the grounds that he didn't like being around women most of the time? Men like this become batterers and rapists instead.

The whole lesbian-feminist phenomenon was observed with amusement by women who had been lesbians all along, who felt that "real lesbians" were those who had risked abuse by the world at large to follow their own preferences before it became fashionable. A "political" lesbian was therefore not a "real" lesbian. If this is true, is it also true that a woman without sexual orientation who chooses to be with men for social acceptability or in order to have children or to have access to a higher income is not a "real" heterosexual? Of course, if the power of the dominant culture to name sexual experience can prevent some genuine lesbians from recognizing their sexual orientation until middle age (as in the Joanna Russ essay mentioned previously), it will certainly prevent women without sexual orientations from recognizing the possibility of relationships with women at all. For this reason, aided by the more direct forms of oppression of sexual nonconformists, most women without sexual orientations think of themselves as heterosexual.

I think that a large number of women who say they are heterosexual are, in fact, women without sexual orientation who are coerced by a repressive patriarchal society into being unaware of, and even actively afraid of, other options. The classic *Lesbian/Woman* has a number of stories about middle-aged "heterosexual" widows or divorcees who meet woman A or B and fall in love.[4] Some clearly feel that they have always been lesbians, but suppressed their true sexual orientation in order to conform and to have children. Others say that, as a result of chemistry with a particular individual, they find themselves feeling for a woman feelings they had previously associated only with men. There wasn't a lot of bisexual awareness back in 1973, so the authors called these latter women "lesbians," too. They are not. They are women without sexual orientation who happen to have primary relationships with other women.

The hostility on the part of lesbians with sexual orientation has been more than amply returned by some lesbian feminists who regard sexual lust for women as tainted with male-identification. It is mainly lesbians without sexual orientation who are hostile to bisexuals as well. The old standard "any woman can be a lesbian" is true for the large number of women who don't have sexual orientations. Therefore being a feminist implies to some lesbians that, on ethical grounds, women should choose to have relationships only with women, the way one would decide to be a vegetarian despite liking meat. I don't see how this attitude differs from that of Phyllis Schlafly, who thinks that I should choose a heterosexual relationship in order to be a good Christian reactionary. Some of the most vicious homophobes around are right-wing women without sexual orientations. The fact that large numbers of women do have such a choice is what makes both attitudes possible.

1980: Sisterhood Has a Few Flies in the Ointment

The phenomenon of "hasbians" in the eighties, i.e. women who first became aware of their sexuality in the lesbian-feminist matrix and later took up with men, indicates again that there are a lot of lesbian feminists who don't really have sexual orientations. It also indicates that the women's community isn't always as supportive as it's cracked up to be. What I am saying here is that there are other reasons that women without sexual orientations might choose to relate to men besides being shoved into it by patriarchal homophobia.

For one thing, the "instant sisterhood" vibes that one can establish with another feminist woman have their down side. Closeness and nurturing coming from other women are often experienced as threatening rather than positive. Margaret Atwood's novel *Cat's Eye* dissects this threat very perceptively.[5] The artist who acquires her audience from the feminist community has a history of emotional manipulation by "best friends" which causes her to rule out any consideration of a close emotional/sexual relationship with another woman. Having problems like that with your mother can lead to the same result.

Being "trashed" is pretty debilitating as well and likely to counteract the emotional advantages of hanging out in the lesbian-feminist community. Jan Clausen describes this experience in a recent issue of *Out/Look*.[6] Her lover was trashed for a book that Clausen wrote to the point of being unable to do her own writing.

Clausen herself became involved with a man she met while working in the Central American support movement. She does not claim the label "bisexual," but her description of her experiences implies to me that she has never had a sexual orientation. Her experience is typical of the "hasbian" phenomenon. Given that radical feminists are radical about everything else as well, they work on anti-apartheid, rain forest action and numerous other progressive causes. They are therefore likely to meet men who are aware of and often committed to working on feminist issues. People choose sexual involvements from the pool of potential partners with whom they spend most of their time. If a large proportion of lesbian feminists in this situation in reality have no sexual orientation, statistical probability dictates that some will establish relationships with men. (Though sexism negatively influences the most liberated heterosexual relationships, trashing in the women's community negatively impacts lesbian relationships. In my experience it's six of one and half a dozen of the other.)

Given that all communities of sexual minorities are currently under serious assault by reactionary thugs, squabbles about who does and who does not belong to "the community" are pointless distractions. It is certainly true that one can gain access to privilege by being closeted, regardless of whether or not you have a sexual orientation. We are divided by class, race and sex privilege as well. We should all be doing constructive work on those issues instead of arguing about who should and should not be included in the work. If you don't happen to have a sexual orientation, that is just a fact. If you do have a sexual orientation, being straight or gay is just another fact.

1990: Queers Sticking Together Is Powerful

On the positive side, there are a lot of folks who accept this and a lot of signs of the emergence of a queer community that is not biphobic. Many people are harking back to the experiences at the beginning of the second wave of feminism and reveling in the power that refusing to lie about your life can bring.

Sexual minorities within minorities, that is leather people and other sex radicals, have become more vocal. I identify with them despite being a total vanilla wimp with a low pain threshold. I like their insistence on writing about and interpreting their own experience, and the comparative absence of biphobia among them.

A number of gay men have written eloquently about feeling alienated among men who are homosexual but not particularly queer. Queer Nation is a wonderful countertrend, consisting mainly of a lot of people young enough to be unsure of exactly what the Stonewall Rebellion was (it happened as they were being born, and it wasn't taught in school) yet who embody that spirit of rebellion far better than the three-piece-suit types who monopolize the "responsible leadership" positions.

In Seattle, the local lesbian/gay pride march is a popular and very open event. Anyone who is willing to comply with traffic and fire safety regulations can have a float or contingent. Inevitably, a few "straight" homosexuals write to the local gay paper demanding that the event organizers eliminate the flakier groups to make the event more "responsible." Fortunately, that has not yet happened, so we can be treated to the sight of a large Queer Nation contingent sashaying down the street shouting, "You say, 'Don't fuck'; we say, 'Fuck you!'" They firmly embrace outrageousness and, significantly, have lots of "Promote Bisexuality" stickers for sale as well as the usual dyke/faggot/queer sort.

Besides the increasingly articulate members of the lesbian/gay community who are in favor of more, not less, queerness and who recognize that bisexual, though not the same as lesbian or gay, is still queer, there are a lot of very weird "straight" people around who also feel that way. It may be stretching the definition of "queer" too far to call them "queer straights," because they don't take the brunt of homophobic harassment, but they can be more fun for bisexuals to hang out with than "straight queers." They can be found (among other places) at pagan gatherings and science fiction conventions, and they are often hassled by Christian fundamentalists in a very familiar way. The powers that be are not fond of imagination and creativity that they don't have under lock and key.

Gloria Anzaldúa calls her community of off-beat friends El Mundo Zurdo, the Left-Handed World, which appeals to me a lot.[7] I think of all the people—both with and without sexual orientations—who don't fit into the neat little rows of square holes, who won't chop themselves down to fit and who won't lie about their lives. Isn't it about time that we dropped the "more-oppressed-than-thou" set pieces and got serious about fighting the world machine that wants us to be sober robots cheerfully beavering away piling up surplus value for the benefit of a very small elite?

*

Endnotes

1. Amber Hollibaugh and Cherríe Moraga, "What We're Rollin' Around in Bed With," *Heresies* 3, no. 4 (1981): pp. 58-62.

2. Joanna Russ, "Not For Years, But For Decades," in *The Coming Out Stories*, ed. Julia Penelope Stanley and Susan J. Wolfe (New York: The Crossing Press, 1980), pp. 103 - 119.

3. Jessie Bernard, *The Future of Marriage* (New York: World Publishers, 1972).

4. Del Martin and Phyllis Lyon, *Lesbian/Woman*, (New York: Bantam Books, 1972).

5. Margaret Atwood, *Cat's Eye* (New York: Doubleday, 1989).

6. Jan Clausen, "My Interesting Condition," *Out/Look* 7 (Winter 1990): pp. 11-21.

7. Gloria Anzaldúa, "La Prieta," *This Bridge Called My Back: Writings by Radical Women of Color*, eds. Cherríe Moraga and Gloria Anzaldúa (New York: Kitchen Table Women of Color Press, 1981), pp. 198-209.

Amanda Udis-Kessler

CLOSER TO HOME:
BISEXUAL FEMINISM AND THE TRANSFORMATION OF
HETERO/SEXISM

The first time I sleep with "Jonathan," it bothers me that he wants to rush through savoring each other's bodies and get on to intercourse. I feel him controlling the tempo of the evening, setting a pace I don't like. I should say something, want to say something, but don't, accepting his expectations without protest. I am usually very direct about my needs and opinions; tonight I cannot bring myself to say anything. Later in the night, after he has fallen asleep, I lie awake, silent, sad, aching fiercely to be with a woman.

One of the great strengths of feminism is its ability to shed light on the social forces acting on our personal lives. This is especially the case when we as women experience ourselves as somehow inadequate; thinking in a feminist way about where the sense of inadequacy comes from leads us to focus on environments in which we are often in no-win situations, and in which doing the best we can under the circumstances is never quite good enough. If feminist analysis only went this far, it would still offer us respite from the self-blame that has, not accidentally, fallen to women in modern Western societies. Yet feminism goes further, asking how it has come to be that our best is never quite good enough, suggesting that our self-blame and sense of inadequacy have been defined, imposed and managed through a set of values that permeate our lives but that have their origins outside of our lives and beyond our full control.

Those of us who identify as bisexual feminists may be politically active in any number of ways, traditional protest strategies and commitment to women's culture and communities being two common approaches. In choosing these forms of activism, we focus on power structures generally understood as separate from our lives and constraining us from the outside: the economy, the political system, the workplace. These structures are important, but they tell only part of the story of our isolation, sense of failure and disempowerment; struggling against their dominance is only part of bringing about long-lasting social change. The structures within us as individuals are as important as those imposed upon us in obvious ways; although these internal structures have not been the subject of that much analysis among bisexual feminists, focusing on them is legitimate and important work. In this essay, I want to consider two arenas of political struggle that are intricately bound up with the internal structures that drive our day-to-day lives: how we relate to our male sexual and romantic partners, and how we respond to heterosexual privilege.[1]

Those are by no means concerns only of bisexual feminists, but we are in a position to bring interesting resources to these inquiries if we wish. When considering our heterosexual relationships, we have our experiences with women available for comparison; we can determine what the similarities and differences are and connect those to the subtle kinds of disempowerment present when we are with men. In this sense, we have access to certain resources that can help us understand the micropolitics of sexism, resources that heterosexual feminists may not be able to draw upon so easily. Yet unlike lesbian feminists, our attempts to transform, rather than reproduce, structures of sexism have an immediate impact on men and can actually directly change their perspectives and behavior. Understandings that enable us to make changes in patterns of heterosexual intimacy, household division of labor, child care and child-rearing, male-female communication patterns, money management and the like, may then become more accessible to heterosexual feminists and play a role in ending the reproduction of sexism that goes well beyond merely those women who identify as bi-feminists.[2]

Similarly, bisexual women experience heterosexual privilege differently than either lesbians or heterosexual women do, given our capacity to be on either end of its effects. We may have a more immediate interest in challenging heterosexism than many heterosexual feminists; we also have more opportunity than lesbians to struggle with our own reproduction of heterosexual privilege. Not only can we address sexism within our relationships with men, but we can also turn those relationships into arenas of struggle against heterosexism as well.

While sexism and heterosexism are generally discussed separately, they reinforce each other and interlock in significant enough ways that it seems reasonable to consider them together. Some bi-feminists and lesbian feminists talk of "heteropatriarchy;" I will use the term hetero/sexism. Although the two forms of oppression cannot be reduced to each other, we can see the overlap in the homophobia behind the enforcement of traditional gender roles and the sexism inherent in heterosexual privilege (a point to which I will return later).[3] Using the term hetero/sexism provides a kind of shorthand for the mutuality of the two systems and may inspire bisexual feminists to look closely at the effects of that mutuality in our lives.

Crucial to any discussion of hetero/sexism as a system is the understanding that gender roles and sexuality are "imposed, managed, organized, propagandized and maintained" and as such are not private concerns (in the sense of being apolitical), nor are they natural ways of being[4]. Once we view hetero/sexism as an institution with a history, form, set of rules and definitions, and arrangement of goods and services, we rightly resist arguments that gender roles are biological and thus immutable; this resistance is necessary if we are to have any reason to hope that sexism can be eradicated. Similarly, although we are deeply accustomed to seeing our sexual orientations as natural, there are important ways in which they are socially constructed rather than simply biologically given; we do not merely engage in heterosexual or homosexual sex, but are understood (and understand ourselves) to *be* bisexuals, heterosexuals, lesbians or gay men. The role that our sexuality plays in our self-identities is not merely a matter of biology; sexual orientation is as carefully managed as gender roles are,[5] and heterosexual privilege provides a structure for this management.

In order to analyze the ways in which hetero/sexism is not merely external to us but also somehow reproduced within our lives, we need an understanding of structure that goes beyond the ways in which the economy or the government works and focuses on how we learn to make sense of reality. Such an understanding must show how hetero/sexism is reproduced regardless of one's intentions not to do so, a crucial point for understanding why men may respond so badly to attempts to challenge sexism, and why heterosexuals (and bisexuals in some cases) are made so uncomfortable by accusations of heterosexual privilege. The perspective sought here is available if we view structure, not as large-scale institutions, but as the rules and resources of a society or social setting.[6] Rules here include both the technical rules (laws among them) about what people may or may not do and the understandings about what is true or good. Political systems, religious values, board games and school curricula are all composed of rules. Resources are any goods, services or ideas made available to (some or all) people that enable social relations to be constantly reproduced and made meaningful and sensible. Resources are not all equal or distributed equally; examples of resources might include money, a computer, a position of authority in some setting, technical or intellectual skills, a building with staff and equipment, access to the media, ownership of coveted fashion or art items, or a strong belief in one's capacity to accomplish something. Structure, then, is generally carried, not behind our backs but in memory traces or emotions, in what we know, in whom we are willing to root for, in what we believe to be possible or desirable.

This way of understanding structure offers a particular explanation as to why and how structural hetero/sexism persists, an explanation that is both realistic and not entirely pessimistic about the chance for change. Hetero/sexism is continually reproduced because people carry certain kinds of "knowledge" about what men and women are like, knowledge that informs their decision-making and behavior,[7] and because some of the people who carry the most problematic (from a feminist perspective) "knowledge" have grossly unequal access to resources such as physical strength, money and control of the media and/or the legislative process. Moreover, if structure is carried in rules about what is and what ought to be—rules that most people obey—one of the important resources to have is the ability to make rules and get them widely accepted; feminism has long pointed to exactly this historical privilege of (some) men: to define what is important, what is good, what is permissible, what God wants or does not want, who governs, who benefits, who wins when rules or the distribution of resources are contested. In this way, certain men have exercised almost complete control over the initial setting up of social structures throughout much of history.

Yet the men who get to make these rules cannot enforce them alone. Even with unequal access to resources, there are too few men to use repression successfully (as police, jailers, thugs) or to run all the mechanisms of manipulation (education, the mass media, child-rearing). The constant reproduction of hetero/sexist structure requires many, most or all people in a society to play a reproductive, rather than a transformative, role. There must be specific mothers who socialize their children in hetero/sexist ways, and specific children who are socialized to be hetero/sexist. There must be specific men who are rapists and gay-bashers, and specific judges who let them off lightly. There must be specific employees who work for companies that provide hetero/sexist educational resources for schools, and specific schools that use the resources. There must be specific mass media consultants, publishers, actors, broadcasters, technicians and the like who participate in reinforcing definitions of appropriate sexual behavior, and specific individuals who watch TV, read the paper or listen to the radio and have their definitions reinforced. There must be specific bosses who underpay or refuse to hire women, and specific women who accept the bosses' authority. It is not necessary that any of these people have bad intentions as they go about their business; it is only necessary that the rules and resources—the structure—of their "business" benefit men at the expense of women, and heterosexuals at the expense of lesbians, gay men and bisexuals. If such inequalities are sufficiently built into the rules and the access to resources, people who consider themselves loving, kind and well-meaning will regularly behave in ways that are deeply hurtful to women and sexual minorities and will become extremely angry and confused when accused of being sexist or homophobic.

It is difficult to see that individuals are ultimately the agents for reproducing or transforming hetero/sexism, because injustice appears in patterns; it is not merely one sportscaster, professor, doctor, mother, man or woman on the street who is hetero/sexist, but many. Observing the patterns and looking for systematic ways to understand them can obscure the role of individuals (in specific social settings, with specific information available to them) in reproducing hetero/sexism. Yet it is possible, even necessary, to grasp how simultaneously individuals reproduce structure and structure reproduces individuals. Even if the people who are maintaining hetero/sexism exist in impossibly large numbers, they (and we) never cease to be specific individuals; hetero/sexist structures are always (literally) in our hands—and minds and hearts.

The idea that structures, including unjust ones, are to be found in the everyday knowledge and routine actions of most people in our society requires us to reconsider the meaning and value of the phrase "the personal is political." Although feminists generally appreciate the ways in which public and private realms are interrelated, we have tended to define political work as organized efforts to change formal and informal institutional rules; our work for safe, legal, funded abortion, the equal rights amendment, and the prosecution of rapists and batterers has been of this sort. An appreciation of both the necessity and the difficulty of transforming hetero/sexist structures in our intimate relationships may get lost in such large-scale mobilization efforts. Nonetheless, challenging the reproduction of hetero/sexism on a routine, daily basis is crucial to any long-term transformation of our society. Laws can be overturned or ignored if they are at odds with enough people's definitions of what is true or good. Only when sufficient numbers of individuals have stopped reproducing inegalitarian structures in taken-for-granted ways will hetero/sexism cease to be possible. I am not for a moment claiming that such a wide-scale transformation is certain or even likely to happen, or that it will be anything other than extremely difficult to accomplish. I am claiming that individual challenges to hetero/sexism, if practiced on a wide and deep enough scale, play a crucial role in ending hetero/sexism.[8] Directing energy toward the transformation of our definitions of the possible and the valued in our personal lives is important and honorable work. It is to this work that I now wish to turn.

Our intimate heterosexual relationships are structured in hetero/sexist ways,[9] and we will need to consider the institution of hetero/sexism in general and the specificities of our relationships simultaneously in order to begin the restructuring process. One important, if often neglected, point to keep in mind is that it is simultaneously easier and harder to be with men as a feminist than it is to be with women. Certainly, there are advantages to being in heterosexual relationships, but we also face educating our companions on the sheer taken-for-grantedness of their privilege, never an easy job. Angela Hamblin comments that:

> when we confront male power in our sexual relationships with individual men, we come up against not only the values of an entire patriarchal culture plus the expectations, pressure . . . and force of

the individual man/men with whom we relate but also our own internalized beliefs and expectations, vulnerabilities and needs. It is a formidable and daunting task.[10]

The daily disparity between our political goals and our body politics, communication styles or sexual desires within heterosexual relationships can seem an unbreachable gulf. Attending a march or rally, writing a letter of protest, boycotting certain products, even engaging in civil disobedience may be easier than attempting to radically change someone about whom we care deeply.

However, the understanding of structure that I have presented leads us to an idea remarkably close to that of loving the sinner and hating the sin. We do not choose to carry the central structures of society; rather, we absorb them or are taught them at a very early age, and they are continually reinforced throughout our youth. The violence that men have visited upon women is unspeakable,[11] and our outrage is a good sign; at the same time, our willingness to trust men with our bodies and emotional lives is not simply a matter of brainwashing or economic need. At some level, we harbor notions of being able to separate our relationships from the sexist violence that has flourished over time and which continues to thrive today. The structure of hetero/sexism offers us both much caution and some hope where that task is concerned; the sin, after all, is deeply built into the sinner, but it is not the final word about who he can be.

Thinking about my discomfort during the sexual experience mentioned earlier, I realize how I took for granted his right to be in control of the evening's sexual tempo. That seemed absolutely normal at the time, as did the greater importance accorded his sexual needs by both of us. How could something so natural make me so uncomfortable? And why was it so natural to remain silent at the time, despite being uncomfortable? Reading stories of other women's experiences,[12] I am struck by similarities. I realize that the scenario was set up in such a way as to define his control of the situation as normal. I remained silent despite my discomfort because that, too, was somehow normal; to do otherwise would have been to challenge unspoken rules, to disrupt the flow, to draw unseemly attention to myself, to be uncool. It was simply easier to go along with the situation, and that it was easier tells me something important about the routineness of sexism. It strikes me that I rarely have these problems with women; our sexual roles are not always clear before sex, so we have to do at least some talking ahead of time. I replay the night with Jonathan in my head, changing moments to add more communication before, during and after the sex, slowing down and taking breaks when I feel like it. Doing this saddens me even as it encourages me; there is something hurt in my life, and I am accepting it and trying to change it. I am angry, too, not at Jonathan, but at commonplace ways of being sexual in which my sexual desires are not as highly valued as his.

Examining how we reproduce hetero/sexism might begin with thinking through the ways in which "normal," "natural" sexual and social interactions with our male companions actually serve to express definitions of heterosexual relationships in areas such as communication, sexuality, the division of household labor, child-rearing and decision-making. How would our definitions be different from those generally taken for granted? What kinds of communication would we like to see? What kinds of sexual interactions? How would our household labor be divided? What are the various ways in which our relationships would be different if rule-making/reality-defining within them involved a completely egalitarian process?

This kind of creative, alternative thinking is not always easy, but we have important resources to draw upon. At some level, we may be quite uncomfortable with heterosexual relations as generally defined; feminist analysis can offer an explanation for our discomfort by helping us to identify the ways in which official definitions of reality in relationships are not in our best interests as full human beings, moral and material agents. Conversations we have had, books and articles we have read, dreams and images of our brokenness and wholeness can aid us in trusting our senses that things are not right as they are.

If such a feminist perspective enables us to clarify some of the limits of our heterosexual relationships, our sexual and romantic experiences with women can offer us hints and hopes of what egalitarian relationships might look like, providing us with energy and ideas.[13] Drawing upon our lesbian relationships to better understand our heterosexual ones needs to be done carefully, of course; the former are not perfect, nor do they always represent exactly what we might want in our relationships with men. I say hints and hopes because I believe that two people who have been historically frozen out of the definitional process can, in some cases, create an environment in which definitions arise mutually, in which the relationship is built equally by both partners. This may actually happen only rarely, given that we bring prior definitions with us when we begin lesbian relationships, but our knowledge that such egalitarianism is possible, as well as our memories or visions of egalitarian moments, may well be one of our most important resources when we turn to address our male companions.

Thinking about my past sexual encounters, I am intrigued to realize my compliance in bed with a system I oppose in most other aspects of my life. How exactly am I complying with hetero/sexism? I realize that several specific actions or lack of actions in my heterosexual encounters enable sexual business as usual to continue. At the first hint of discomfort during sex, I wonder whether I should say anything but always just let it go. Instead, I resist with my body or face momentarily—not terribly effective in a dark room at night. Nor is the physical resistance particularly strong; my partner may well not notice it. If he notices it, he may think nothing of it since folk wisdom says that women are supposed to resist. I rarely say anything ahead of time about my sexual tastes, and if I do, it is too far ahead of time to remain in context and I do not offer reminders later. Once the situation has gone far enough for me to be uncomfortable, my mental focus shifts away from the experience; I watch, detached, like a third party. I do not say anything, not then, not later. If I am cold or distant in the morning, it goes unnoticed by my partner.

The next step in the process of structural change might be to examine our day-to-day, face-to-face encounters with our male companions to identify minute ways in which we are reproducing, rather than transforming, hetero/sexist structures. What are the words spoken or not spoken that identify us as agents of our own lives or as dependent on male decision-making? How does our body language aid and abet inegalitarian structures? When and how is emotion expressed, and is its expression defined as a weakness or strength? How do we communicate our discomfort about a sexual request? When we are asked for a favor that would needlessly inconvenience us, what is our response and how is it made? The more we can identify the minutiae of hetero/sexism, and the more we can identify what an egalitarian version of the encounter would look like, the closer we are to taking steps toward putting this vision into place in our lives and offering it as a possibility for other women.

I think about ways to break the natural flow of male-defined sexual encounters: things to say, body motions that cannot be ignored. I begin to test some of them out during sexual encounters with men. This is difficult, perhaps the most difficult kind of communication I have ever tried. I find that I must wrestle deeply with the image of being uncool and do not always succeed in speaking up. Sometimes I can say something directly in a clear voice; sometimes I can stammer out what I need to; sometimes my voice fails me entirely. I find that trying to speak with my body on these occasions simply does not work; somehow, it has been too co-opted to be helpful. I am left with my voice and its mumbles, cracks, nervous giggles and occasional complete sentences.

I can't explain to my male partners how this need to play an equal role during sex is connected to feminism, at least not yet. At first, I think that I just don't want to bother them with such conversations. Later, I realize why: that is the true challenge, the clash of perspectives on reality. Men who are willing to be somewhat more egalitarian about sex are not likely to want their basic definitions of male-female interaction to be challenged. Nor are they likely to appreciate being told how their habits and patterns sustain and reproduce hetero/sexism. They will argue about meaning well. How can I tell them that is not the point? How can I present this way of understanding society so that it will become real for them, real in their minds, real in their guts? I am only now coming to accept that this conversation is the next step, that it is not sufficient to request an isolated change ("request"—as though it were a favor to be granted if he so deigned). My commitment to transform hetero/sexist structures requires me to find ways to express my perspective and engage in dialogues complete with compromises, endlessly shifting boundaries and most likely a permanent sense of incompleteness. Getting laws changed seems so much easier in comparison—but it is not sufficient.

Up to this point, the primary requirements of change have been the courage to explore hetero/sexism in our lives and the creativity to imagine alternative ways of being. The requirements shift when we confront our partners on the ways in which their behavior, as well as our own, is maintaining hetero/sexism. Courage is needed, and lots of it, but clear thinking, tact and negotiating skills come into play as well. For example, openly addressing hetero/sexism is made more difficult by the fact that it is not merely what we say or do but how we say or do it that is crucial. A hesitant, questioning protest is not likely to help our cause, though there is a good deal of evidence showing that women often address men, or for that matter simply put forth our opinions, in tentative ways.[14] Other less than helpful approaches might involve lobbying for change during arguments or in manipulative ways. Challenging hetero/sexism is likely to require the same forethought and careful choice of method and timing needed in coming out to one's family, and the similarity is not coincidental; both processes involve the task of giving new information to someone important to you, information that will challenge—sometimes deeply—their prior understanding of reality.

Our attempts at change will sometimes lead to deep and fruitful restructurings in ourselves and our partners, but there is a great deal of room for tension and stagnation as well. We may fail to follow through with a planned change, or we may succeed in carrying out a plan but be dismayed by a partner's reaction, or a partner may respond with equanimity to one aspect of breaking hetero/sexist patterns but with defensiveness, hostility, manipulation or even violence to another aspect. If men respond poorly to our attempts at change, it is likely to be because they are protective of what they have always experienced as reality and (like most of us) are afraid of change, not because men are born with genes for evil. We must, to some extent, expect powerful resistance, and we may, at some points, simply give up on a particular issue.[15] Male privilege, especially male power to define, is likely to have been taken entirely for granted as the natural right that "comes with the plumbing," and our assertions that this "natural right" is a social wrong are not likely to make for comfortable relationships.

Two especially difficult scenarios strike me, though I am not sure how common they are. The first involves a man who is willing to make changes because he cares about his lover and wants her to be happy. Although any willingness to change is helpful and good intentions are certainly welcome, this situation brings with it certain problems. First, it implies that the woman is the one with the problem (she is the problem), not the man; his willingness to change out of generosity may involve a roundabout "blaming the victim" and a belittling or demeaning attitude. Second, men and women tend to define the expression of love in different ways,[16] women focusing on emotional closeness and affection and men on instrumentality and sex; this difference can play a significant role in what a man will "instinctively" do in the name of love. Third, as long as a man fails to take seriously the extent to which "the problem" is a large-scale structural issue and not "merely" an idiosyncrasy of "his woman," the degree to which he will be willing to change is necessarily limited. Although willing to rethink a certain issue such as sexual initiative or child care, he may not understand when one change does not satisfy his partner and may become quite alarmed and threatened once he sees what she "really" has in mind. It may be that the only way to forestall this at all is to be consistently as clear as possible about the motives and perspectives behind attempts at change.

The second scenario involves a man who identifies as a feminist. Although many such men may listen and learn carefully, providing support and becoming radicalized themselves in the process, others may respond, in anger, that their identification "as a feminist" is sufficient, or they may twist the male power to define by defining for their partners what feminism is "really" about (which presumably will not include challenging one's male companion on his routine hetero/sexism). This latter response is, of course, just another version of telling women what we "really" want and once we recognize it as such, we will likely (and rightly) reject it immediately.

Throughout this process, the love and support of our feminist, bisexual and bi-feminist friends are crucial. Maintaining the energy and courage to challenge the meanings and practices taken for granted in our heterosexual relationships may be impossible without encouragement from others in similar situations; should this approach to political activism become common, it seems likely to me that there would be a call for support groups that could draw on the insights of second-wave feminist consciousness-raising as well as more recent self-help approaches. Yet regardless of whether encouragement comes from individual friends or an organized group, it will play a vital role in refreshing and restoring our energy and creativity.

At this point, bisexual (and heterosexual) feminists may well protest that we do not get into relationships with men in order to spend all of our time wrangling with them over seemingly impossible goals of social change, a protest with which I have no disagreement. All of us feel the "need of a [private] zone of experience off limits to instant political critique at various times,"[17] and if the personal is political, it does not cease being personal as well. My point here is simply that our relationships with men always contain opportunities to work against hetero/sexism, that these relationships represent an appropriate and important locus of struggle and that our experiences as bisexual feminists can offer crucial resources, should we want to take up these particular struggles.

If addressing the hetero/sexism of gender roles in our heterosexual relationships seems difficult, addressing the hetero/sexism of heterosexual privilege may be more so, and there are a number of reasons why that would be the case. First, there is a great lack of clarity about what the privilege actually consists of. Second, bisexuals tend to be defensive about the term when lesbians and gay men use it about us (and we certainly seem to be the people in honor of whom it was coined). Finally, we benefit as well as suffer from heterosexual privilege, and addressing one's privilege in this period of identity politics seems invariably to lead to immobilizing guilt or an abrupt changing of the subject. My discussion here is intended only to start opening up some ways of approaching this topic without confusion, defensiveness or guilt.

The first order of business in understanding heterosexual privilege is to distinguish between what Lenore Norrgard calls its intangible and tangible aspects.[18] Tangible heterosexual privilege refers to the economic and legal discrimination against lesbians, gay men and bisexuals held in place by the inability of same-sex couples to marry legally. Tax breaks, insurance coverage, inheritance rights and child custody rights are only some of the advantages offered to married heterosexual couples and denied to other couples. (Some legal housing discrimination can be listed here as well.) Norrgard argues (correctly, I think) that the tangible aspects of heterosexual privilege are more appropriately understood as benefiting men—and the women who marry them—of a certain socioeconomic class. To understand how this inequality is maintained, then, we need to take seriously the intersection of sexism, heterosexism and classism in our society.[19]

Intangible heterosexual privilege refers to the lack of safety and inclusion offered to those who are openly queer or in same-sex relationships. Under this kind of inequality we might list the danger of being called names or bashed while walking with a same-sex lover or leaving a lesbian or gay social space; nonlegal discrimination and harassment in living arrangements ranging from college campuses to apartment rentals; and the need for keeping one's love life hidden from friends, family, co-workers and other important people.

Because these two forms of heterosexual privilege are enforced in different ways (official versus unofficial rules), they need to be challenged in different ways. People primarily concerned with tangible heterosexual privilege will rightly focus their energy on confronting legal and political institutions. Those who are more concerned with the intangible aspects can benefit from a strategy that takes into account the idea of structure and face-to-face transformation that I have been discussing.

It is not merely gender roles that must be reproduced to maintain hetero/sexism, but a set of understandings about sexuality as well. Basic, of course, is the idea that homosexuality is immoral, psychologically unhealthy, criminal or just plain weird, along with the attendant anger, fear and disgust. But because same-sex sexual acts are not generally practiced in front of family members, co-workers or hostile passers-by on the street, there must be other ways for one's sexuality to become public knowledge. Thus, there are two kinds of "folk knowledge" (informal rules) at play here, one focusing on values (homosexuality is bad), one focusing on truth (this is who and how homosexuals are). In order for intangible heterosexual privilege to be possible, there must be ways to identify a queer, or a pair of queers, as such,[20] as well as a particular kind of unthinking response to said queers. We are very familiar with the ways in which the unthinking response is learned, but have not focused much on the folk knowledge required to define situations in which heterosexual privilege can play itself out. This information includes physical (or at least visible) stereotypes, knowledge about gay and lesbian social settings, "understandings" about single men over a certain age renting a room together, and the like. Such folk knowledge functions similarly whether the heterosexual privilege is operating through secrecy and shame or through violence; the same information about homosexuality creates a diverse range of problematic situations for bisexuals, lesbians and gay men, whether open or closeted, as well as for heterosexuals who "look" or "act" queer.

Where does this folk knowledge come from, and how is it maintained? Here, the analysis of hetero/sexist structures above provides useful insight. Initially certain decrees about the value of same-sex sexuality were enacted—primarily by white men in leadership positions, but at this point in time, sodomy laws are not required to maintain hetero/sexism. Most people in our society simply carry the folk knowledge described above and unthinkingly apply their definitions of normality in ways detrimental to lesbians, gay men and bisexuals. Understandings of "real" and "good" sexuality are reproduced regularly in a thousand small ways: locker room conversations; the absence of positive images of us in the media; passive acceptance by parents, teachers and other adults when children call each other "fags" in a derogatory way; Top-Forty love songs extolling boy-girl romance and (recently) advocating violence against gays; homophobic sexual humor; homophobic sermons and religious education in churches and synagogues; heterosexual-only educational materials; and the list goes on. Gender roles play an important part here as well: a "sissy" is probably a "homo," and vice versa. Nor are heterosexuals the only people who reinforce these stereotypes; gay men, lesbians and bisexuals who have certain information about what it means to be queer may well shape themselves around that information even if such shaping (like the aforementioned sexual encounters) is initially uncomfortable.[21] Alternatively, those who do not shape themselves around that information may deny their homosexuality (since "I'm not a sissy") or may take advantage of their invisibility and remain closeted. In either case, the stereotypes are reinforced; the vicious cycle continues.

If this identification of folk knowledge as a prerequisite for intangible heterosexual privilege is on target, routine, face-to-face challenges to the informal rules will play a vital part in transforming hetero/sexist structures.[22] As with the attempt to transform hetero/sexist structures in our intimate relationships, a combination of critical analysis and reflection on our experiences as bisexuals of both suffering from and benefiting from heterosexual privilege will provide crucial ideas and energy. We may work for transformation by correcting stereotypes and confronting derogatory comments, offering new information about the "truth" and "value" of homosexuality and bisexuality. We may use our positions as parents, teachers, consumers, ministers, landlords, friends, supervisors or adults to break into the taken-for-granted definitions of sexual reality, whether that means rewriting the Sunday school lesson, requesting more queer-positive music on a radio station, renting to that female couple or offering time off from work to a man whose lover has just died. We may work to change our patterns of public affection with women and with men, refusing certain aspects of heterosexual privilege where this seems important.[23] These are only a few of the transformative tasks that people of all sexualities can take on.[24] Hetero/sexism is not a matter of ill-wishes but of structures carried within our hearts and minds; as the information fueling our behavior changes, so too will our behavior change. Concrete processes of change can be thought up by individuals, and suggestions can be found in any number of educational materials devoted to ending homophobia. Thankfully, we have plenty of resources available to challenge the folk knowledge behind intangible heterosexual privilege.

This way of analyzing and responding to heterosexual privilege has a number of advantages. It targets hetero/sex*ism*, not heterosexuals or bisexuals, as the problem, a move that we may hope will free up bisexuals from our defensiveness, guilt and immobilization. Our experiences on both ends of the inequality can fuel our creativity in challenging taken-for-granted information in our various communities, and we can draw on both our bisexuality and our feminism in transforming hetero/sexism, within and outside of our heterosexual relationships. Moreover, if most or all people in our society carry hetero/sexism in emotions and knowledge, bisexuals are not somehow especially to blame for "taking advantage" of the system; we are as guilty (and as innocent) as everyone else, sinners along with the rest of society. We can play a powerful transformative role (sometimes, let it be admitted, at personal risk) through the various sexual, occupational and other social roles we play daily, without being solely responsible for changing the system.

The work I have described in this essay is not any easier for taking place close to home; in fact, it may be much harder than lobbying, voting, marching, writing and the other generally accepted forms of political activism that bisexual feminists may engage in. It does not bring the gratification of getting a law changed. It may, however, ultimately bring the gratification of getting many lives changed—piece by piece, moment by moment, with success and setback. Taking on the transformation of routine, taken-for-granted structures of hetero/sexism means challenging the definitions that have disempowered us as women and sexual minorities and instead building structures of mutuality, togetherness and justice—structures that we can hold in our heads, hearts and hands with pride.

Endnotes

Warm thanks to Elizabeth Reba Weise for her seemingly unending faith in this paper and to Sarah Murray for her continual support and excellent suggestions.

1. I should note here that these ideas, at least at this point, are primarily addressed to women, though bisexual-feminist (and other) men may find them interesting and challenging.

2. However, to the extent that our arrangements reflect the privilege of being white and middle- or upper-class, they will need significant tempering and rethinking if they are to be useful for poor or working-class women and women of color. There has been a tremendous outburst of important writing by women of color, especially in the last decade, that speaks eloquently to these concerns. Some introductions to this literature include bell hooks, *Feminist Theory: From Margin to Center* (Boston: South End Press, 1984); Audre Lorde, *Sister Outsider* (Trumansburg, N.Y., The Crossing Press, 1984); Cherríe Moraga and Gloria Anzaldua, eds., *This Bridge Called My Back: Writings By Radical Women of Color* (Watertown, Mass.: Persephone Press, 1981); and Barbara Smith, ed., *Home Girls: A Black Feminist Anthology* (New York: Kitchen Table/Women of Color Press, 1983).

3. See Lenore Norrgard, "The Myth of Heterosexual Privilege, *North Bi Northwest* (June/July 1990); and "The Reality of Heterosexual Privilege," *North Bi Northwest* (August/September 1990); Suzanne Pharr, *Homophobia: A Weapon of Sexism* (Inverness, Calif.: Chardon Press, 1988).

4. Adrienne Rich, "Compulsory Heterosexuality and Lesbian Existence," *Signs: Journal of Women in Culture and Society* 5, no. 4 (1977), p. 648.

5. Because this point is so important and at the same time so counterintuitive, I want to take care to suggest some useful and accessible writings on the subject. The following differ in their reliance on academic jargon, but all are worth reading: Michel Foucault, *The History of Sexuality, Vol. 1,* trans. Robert Hurley (New York: Pantheon Books, 1978); Jonathan Katz, "The Invention of Heterosexuality," *Socialist Review* 20 (January-March 1990), pp. 7-34; William Simon and John Gagnon, "Sexual Scripts," *Society* 53 vol. 22 (1984), pp. 53-60; John Stoltenberg, *Refusing to Be a Man: Essays on Sex and Justice* (Portland, Ore.: Breitenbush Books, 1989); Lorna Weir and Leo Casey, "Subverting Power in Sexuality," *Socialist Review* 13 (May-August, 1984): pp. 139-57.

6. The following ideas draw heavily on the work of sociologist Anthony Giddens, especially pages 64-73 of *Central Problems in Social Theory* (Berkeley: University of California Press, 1979) and pages 16-34 of *The Constitution of Society* (Berkeley: Uni-

versity of California Press, 1984).

7. These "kinds" of knowledge include all the information about "natural," "normal" and "desirable" sexuality that we learn; that this specific knowledge exists *within* our understanding of gender roles is yet another argument for analytically linking sexism and heterosexism.

8. The other crucial aspect is reallocating resources fairly; individual change alone will not suffice as long as there are people with the resources to keep defining what is and what ought to be in ways that reinforce hetero/sexism. This is also no easy task, but it directs us to consider the ways in which the current class structure intersects with hetero/sexism.

9. As are our lesbian relationships. If we carry hetero/sexist structure within us, it inevitably colors our relationships. I choose not to focus on lesbian relationships here because there are various resources within women's communities upon which we may draw, whereas there are not many guides for transforming heterosexual relationships.

10. Angela Hamblin, "Is a Feminist Heterosexuality Possible?" in *Sex and Love: New Thoughts on Old Contradictions*, eds. Sue Cartledge and Joanna Ryan (London: The Women's Press, 1983), pp. 105-123.

11. Op. cit. Rich "Compulsory Heterosexuality and Lesbian Existence"; see pages 638-40 for a list of some of the mechanisms by which women have been silenced, controlled and excluded.

12. Op. cit. Hamblin, "Is a Feminist Heterosexuality Possible?"; see pages 108-110 for an extremely helpful list of male definitions of "normal" sexuality, and pages 116-117 for some preliminary redefining of heterosexuality that women can do.

13. I want to be careful in my use of the word "egalitarianism." I am not proposing that all interactions should be completely even and equal, that power struggles will disappear from our relationships, or for that matter that power imbalances are always equally undesirable. I mean by egalitarianism only that both partners have equal say in defining what the rules of the relationship are to be, including how resources are to be divided, how conflicts are to be handled and who gets to make various decisions. A sexual analogy to this might involve completely mutual sadomasochism (s/m) or other role-playing; the crucial factor is that both parties equally define the setting, not that both parties are necessarily always defined as equals within it.

14. Sandra L. Bartky, Chapter 6 "Shame and Gender", *Femininity and Domination: Studies in the Phenomenology of Oppression* (New York: Routledge, 1990), pp. 83-98; Laurel W. Richardson and Verta Taylor, eds., *Feminist Frontiers: Rethinking Sex, Gender and Society* (Reading, Mass.: Addison-Wesley, 1983).

15. It is also, of course, conceivable that we will give up on particular men at times.

16. See Frances Cancian, "Gender Politics: Love and Power in the Public and Private

Spheres," in *Family in Transition*, ed. Arlene Skolnick and Jerome Skolnick (Boston: Scott Foresman and Company, 1989), pp. 219-230; Lillian Rubin, "Changing Expectations: New Sources of Strain" and "The Marriage Bed," *Worlds of Pain* (New York: Basic Books, 1976), pp. 114-154.

17. Jan Clausen, "My Interesting Condition," *Out/Look* 7 (Winter 1990): p. 13.

18. Op cit. Norrgard, "The Myth of Heterosexual Privilege"; "The Reality of Heterosexual Privilege." I will rely on her analysis throughout much of this section.

19. Although I will not discuss the sexism behind intangible heterosexual privilege, it can be argued that much of the discrimination is based on stereotypes that conflate what a "real man" or "real woman" is with certain images of (hetero)sexuality.

20. Op. cit. Clausen, "My Interesting Condition," pp. 20-21; Clausen discusses the way in which being able to pass because of one's appearance plays a role in lesbian-bisexual tensions; her point is particularly useful here, given that the rules that have been set up miss a number of queers and mistakenly identify as queer a number of heterosexuals. See also Amanda Udis-Kessler, "Culture and Community: Thoughts on Lesbian-Bisexual Relations," *Sojourner: The Women's Forum* (December 1990, Vol 16 No. 4): pp. 11-12.

21. It also may not be uncomfortable at all. If folk knowledge about homosexuality is deeply ingrained enough, fitting queer stereotypes and devaluing homosexuality will be entirely "natural" in the same way that the male power to define is "natural."

22. Once again, the question of resource allocation should not be ignored, though I am not directly covering it here.

23. This approach to heterosexual privilege is not a particularly popular one, but if our routine public interactions with (or discussions about) our opposite-sex lovers are contributing to hetero/sexism, they represent an arena of potential change. I am not suggesting that we take risks with our same-sex lovers that endanger our lives or that we simply avoid all public displays of affection with our opposite-sex lovers. It does seem to me, however, that taking this aspect of heterosexual privilege seriously requires some thought and can clarify our commitment to transforming hetero/sexism. There is certainly room and necessity for creative strategizing on the subject.

24. It is particularly important that heterosexuals engage in this work, since they are seen as more neutral than sexual minorities with "special interests."

THE QUESTION OF COMMUNITY

Kathleen Bennett

FEMINIST BISEXUALITY:
A BOTH/AND OPTION FOR AN EITHER/OR WORLD

"I'm simply trying to live a both/and life in an either/or world."
—Tom Robinson, *Bisexuality: A Reader and Sourcebook*

In the 1990s, the bisexual community is speaking out, organizing and becoming increasingly visible. We strengthen each other in our commitment to live proudly and honestly in our belief that our affection, love and desire cannot be restricted to one gender alone. To share our experiences as unique and diverse bisexual people makes it possible to begin to create and foster a larger vision of a world aware of and accepting of the potential for multidirectional attraction, affection, desire, love and bonding. Our alternative vision must struggle for validity, however, against the misperceptions and vicious untruths of biphobia (prejudice against bisexuality) and monosexism (the privileging of single-gender orientation).

Denigration of our bisexuality may be directed at us by both heterosexuals and gays/lesbians. To some degree, we may also have internalized these negative images. We, like everyone else, are profoundly influenced by the attitudes and structures of the culture of which we are a part. The mindset of Western society tends to divide the world into dichotomies. This "either/or" structure is pervasive in modern Western culture and certainly is present in other cultures as well.

The supposed requirement to choose one sexual/affectional "direction" or another, which is at the heart of biphobia, is clearly a result of this dichotomizing tendency. The either/or mentality is also a basic source of the way our culture organizes and perceives sex and gender. Sexism shapes our views of the differentiation between humans. Sexism is also one of the major sources of the culture's assumption that heterosexuality is more natural than other sexualities. This attitude comes about because the central significance of gender differentiation colors social norms for human interaction and connection. Biphobia results from the application of the either/or mentality in turn to the heterosexist distinction between straight and gay.

To challenge biphobia more than superficially, we must take on a fight against the either/or mentality itself. In a very important way, just being bisexual can itself do this. Bisexuals make erotic connections across lines of gender and sexual orientation, rejecting the concept that love and, by extension, life, is an either/or proposition. We subvert the dominant culture's paralyzing dichotomies through being open to constant reinvention of our diverse and unique lives and experiences. We wiggle out from under references to "natural" essences of sex, gender and sexuality. We often resist the use of sex and sex roles as an instrument of social control. We aspire to live by the standards of flexibility, ambiguity, creativity and truth to the self rather than by simplistic social definitions, categorizations and roles.

Although claiming bisexual experience and identity has an important effect in that it reveals a truth that does not fit the myths of biphobia, this is not enough. For the myths—and the ignorance and bigotry they bring about—will continue to mask our truth if we do not challenge them at the roots. We must make alliances with others who are attempting to bring about a shift away from the either/or paradigm. The recognition and acceptance of bisexuality for which we strive must, and inevitably will, bring about deeper change closely related to the goals of these other forward-looking liberation movements. Challenges to the either/or mentality on a local basis will foster a more global questioning of its appropriateness, which in turn will strengthen specific struggles.

We must ally ourselves first with the lesbian and gay movements, because they fight against the heterosexism and homophobia that oppress all sexual minorities. We must ally ourselves also with feminism, because feminism struggles against arbitrary categorizations and divisions on the basis of gender. In addition, our goals are linked with those of any other movement, segment of a movement, or ideal that rejects dichotomizing and replaces it with a vision of unity-in-diversity. However, we must maintain our ability to sympathetically criticize problematic tenets of these same movements when they fall prey themselves to the internalized cultural message to dichotomize. Adding a bisexual understanding to other movements can help call attention to and counteract this danger. As a result, both our progress and that of our allies will be strengthened. Bisexuals' recognition of our common ground with these movements is crucial to our own movement. The bisexual movement stands ready to benefit from the previous advances of our chosen allies, both in extending their gains to ourselves and in being aware of and avoiding their mistakes.

A feminist theory of bisexuality can be part of this process of connection-building, web-weaving. The effectiveness of this theory is greatly strengthened by a critical analysis of the either/or mindset of Western culture. This essay attempts to formulate and present such a theory.

Biphobia and the Myths of Sex, Gender and Sexual Identity

Why have bisexuals been simultaneously criticized by straight society for being too queer and by gay society for being too straight? The either/or mindset of Western culture is the basic source of this criticism. Bisexuality is far too often characterized as immature indecision or hypocritical fence-sitting, rather than as flexibility of affiliation and love.

Biphobia, the denigration of bisexuality as a valid life choice, depends on either/or attitudes as they apply to both gender and choice of partners. Cultural antagonism to bisexuality occurs because attraction to both men and women threatens the prevalent social myth of either/or in its various versions. One of these versions is heterosexism, which is based on the assumption that there is something by nature complementary about masculinity and femininity. Another is monosexism, the idea on the part of heterosexuals and gays that a unidirectional sexual orientation is more natural than bisexuality. Both of these attitudes are upheld by a sexist myth that the genders are mutually exclusive—thus, anything other than a clear preference for one or the other must be a phase or a pathology of identity confusion. In contrast, some bisexuals say that they are blind to the gender of their potential lovers and that they love people as people; others are aware of differences between their female and male partners but are able to be attracted to each in different (but overlapping) ways. For the first group, a dichotomy of genders between which to choose doesn't seem to exist; the second group simply disregards the social obligation to choose.

Nothing inherent in the character of sex, gender or sexuality determines how one's *own sex* or gender influences one's choice regarding
the sex or gender of *one's lovers.* Contemporary feminist scholarship
has demonstrated that delineations of masculine and feminine gender
identification vary from culture to culture, are guided by the social
forms male domination takes in each culture and have only marginally
to do with our biological character as male and female human animals.
The increased occurrence of androgyny in people's appearance and
behavior, as well as the growing visibility of transsexuals and others
who are migrating away from the gender that accompanies their biological sex, is evidence for a modern-day transformation in the sex/
gender system. This transformation is in large part a result of thinking
and activism on the part of both feminism and the gay liberation
movement.

"Sexual identity," a concept bisexuals have alternately clung to and
shrunk from, is itself culturally created. Before the psychiatric estab-
lishment recorded and codified "the perversions," sex was merely a
group of activities involving pleasure and the body. Medicalized, sex
became "sexuality" and categories of acts were linked with the idea of
an individual's character or identity.[1] Because our culture has such a
high stake in gender differentiation, one of the major determinants of
sexual identity has been opposite-gender or same-gender object
choice.

The very concept of sexual identity is problematic for those who
wish to challenge the sexual status quo, and I believe this is so especially for bisexuals. The linking of one's choice of pleasures to some
inherent individual identity is threatening in that it attempts to reduce
a lifetime of erotic experiences and decisions to a static label. On the
other hand, self-identification as a sexual minority also empowers us in
that "it is about affinities based on selection, self-actualization, and
choice,"[2] allowing us to discover, affirm and be affirmed by other "differently pleasured" people. Without our communities, however re-
strictively labeled they may feel at times, the negative messages of the
dominant culture would surely overpower the small voice of our own
isolated affirmation of self.

Either/or myths of both gender and object choice are part of an
even more widespread dualistic belief system. This system is at the
root of the power structures of Western culture that practice "divide

and conquer" between different peoples, people and their environment and even within individuals themselves. Gender opposition is a primary metaphor influencing most oppressions based on mutually exclusive divisions.[3] Although such division harms us in many ways, for instance in the forms of racism, ecological degradation and spiritual alienation, I wish to deal with it here specifically in terms of how dualism in the sex/gender system influences the Western approach to the question of bisexuality.

Within this dualistic system, men and women internalize divergent expectations of their own and others' gender identity and sexual behavior long before the issue of sexual/affectional object choice ever arises. We bring these attitudes with us when we come together with our lovers. To live a healthy bisexual life, not clouded by veils of self-denial and internalized homophobia/heterophobia, is itself a process of refusing to buy into the "logical" conclusions of these ingrained attitudes.

Many bisexuals wish the either/or mentality, and the labeling it requires, would just disappear so that we would not have to continue explaining and justifying our choices, selves and lives. If we hope to eliminate it, however, we need to explore its deep-seated links with other divisions and dualities in our culture. To claim that we can do away with labels without seeking out and attempting to destroy the roots of the labeling attitude leads only to futility and frustration.

The Unmasking of the Either/Or Mentality

The human process of knowing is fundamentally based on the fact that our minds structure ideas about the world into categories. The specific categories we use and the way we organize them vary among cultures. The processes of thought and understanding typical of Western society are structured around mutually exclusive dichotomies. These include such familiar binary oppositions as male/female, masculine/feminine, nature/culture, self/other, us/them, body/spirit, intellect/emotion, as well as the more recent distinction between legitimate and unsanctioned sexualities. Of each polarity, one side is often judged to be inherently better or more important than the other, according to what will best serve the mechanisms of power structures. The dual opposition and the hierarchical ranking of its parts are justified as being "natural," making such a construction impervious to criticism, much less to clear analysis. Hierarchical dualism, this division and ranking, is so pervasive that it is difficult to understand that it might be possible, in fact necessary, to balance, integrate or even transcend "opposite" sides of such socially constructed dichotomies.

Hierarchical dualism is a process intimately linked with the evolution of patriarchy. It is a history of power dynamics that divide and organize people along gender lines and give determination of cultural meaning and control of material resources to (some) males only. Hierarchical dualism is a broad streak running through Western civilization, deeply ingrained in our political history and in our internalized view of our self and its environment. It is a philosophy which both grows out of and influences the history of culture, a structure reinforced by and bolstering millennia of social control by dominant classes.[4] It favors exclusion and domination in cultural and political systems, and ignorance and dogmatism in ethical and spiritual arenas. It has obscured and marginalized the connectedness between diverse beings, the equal value-in-themselves of all beings, and the possibility for personal fluidity and transformation.

Several different traditions of radical theory are part of the project to unmask the workings of hierarchical dualism and bring about a paradigm shift through which it might no longer be taken for granted that differences obscure and overcome similarities. One of the central mytho-philosophical structures that gives hierarchical dualism its form is the social discourse through which gender is constructed. Through this social interpretation of sex, physiological differences between men and women have come to determine masculine and feminine emotional and intellectual characteristics, material and spiritual social roles, arenas of power and powerlessness and practically everything else in the way we live our lives. Accepting this does not mean accepting the ideology of radical feminism, that the sex/gender system is the "most important" or the "only real" division and oppression. Such a view is as misguided as the view of non-feminist theorists who try to analyze nature/culture or mind/body dualities without any reference at all to the structures of gender that support and perpetuate them.

An understanding of the sex/gender system, *in connection with other forms* of division and oppression, is central to any exploration of hierarchical dualism. Feminist thinkers in many schools of thought are doing this work of making the connections. They draw on a variety of background ideas, as is apparent in the names of their philosophies, including black feminism/womanism, socialist feminism, anarchist feminism, eco-feminism, feminist ethics and women's spirituality.

Hierarchical Dualism, Essentialism and Heteropatriarchal Oppression

The thought explorations of these feminists and their allies provide a multifaceted account of the system of male dominance, or patriarchy. It was patriarchy that shaped sex into gender and defined gender as an inherence in biological sex. The reification (thing-making) of gender functions by instilling the belief that biological differences and social roles and power differentials are intrinsically linked. The historical beginnings of the ascendancy of the hierarchical dualist mindset are directly linked to the origins of patriarchy.

No primary written record of any pre-patriarchal culture exists. An important new movement in feminist scholarship is attempting to reconstruct a description of a past world without male domination through research and writing in anthropology, archaeology, art history and history of religion.[5] These earlier civilizations, in the prehistoric Paleolithic through Neolithic eras of human history, were far from "primitive." They developed agriculture, metalworking, art, architecture, commerce and a rudimentary form of script. As tribal elders, clan mothers and shamans, women made many of the important sociopolitical and family decisions. A sexual division of labor most likely existed, but the sexes were in partnership. A system of dominance whereby one sex controlled the labor power and self-determination of the other had not been developed. [6] Their nature-reverent religious tradition was based on the vision of a nurturing and immanent goddess (as contrasted with the aloof and often violent gods of later patriarchal civilizations), and the ritual practices of their culture reflected an appreciation of diversity and mutuality. The mother's cyclic power of life and death was the center of religion, and women were respected as holding great spiritual strength. The social vision of these cultures relied upon the ideals of cooperation between necessarily diverse parts of an interconnected whole, rather than upon power struggles between exclusive opposites.[7]

To say that patriarchy originated when men realized that it was in their interest to wrest power from the female sex would be simplistic and inaccurate. The increase in violence, slavery and ecological exploitation that grew up around the domination-culture that was patriarchy was certainly less in the interests of all people than the partnership-oriented practices of the earlier society had been. The dominator/dominated model of social organization both served and perpetuated new modes of economic production and newly centralized loci of political power, but it could not have flourished as it did without the ideology of hierarchical dualism. Patriarchy was made possible by the acceptance of categories of opposition setting people against one another along socially constructed lines, most importantly the distinction of gender.

Western culture underwent a deep and pervasive change in character at this time. Spiritual views that held the divine to be separate from human experience and from the earth and characterized divinity as an idealized form of the human male accompanied the burgeoning and institutionalization of structures that reflected and reinforced the idea that men had rights of self, property and leadership over women, who had little or none. The patriarchal ideologies of hierarchical dualism were so fundamentally opposed to the pre-patriarchal vision of self and society, which valued immanence and connectedness, that patriarchy needed to infect basically every area of life in order to further itself. We still suffer under the legacy of this transition today, as this philosophy has been growing more pervasive and sophisticated for thousands of years. However many times it has been challenged, it has been able to gain strength by adapting and evolving, preserving its core ideas of dualism and dominance. It has had lasting impact on the deep-seated categorizations that shape the Western mindset, most notably through the influence of the Greek philosopher Aristotle, the Hebrew scriptures, the Christian theologians and the Enlightenment rationalists.

At the core of this mindset of division and domination lies the structuring metaphor of gender and the necessarily correlative belief in the unchanging, essential natures of men and women. The belief that the sexes are inherently different in character, because of their biological difference, has made it possible for men to exploit, own, exchange and govern women solely on the basis of sexual difference and reproductive capacity. People have been denied empowerment and self-determination by the attribution of dichotomized social roles and emotional qualities to masculine and feminine "natures." The naming and structuring are enforced by the denigration of those who do not conform to cultural expectations.

This process has functioned from ancient times to today, making men and women into an agglomeration of masks, roles and armor, rather than fully realized human beings. It is difficult for women to question the workings and roots of our subordination or for men to question their own expected role of brutality, cruelty and dominance. All are kept ignorant of our cultural history and our potential to change. We are not even allowed to own our own bodies. The separation of intellect from emotion and of spirit from flesh, again largely characterized along metaphors of gender, reinforces the denigration of the flesh and of lived human experience. It keeps us from knowing and honoring our deepest passions. The special subjection of woman is facilitated by the identification of the female with nature and the degraded flesh.

The dualistic Western conception of masculinity and femininity depends for its survival on the ideology of gender essentialism: the description of the gender split as inherent in human nature. Acceptable personality traits, behavior and social roles for men and women are defined in terms of how they fit putative male and female "essences" that are considered universal and transhistorical. This reification of culturally constructed gender characteristics into sexual "nature" inherently sets up structures of "otherness," denying the potential for change. Through this process, it becomes true that our anatomy determines our destiny. We lose the knowledge that cultures in other times and places have had definitions of male and female different from ours. This perpetuates the ethnocentric notion that the way of Western culture is the right way, the only way. The possibility of alternatives is hidden, and the potential for self-determination for oppressed gender and sexual minority groups is quashed.

Sexuality holds a central position in the perpetuation of hierarchical dualism by sex and gender. For the patriarchal family to maintain its functions of kinship and property transfer, a patriarch needs to be certain that the children in his family "belong" to him.[8] It must thus be rendered acceptable for man to be able to "own" both his sexuality and that of woman, and for woman to have no right to any sexuality at all. For this to be possible, people must believe that men and women have different sexual "natures."

Such gender essentialism links, by means of the procreative myths of heterosexism, our sexuality to our supposed need to reproduce our "self" and our labor power. Heterosexism links sexuality with gender through the essentialist myth of "correct" choice of lovers; preferences for sexual activities become named as inherent individual identities, and a spectrum of "naturalness" is drawn up based on those identities. "Correct heterosexual object choice" is maintained not only by essentialism of sexual identity, but by the more basic fact of gender essentialism: that the appropriate object of desire, the "opposite" sex, is named "other" in the first place.

This assumption that the essential male and female must by nature be drawn together into a complementary unit forms the basis of the system of compulsory heterosexuality. Under this system, it becomes possible to ask of same-sex attraction; "What is this thing called homosexuality, and where did it come from?" Like homosexuality, heterosexuality is seen as an unchanging state, but no one asks to know its origin. Its etiology is not demanded, because heterosexuality is the assumed, "natural" backdrop that permeates all of our other perceptions of sexual orientation. Gender essentialism limits us in how we perceive our own sexual bodies; essentialism of sexuality limits our options regarding the sexual bodies we may be attracted to. The essentialist jaw of the patriarchal trap distorts a wide range of sexual experiences and potentials into simplified, reductionist gender codes, and constructs from them a hierarchy of accepted sexual behaviors. The dualist jaw of the trap posits difference as the primary category of definition rather than valuing connectedness-within-diversity. Imprisoned between these jaws, we are denied the liberating knowledge that sexuality is also a locus where we can transcend the artificial boundaries between spirit and flesh, self and other.

Hierarchical dualism and its essentialist supports guide our culture's processes whereby dominant power interests name and create "the other" in order to control and suppress it. The power structures of the patriarchy are reinforced both by the individual's fear of not conforming to cultural expectations—of being the other—and by group-instilled hatred of those who are visible as or suspected to be "other." The deep-seated and disproportionate fear of socially non-sanctioned sexualities is an especially unchallenged form of such other-izing; the specific fear of homosexuality is a crucial factor in this social mechanism precisely because same-gender love challenges the essentialist vision of the complementarity of "opposite sexes."

Ambiguity and the Erotic: A Feminist Theory of Bisexuality

Straight society's fear of gender transgression affects bisexual and monosexual queers alike. To fight biphobia, we must fight the cultural hatred of homosexuality. However, biphobia is indeed a special species of homophobic oppression, as is clear when we view the meta-ideological structure underlying such ideology. Bisexuality has the potential to challenge essentialist hierarchical dualism at its very roots by refusing to accept the necessity to dichotomize.

Essentialist/hierarchical-dualistic structures of sexism and heterosexism are supported by patriarchal attitudes about sexuality. Breaking down the next barrier of dualism, within the categories of sexual identity and sexuality themselves, is a task for which a feminist theory of bisexuality is well prepared. This is not simply a theoretical task. A revised picture of the realities and potentials of sexuality can serve as a template for social change of institutions that attempt to preserve the old order of patriarchal oppression organized around the social naming and control of human impulses and pleasures. It can show us how to tear off the masks forced upon us by patriarchal society and begin to name our own experience. For as Starhawk notes, "erotic energy is a manifestation of the sacred.... Control of sexuality by others is a primary way in which our sense of worth is undermined, and is a cornerstone of the structures of domination."[9]

Our sexuality is a very deep part of our self. Many of us may have felt that we come closest to some deeper truth through the exercise of our sexuality in connection with self and others. Hierarchical dualism and sex/gender essentialism threaten such self-realization on our part. They answer our individual searches for pleasure and meaning with categories fabricated long before our birth to uphold and replicate a system that intends to long outlive us. Instead of juiciness and energy, we are given cardboard and chains.

Essentialist hierarchical dualism is not merely a free-floating philosophy in the cultural landscape. It is the guiding force behind very real and very familiar institutions of social control. Most notable among these institutions is the conventional, predictable and socially isolated nuclear family. However, the control also extends outward into our systems of law and economics and inward into our very self-images. Institutions of sexual power-over[10] preserve the status quo by "defining the boundaries." In a patriarchal system whose power rests on keeping women ignorant of the strength of their own experience, the manipulation of women's self-image, knowledge and sexuality is a top priority. In a hierarchical system whose power rests on making distinctions and judgments based on culturally determined characteristics, the fiction that those characteristics and the gulfs between them are natural must be maintained. Essentialism defines by exclusion, grants "natural" status to those who conform to the dominant paradigm by defining what a man and a woman "should" be, tells us how they should interact and oppresses those named "other."

It is crucial to a bisexual theory to note that the very structure of a system of hierarchized essentials requires the denigration of any concept of ambiguity. Mariana Valverde writes:

> If the goals of feminism and gay liberation include the abolition of the gay/straight split, and its replacement by a social system which does not label and categorize people according to whom they are attracted, then bisexuality is an important part of the challenge to the status quo. Its role could involve vindicating and affirming sexual ambiguity, in a world which is presently extremely uncomfortable with *any* ambiguity.[11]

The coming-out stories of so many bisexuals speak of bisexual people's realization of the truth of their polyvalent attraction.[12] They did not originally intend to be crusaders against dualism. They began their quest for a bisexual identity with the raw data of their own emotions, urges and experiences. Only after that, if at all, did they face the understanding that our culture requires too many either/or choices for it to accept that a bisexual life even existed, much less was a worthy one. The realities of bi-oriented love and lust speak to our souls long before we become inclined to theorize about them. However, in the face of institutions of social control that wish to hide, deny and eradicate that reality, a boundary-breaking theory is necessary if our ability to make our own erotic choices is to be truly ours rather than a mirage or a sin.

A bi-positive, feminist view of sexuality as integral to self-knowledge can be inspired by a connection-valuing, life-affirming spirituality reflecting our visions of pre-patriarchal cultures. The centrality of the erotic to systems of social control in Western patriarchy is ironic by contrast. It certainly follows that if "the man" in power can make us doubtful of the erotic core energy of our own being, he can control other elements of our lives accordingly.

It was hierarchical dualism that first stood the erotic on its head. When the first philosophers and theologians who separated spirit and flesh concluded that the sacred resided only in the spirit, sacredness was denied to the body (associated with the female, the earthly, as the spirit was with the male, the eternal); the body came to be scapegoated as the source of sin and filth. These sex-negative "notions have by now acquired a life of their own and no longer depend solely on religion for their perseverance."[13] We feel the effects of the powerful history of sex negativity "in our body hatred and our experience of sex as sick, shameful and dirty, something done secretly and furtively."[14] The disproportionate effect of sex and body negativity on women clearly shows how this system functions in favor of male dominance. Women's body image is almost always evaluated in relation to an ideal image, and women suffer the effects of body negativity far more than men do, suffering from ignorance and hatred of ourselves, and socially sanctioned or self-inflicted mutilations. Closely related to this are the silence and misinformation about women's sexual pleasure and orgasm, which have only within the last thirty years begun to be discussed accurately among sexologists and popular literature, and only within the last several years in erotica.[15]

This profound untruth and insecurity on the subject of sex allows the defenders of the patriarchal system to use sex as an instrument to keep down potential questioners or underminers of the sex/gender status quo. In Western culture, "Sex is presumed guilty until proven innocent."[16] This attitude keeps us from listening to our bodies, emotions and pleasures, as well as those of our lovers. It tells us what we should be feeling and with whom. The sexual freedom that bisexuals seek to love whom they choose comes under special scrutiny, but this occurs under the aegis of anti-sex attitudes and homophobia.

In a sex-negative culture, deviant sexuality (any sexuality that threatens heteropatriarchy) is kept in check by a series of mechanisms.[17] Different sex acts, and the corresponding essentialist "identities" that are linked to preferences for certain acts, are valued on a hierarchy from good to bad, with an invisible, culturally relative, constantly shifting line marking the boundary whose crossing implies perversion and perhaps eternal perdition. The "domino theory of sexual peril" is illustrated by the conservative contention that any straying from monogamous "vanilla" (non-kinky) heterosexuality is only the first step of a slide down the slippery slope into a nation of family-destroying perverts.

> The line appears to stand between sexual order and chaos. It expresses the fear that if anything is permitted to cross this erotic DMZ [demilitarized zone], the barrier against scary sex will crumble and something unspeakable will skitter across.[18]

A tellingly disproportionate focus on object gender choice in determining the "badness" of an act accompanies the mechanisms of sexual control. For example, heterosexuals who practice sadomasochism are not nearly as visible nor as reviled as people in queer leather subcultures. By contrast, a monogamous lesbian couple, however vanilla their sex life may be, are far less socially acceptable than a heterosexual couple who do the exact same acts, merely because the latter have "complementary" genders.

Western society's lack of a "concept of benign sexual variation,"[19] combined with its obsessive attention to "correct" sex as an upholder of all that is important, has brought about a system of sex law that may be said to resemble apartheid in that some people are oppressed as a result of their liking for the "wrong" gender. These laws ostensibly keep people in their place because of what they *do* rather than what they *are*, but in a system where essentialism colors our image of sexual self-identification and object choice, the distinction becomes all but irrelevant.

> All these hierarchies of sexual value . . . function in much the same ways as do ideological systems of racism, ethnocentrism, and religious chauvinism. They rationalize the well-being of the sexually privileged and the adversity of the sexual rabble.[20]

In a community where police can enter a man's room and arrest him for engaging in oral sex with another man, both gay-identified people and all who have homosexual sex are stripped of their rights.[21] Just as abortion laws dehumanize women by taking away from us the human right to be full moral agents in our own bodies, sex laws indicate that some people have rights to do what they want with their own bodies and their own lives, and other people don't. They classify and control people, not just acts.

Sex as an instrument of social control affects far more than simply the way sexual minority people are treated in our legal system, church, educational system, health care system and other social institutions. The dominant paradigm is so pervasive that it affects, as well, our internalized images of self. Collective cultural myths of "the way it is" serve to keep knowledge about different ways of living from people who may need or want to live apart from the norm. In keeping our history from us, this system has forced deviants to reinvent our own lives at every moment. Ugly stereotypes conspire with the silence about our diverse realities to keep us in constant ignorance, self-doubt and self-hatred. To be happily deviant, we must manage the dialectical balance between reinventing our lives from our own experience and dealing with negative images of ourselves that stem from deeply held cultural myths. Strengthening our own communities is a tool in this struggle, but this task as well is inhibited by negative stereotypes.

Visions of Struggle: Avoiding the Traps of the Dualist Mindset

To fight the poisonous stories and oppressive institutions of heteropatriarchy, we must fight both sexism and heterosexism. In fact, we must fight any cultural ideology that separates and stigmatizes people, because although gender and sexuality are the specific loci of oppression of those considered "queer," it is hierarchical dualism that underlies the form of such oppressions, as a feminist bisexual theory makes abundantly clear.

The struggle against biphobia is linked with the struggles against homophobia and male domination because of both the overlap in constituency and the links between ideological goals. The bisexual movement shares with feminism and gay liberation the combined objective of making visible the social and cultural realities of its oppressed constituents while acting to change the dominant social and cultural realities that bring about that oppression. Such movements change our internalized view of our own nature as well as affecting the structure of society toward greater inclusiveness and freedom.

To combat these mingled oppressions, as well as all others that are so inextricably linked, we must base our struggle on a vision of unity-in-diversity that can counteract the insidious effects of hierarchical dualism. Such a theory, elements of which occur not only in feminism but also in the thought of some anarchists, neo-pagans, sex radicals and ecologists, embraces the following central commitments:

- The self-determination of and pride in personal and community identity
- The necessity, right and power of all people to seek and make their own authentic choices and judgments
- The objective and subjective equality of all people (or all beings)
- The realization of the fundamental connection between all people (or all beings)
- The realization of and respect for the positive, creative power that comes from within ourselves, individually and collectively; distinguished from the abstract, external power-over that acts in the interest of dominance.[22]

Other-izing and domination have escalated to such a point that a counter-vision and movement are crucial to our well-being and, indeed, the survival of our planet. Whereas various movements have worked to spin threads of the web of ideas and action that challenge the deadly system of hierarchical dualism, a feminist perspective makes the root connections between the dualisms of self/other, nature/culture, spirit/intellect and mind/body and the pervasive mindset of patriarchal domination. This makes it even more clear that the solutions to all of these problems are and must be connected. A movement for sexual self-determination must be seen as a part, an integral part, of this linked struggle, since our sexuality is so deeply conditioned by metaphors of gender. We cannot be free in the world until we are free to be who we are and love how we please.

Such a radical philosophy is clearly of benefit to a movement to end biphobia and bisexual invisibility. We wish society to see people as the diverse creatures that we are instead of evaluating us on how well we fill social roles. However, even while the bisexual movement avoids reinventing the wheel by following the accomplishments and example

of the feminist and lesbian/gay liberation movements, we must be at-
tentive to some of the design flaws in that wheel that have caused it to
run over us at times. These problems arise particularly in areas where
the feminist, lesbian and gay movements succumb to hierarchical dualism and essentialism in their own thinking.

Many of the historical schisms within the feminist movement have
occurred when it was unable to see the interconnected effects that dualism has had on human thought, including feminist thought. For
instance, feminism has historically suffered from a split between those
who claimed that women were fundamentally different from (and
even superior to) men and those who argued for equality on the basis
that the genders were basically the same. The first group has suffered
through being belittled or subjected to protectionism as the dominant
society continued to degrade the very "eternal" feminine qualities that
the feminists were trying to exalt. The second group has often been
co-opted and has suffered from ignoring the diverse intrinsic qualities
of women in favor of what they conceived to be a "gender-free" model,
which, because patriarchy dominates the discourse of the generic, is
still based on maleness. Both sides of this split neglect the possibility
that dualism itself is an unnecessary confounder of the truth: that what
is human can encompass many aspects that have been categorized as
mutually exclusive.

Divisions in the feminist movement concerning whether gender is innate (essentialism) or a creation of social conditioning (constructionism)
have continued from the nineteenth century to today. They can be seen in
contemporary arguments in the areas of political activism (separatism as
opposed to working with men or otherwise within "the system"); theory
("cultural" feminism's elevation of the "innate" good of femaleness as opposed to the historical-materialist analytic focus of Marxist/socialist feminism); and sexuality (viewing women as victims of male sexuality and pornography as opposed to calling for women to take pride in and control of
diverse erotic fantasies, acts and representations). Where does this put
those of us who wish to be neither other-worldly farm amazons nor stock-
portfolio-toting corporate climbers? Who reject the Victorian over-
simplifications of "new age" feminism as well as the unfeeling mecha-
nization of Marxism? Who are left cold by the shallowness and con-
sumerism of mass pornography but also reject the "thought policing"
of puritanical feminists who would institute an unattainable sexual

standard of behavior for "political correctness"? Crucial to us as bisexual feminists, in addition, is the question of how we can criticize the evil that men do and become under patriarchy while still being able to love men and have faith in their humanity.

Feminism is hard-pressed to live up to its own tenet of giving validity to women's experience when such experiences appear to threaten its basic principles and tactics of opposition to patriarchal domination, as it has formulated them. Such threatening factors include "sleeping with the enemy" — bisexuality and feminist heterosexuality. For instance, a well-known (although misquoted) radical feminist saying, "Feminism is the theory, lesbianism is the practice," self-righteously rejects alliance with non-lesbian-supremacist women.[23]

Adrienne Rich has introduced the terms "lesbian existence" and "lesbian continuum" to describe the experience of women who resist the assumption that heterosexuality and relations dependent on men are the norm.

> If we consider the possibility that all women . . . exist on a lesbian continuum, we can see ourselves as moving in and out of this continuum, whether we identify ourselves as lesbian or not. It allows us to connect [diverse] aspects of woman-identification. . . .[24]

Bisexual women should be able to find welcome in this concept. We do so when we realize that many famous lovers of women honored in lesbian culture as foremothers, such as Virginia Woolf, Colette and Georgia O'Keeffe, were, by these lights, bisexual. They were woman-identified even while sharing strong bonds of affection, eroticism and commitment with men. But even as we are feeling a breath of fresh air at this inclusivity on the part of the lesbian-feminist canon to bisexual experience, we notice that these descriptions usually ignore, downplay, or explain away as "false consciousness" the relations that women-on-the-continuum had or have with men.

Rich's position can be interpreted as stepping dangerously close to an essentialist assertion that all women who desire connection with other women are truly lesbian. For many bisexual women, woman-identification is a crucial part of our experience. If feminism claims to speak of and value the authentically-lived experiences of women, it should grant as much validity to other facets of our experience as it does to our "lesbian side."

However much bisexual women feel gladdened and nourished by their sexual attachment to women and their sexual identification with women in general, they do not feel complete in that lesbian identification. . . . We would experience more draining of psychic energy by cutting off from our own possibilities than we do from accepting them and working from there. . . . The whole point of why bisexual feminists embrace our heterosexual component is that we see it as more about *us* than about men. We would feel diminished and crippled without that part of ourselves.[25]

The lesbian essentialism of Rich's metaphor has its roots in the general gay/lesbian liberation movement. While for most of history, what we call homosexuality was seen merely as a penchant for certain sexual acts, rather than an identity, "the homosexual" is a recent phenomenon. There was a point at which gayness itself was reified, turned into a thing.[26]

Bisexual theorist Amanda Udis-Kessler writes of the post-Stonewall gay movement's use of that identity as an "ethnic self-conception," as well as their drawing on the black civil rights movement and the feminist movement for political inspiration. Just as blackness and femaleness were seen as unchanging qualities, and it was argued that racism and sexism should end because blacks and women could not become the more privileged whites and men, the thrust of gay rights was that homosexuals should be given rights and acceptance because they, too, could not change.[27] This ethnic model of homosexuality stemmed from the history of the formation of gay communities. In the late nineteenth and twentieth centuries, homosexuals began to live together in selected neighborhoods in large cities, and began the "sexually-motivated migration" of other homosexuals to those ghettos (which presumably resembled ethnic ghettos).[28]

Udis-Kessler argues that biphobia within the lesbian/gay communities with which we seek to affiliate is largely due to the symbolic threat that bisexual ambiguity and flexibility present to this conception of permanent gay identity. Because of the way gays have struggled to exist and join together, "the collective myth and the community . . . can only remain intact if the pain which built the community was in some way the inevitable product of being oneself in a heterosexist society."[29]

But, as Deborah Gregory argues above, bisexuals are also only being ourselves. Only under the influence of dualism is it necessary for a Kinsey 6 gay person (See appendix, "The Kinsey Scale"), to be true to him/herself, to reject the possibility of a continuum of queerness. Bisexuals must continue to challenge the gay and lesbian communities to face up to the claims that they have built in support of their own freedom and to question the ways in which they argue from essentialism. Feminists and gay liberationists used to great effect the tactic of arguing that, if there are indeed two unchanging sides to a dualism, it is only ethical to grant full humanity to the traditionally denigrated side. But there are other ways to argue for liberation. Unity-in-diversity represents a quite powerful alternative and one that speaks to our self-determination of our own future rather than dependence on the goodwill of our oppressors.

While essentialism may have served to build a basis from which to argue to women's and gay rights, we can no longer afford to fail to recognize its inherent dangers. For the flip side of the argument that gayness is innate and therefore gays should be given rights is that gayness is innate and therefore gays should be ostracized or eliminated. The flip side of the argument that women hold a crucial card in the salvation of the human race due to our natural capacity for nurturance and our special grasp of interconnectedness is that women are innately inferior to men because we are equipped to take care of husband, home and children rather than to think abstractly in the world of commerce and politics.

When the gay liberation and feminist movements ask for rights and not for liberation, when they do not liberate themselves from sex and gender dualities that uphold social power relations, they leave themselves open to continued repression based on the very attributes that they assert to be a basis for freedom. The liberal model of social reform based on ethnicities and rights is based on the assumption that the struggle begins and ends with petitions by subordinate groups to the dominant class for the incremental expansion of previously denied human rights. However necessary reformist action is, it is not sufficient for liberation. It neglects to challenge the fact of there being a dominant class at all in the first place.

*

Feminist Bisexuality: Cautions and Clarion Calls
—An Alternative Paradigm for a Diverse Future

Feminist theory is facing new questions that come with new paradigms of thought. Unity-in-diversity, multiculturalism, and power-from-within are among those issues. If feminism is to live up to its own standards for liberation, some of the dogmas that it has found useful in the past must be transformed. For instance:

> • It must abandon "cultural feminist" viewpoints that merely reverse the superior/inferior dualism of the genders, and are reluctant to consider that so-called "masculine" and "feminine" characteristics may be complementary within one personality;
> • It must transcend the simplistic perspective on the development of patriarchy which blames men as an eternal class for all oppression;
> • It must reject the assumption that a fight against heterosexism necessarily implies accepting an exclusively (and militantly) homosexual identity and practice;
> • It must refuse the dogma that an egalitarian erotics is monolithic and that personal sexual desire should be subsumed to an arbitrary ideal.

In contrast, a deeper, broader cultural vision is being added to the political model by some newer elements of the feminist and sexual minority movements. Thinkers in this new sphere see that we are divided by dualisms which are socially located and which obscure the truth of the interconnectedness of diverse beings and actions. The bisexual movement can bring its unique and eclectic experiential insights to this vision and struggle. Those who reject the requirement that they choose from an either/or set of choices already have the potential for penetrating wisdom about other ways in which the either/or mentality is oppressive. Members of bisexual organizations are not only those "perfect middles" whose orientation is equally balanced between same-sex and opposite-sex leanings. We have no criterion, no clear line, to determine who is bisexual and who is not — nor, I think, do we desire one. Bisexuality is an orientation composed of shades of meaning, shifting vectors of love and lust. It is named only through self-identification, which itself may be none too easy to pin down. In this way, a bisexual identity is one that challenges dualisms. Any movement for true bisexual liberation must follow the paths of the interconnected movements for unity-in-diversity, rather than the divisive tactics that attempt to liberate some to the exclusion of others.

As bisexuals, our awareness of the culturally pervasive nature of essentialized hierarchical dualism is crucial. We face it when we argue that our love for men and women may be different in some ways, but that we basically love them as human beings. We confront it most directly when we argue that we share characteristics with both homosexuals and heterosexuals, but that we are both and neither. As Mariana Valverde writes,

> Although bisexuality, like homosexuality, is just another deviant identity, it also functions as a rejection of the norm/deviance model.... What bisexuals do is not so much escape the gay/straight split, but rather *manage* it.[30]

Our very commitment to realizing the fluid and transformative nature of sexual "identity" may make it easier to make the connections with the functioning of dualism in other areas of our lives and our culture. This is a process by which we transform a very personal realization of the non-essential character of sexuality into a wider and deeper spiritual and political understanding. Our "mixed" heritage and erotic inclusiveness can serve as a basis for increasing our multicultural awareness and openness to a variety of viewpoints. Our lives make it necessary to critique (however sympathetically) the separatism that occurs in other liberation movements.

We are in a key position to undermine the infiltration of hierarchical dualism into liberation politics. Like the groundbreaking early feminists, we speak from personal experience, from our individual minds, bodies, hearts and souls. We speak of bridge-building. We say that what the male and female halves of humanity have in common is more important than what differentiates them. We recognize that love is love for a person, not their gender. We believe that all people are unique and different *and* that all people have basic and deep commonalities.

Acceptance of the gray areas, of the flexibility of the human spirit and eros, in the end will benefit gays, lesbians, feminists — indeed, all people — not just bisexuals. Challenging hierarchical dualism presents a definite challenge to established cultural relations, in areas far beyond sexuality alone. This is why we can expect, as our movement gets stronger, to be a particular target of those who most wish to preserve the status quo. This also explains why we have been denigrated even by movements that clash with the status quo — because some of their system-challenging precepts are themselves based upon ideologies that ultimately uphold that system. In challenging binary classification itself, we upset those who have gotten some crumbs from their oppressors by classifying themselves. Perhaps we can see more clearly now why, as Audre Lorde has said, "the master's tools will never dismantle the master's house."[31]

In light of the insidious effect of hierarchical dualism and essentialism on the feminist and gay movements, we must keep in mind important cautions for our own. A decisive part of how we deal with the bisexual label involves our attitude toward heterosexual privilege. While working with gays and lesbians to fight heterosexism, we must acknowledge the truth that they are far less likely to find themselves in a societally-approved relationship than we are. Our own potential to find such approval, in addition, depends completely on the chance occurrence of whom we happen to fall in love with. The ethical response to this is to live our commitment to fighting heterosexual privilege even, indeed especially, when we are in ostensibly heterosexual relationships. We cannot take safe haven in the "acceptable" portion of our experience, for our bisexual identity as a whole is socially unacceptable.

We must judge ourselves by the same standards with which we sympathetically critique our allies. The bisexual movement must not yield to the faulty thinking of "vanguardism" just because of our potential to have a special perspective on dualism. We must reject the idea that some people are clearly more oppressed than others. Believing in a "hierarchy of oppressions" turns us against each other when we should be realizing that our struggles are fundamentally interconnected. This realization is especially important if the bisexual movement is to be truly multicultural, seeking racial and religious as well as sexual and gender justice. We must not treat other movements as though they are competing with us for scarce resources, because the freedom that we all seek is an unlimited ocean of possibility.

While we reject ethnic conceptions of gayness and lesbian-feminist superiority complexes, we must also reject the easy answer of stating

that "everyone is really bisexual." The claim that everyone's orientation is flexible is as fallacious as it is to say that everyone's orientation
is rigidly defined. Neither may we say that one is bisexual only if one
is actually sexually active with both men and women.

> Consider that heterosexuality and homosexuality would be easy to
> reify compared to bisexuality. They seem to make sense as catego-
> ries. But how does one reify fluidity. . . ? The essentialist answer
> is to change bisexuality from a potential-for-either to a require-
> ment-for-both identity. . . .[32]

We cannot in truth claim that men and women are exactly alike,
and that therefore whom one loves or has sex with does not matter. In
doing so, we succumb to a homogeneity of love that denies the very
real variety of sexual experiences with men and women.

We must also be aware that bisexuals are not ourselves "inherently" in tune with the virtues of ambiguity and flexibility — while we
may strive to achieve them, our personalities are also held back by the
dominant cultural paradigms we have internalized. While we constantly try to listen to and value our own experience, to "live our bisexuality *in the present tense*,"[33] we must fight against the systems that
attempt to control and define that experience. The ideologies of
domination are interconnected in working against *us all*, keeping down
everyone who threatens the patriarchal status quo. A bisexual liberation movement cannot exist without attacking at the root sexism,
heterosexism, ethnocentrism, and all other such ideologies of hierarchical dualism and essentialism.

Along with feminists and gay liberationists, we question the construction of sexuality based on irreconcilable gender differences and its
use as an instrument of social control. In basing our identity not only
on fluidity, but on *fluidity of sexuality*, we perform the radical act of
challenging the segregation and denigration of human erotic energy.

Many bisexuals wish to "do away with labels," to surpass the binary opposition and the compartmentalization that requires us to sub-
sume our overall commitment to our diverse and flexible affiliations
under the name "bi-sexual." However, while we live under today's
culture of hierarchical oppression, we must fight against sexism and
heterosexism before we can simply walk away from the boxes they put
us in. Before we can reject the "primary colors," we need to explore

how the color palette came to be arranged the way it did. We must do the best we can to create beautiful and visionary works of art with the colors available. We must take the power of *claiming* and *changing* our identity-label before we will be truly able to *chuck it.*[34]

Endnotes

1. See Michel Foucault, *The History of Sexuality, Vol. 1: An Introduction*, trans. Robert Hurley (New York: Vintage Books, 1978, 1990), especially pages 42-44, 101-02. See also Lisa Orlando, "Loving Whom We Choose," in eds. Loraine Hutchins and Lani Kaahumanu; *Bi Any Other Name: Bisexual People Speak Out* (Boston: Alyson Publications, 1991), pp. 223-32, especially pp. 227-28.

2. Jeffrey Weeks, *Sexuality and Its Discontents* (London: Routledge and Kegan Paul, 1985), p. 188.

3. Ideas in this section regarding the nature, origin and workings of hierarchical dualism stem from and are more fully described in Kathleen Bennett, "Ecology and the Promise of Feminism: Theoretical Connections" (unpublished, 1987, revised 1989).

4. It is telling that hierarchical dualism itself cannot be adequately analyzed without the use of a plethora of "both/and" sentence structures in order to avoid the truth-obscuring what-caused-what arguments between materialistic and "cultural" methods of analysis.

5. The following works on pre-patriarchal culture are both incredibly diverse in approach and thought-provoking in their consistencies. My interpretations of the origin of patriarchy is largely drawn from this scholarship: Riane Eisler, *The Chalice and the Blade: Our History, Our Future* (San Francisco: Harper and Row, 1989); Elinor Gadon, *The Once and Future Goddess* (San Francisco: Harper and Row, 1989); Gerda Lerner, *The Creation of Patriarchy* (New York: Oxford University Press, 1986); Starhawk, *Dreaming the Dark: Magic, Sex and Politics* (new edition) (Boston: Beacon Press, 1982, 1988); Starhawk, *Truth or Dare* (San Francisco: Harper and Row, 1987), especially Chapter 2, "The Dismembering of the World."

6. Sherry B. Ortner, "Is Female to Male as Nature is to Culture?" in *Woman, Culture and Society*, eds. Michelle Rosaldo and Louise Lamphere (Stanford: Stanford University Press, 1974), pp. 67-88.

7. To call these cultures "matriarchies," as many have (often in the process of belittling the cultures' proponents as unscholarly), is incorrect and reflects hierarchical dualism, as the term assumes that women must have ruled over men.

8. See Fredrick Engels, *The Origin of the Family, Private Property and the State*, edited and with an introduction by Eleanor Burke Leacock (New York: International Publishers 1972). See also Gayle Rubin, "The Traffic in Women: Notes on the Political

Economy of Sex" in *Women, Class, and the Feminist Imagination: A Socialist-Feminist Reader,* eds. Karen V. Hansen and Ilene J. Philipson (Philadelphia: Temple University Press, 1990), pp. 74-113.

9. Op. cit. Starhawk, *Truth or Dare,* p. 25.

10. The feminist witch/philosopher Starhawk discusses two different aspects of power (*Dreaming the Dark,* op. cit., Chapter 1, and *Truth or Dare,* op. cit., Chapter 1 "Power-over is linked to domination and control...we live embedded in systems of power-over and are indoctrinated into them. Power-over enables one individual or group to make the decisions that affect others, and to enforce control." (*Truth or Dare,* p. 9) Power-over is contrasted with power-from-within, which is "akin to our sense of mastery [and also] something deeper...our sense of connection, our bonding with other human beings, and with the environment. Although power-over rules the systems we live in, power-from-within sustains our lives." (*Truth or Dare,* p. 10)

11. Mariana Valverde, *Sex, Power, and Pleasure* (Philadelphia: New Society Publishers, 1987), p. 118. (Italics in text.)

12. For instance, see the stories in Hutchins and Kaahumanu, *Bi Any Other Name: Bisexual People Speak Out.*

13. Gayle Rubin, "Thinking Sex," in *Pleasure and Danger: Exploring Female Sexuality,* ed. Carole Vance (Boston: Routledge and Kegan Paul, 1984), p. 278.

14. Amanda Udis-Kessler, "Present Tense: Biphobia as a Crisis of Meaning," in Hutchins and Kaahumanu, *Bi Any Other Name,* p. 354.

15. Barbara Ehrenreich, Elizabeth Hess and Gloria Jacobs, *Re-Making Love: The Feminization of Sex* (Garden City, New Jersey: Anchor Books, 1987); Steve Chapple and David Talbot, *Burning Desires: Sex in America* (New York: Doubleday, 1989), especially Chapter 7, "Pandora's Mirror: The Rise of Fem Porn."

16. Op. cit. Rubin, "Thinking Sex," p. 278.

17. The description of these mechanisms owes greatly to Rubin. "Thinking Sex." pp. 278-82.

18. Ibid., p. 282.

19. Ibid., p. 280.

20. Ibid. p. 281.

21. The *Bowers v. Hardwick* case before the Supreme Court resulted in the upholding of an anti-sodomy law used specifically to persecute homosexual acts. The courts specifically gave states the right to exclude heterosexuals engaging in sodomy from its laws.

22. The last topic is consistently elaborated by Starhawk throughout her work.

23. The original quotation from Ti-Grace Atkinson is the far less judgmental "Feminism is a theory; lesbianism is a practice." The fact that the misquotation is far better known is no fault of Atkinson's, but reflects a political prejudice that has had far-reaching effects on the lesbian movement.

24. Adrienne Rich, "Compulsory Heterosexuality and Lesbian Existence," *Signs: A Journal of Women in Culture and Society* 5, no. 4 (1980): 650-51.

25. Deborah Gregory, "From Where I Stand: A Case for Feminist Bisexuality," in *Sex and Love: New Thoughts on Old Contradictions*, eds. Sue Cartledge and Joanna Ryan, (London: The Women's Press, 1983), pp. 145-49.

26. Op. cit. See Foucault, *The History of Sexuality, Vol. 1*, especially Chapter 1, and Weeks, *Sexuality and Its Discontents*, especially Chapter 4.

27. Udis-Kessler, "Present Tense," See also Udis-Kessler, "Bisexuality in an Essentialist World: Toward an Understanding of Biphobia," in Tom Geller; ed., *Bisexuality: A Reader and Sourcebook*, (Ojai, Calif.: Times Change Press, 1990), pp. 51-63.

28. Op. cit. Rubin, "Thinking Sex," pp. 286-87.

29. Op. cit. Udis-Kessler, "Present Tense," p. 353.

30. Valverde, *Sex, Power and Pleasure*, p. 115. (Italics in text.)

31. "The Master's Tools Will Never Dismantle the Master's House," in *This Bridge Called My Back: Writings by Radical Women of Color*, eds. Cherríe Moraga and Gloria Anzaldúa, Watertown, Massachusetts: Persephone Press (1981), pp. 98-101.

32. Op. cit. Udis-Kessler, "Bisexuality in an Essentialist World," pp. 59-60.

33. Op. cit. Udis-Kessler, "Present Tense," p. 356, (Italics in text)

34. Clare Thompson, "Speech to Bicon 1990" (First National Bisexual Conference, San Francisco), *North Bi Northwest*, Volume 3, Number 4 (August/September 1990), p. 1.

Beth Elliott

Holly Near
And Yet So Far

It was too good to be true: Holly Near—courageous and outspoken (and deservedly beloved) lesbian feminist, and perhaps the very embodiment of women's music—speaking in her autobiography[1] about both her "passion for women" and her conviction that closing the door to heterosexual affairs would make her life so unauthentic that she would no longer be able to write or sing.[2] For bisexual feminists, especially those of us with "women's community" backgrounds, Near's statements could have been validation of the highest order. Even more, they could have been an incredible breakthrough in raising the lesbian community's consciousness about the lives of bisexual feminists (especially those lesbian-identified feminists who own their bisexuality) and the power of our presence in the larger world. It would have been a dream come true.

Dream on. Though bravely voicing her determination to love and sleep with whomever she chooses, woman or man, Holly Near declines to call herself bisexual because, one, she "doesn't feel like a bisexual"[3] and, two, her lesbianism is "linked to [a] political perspective" rather than mere "sexual preference"[4]—unlike, presumably, her bisexuality. How very sad that a woman who has done (and risked) so much for women's and lesbian liberation is so unaware of all the support and admiration she has for daring to follow her passion with whomever she chooses, so unaware of all the women who believe doing so can indeed be a bold and principled feminist action.

Talking About My Generation

At one end of the broad spectrum of bisexual feminists is a large group of women who are lesbians (the noun) and bisexual (the adjective). Many of these women, like myself, came of age and/or came out in time to help create the "women's community" groundswell of the 1970s. We, too, have a keen appreciation of the political import and power of our lesbianism. We know too well the misconceptions many lesbians have about bisexual women, and we understand both how a lesbian feminist could be involved with a man and how reluctant she could be to name this as bisexuality. We cherish our place in the women's community, a community many of us have worked strenuously to build, and we care passionately about maintaining our connection with it. We realize that to do so, we must combat homosexism in the women's community—in addition to the ongoing challenge of fighting sexism, biphobia and homophobia in society at large. To the extent we overcome biphobia—wherever we find it—we liberate women by expanding the range of life choices by which we can empower ourselves and each other.

Some of the bisexual lesbians from my "aging hippie" cohort have fallen head-over-heels in love with another outspoken woman musician, Gretchen Phillips of Two Nice Girls. Phillips not only sings proudly of being a lesbian and bisexual, but rocks on out in the process. Ah, but she warms the hearts of those of us who built a woman-loving-women's community post-Stonewall but pre-"political lesbians" (that is, women whose lesbian identity is based more on feminist politics than on sexual attraction to women).

Phillips personifies the freedom to be whatever kind of woman-loving woman one chooses, the freedom around which we "pre-PC" lesbian feminists attempted to build a community and movement. We were stopped when separatism and other forms of political correctness became the dominant and exclusive women's community paradigm; perhaps the success of Phillips and Two Nice Girls is an indication that politically correct lesbian feminism has run its course as an ideology that can be successfully enforced community-wide. I, for one, am thrilled by the emergence of a generation who can take the fall of political correctness for granted. Still, it is Holly Near and not Gretchen Phillips who has the credentials to be a spokesperson or role model attractive to seventies lesbian feminists and the younger women who identify with their left-oriented community—thus my disappointment at coming so close, without success, to having a Holly Near-type/era bisexual feminist role model to go along with the Gretchen Phillips-type/era bisexual feminist role model.

Make no mistake: in writing frankly of her refusal to swear allegiance to either sex, and to be sexually involved with individuals of her own choosing, male or female, Holly Near has knowingly braved the wrath of her most devoted audience in order to speak the truth of her life. This is the kind of courageous act on which she has built her reputation and is in marked contrast to the silence of the many closeted bisexuals in the lesbian community. I admire her for speaking out at all. Sure, I wish she were more comfortable with the "B-word," because I wish someone like her would convincingly embody, within the (political) lesbian community, the truth that one can promote lesbian feminism without sexual exclusivity. I also wish Gretchen Phillips were admired by more thirty- and forty-something lesbians—the generation who, alas, equated rock 'n' roll with sexism.

And so, for us bisexual lesbian feminists to have this kind of role model to present to the lesbian community, we may have to aspire to being that kind of role model ourselves. The potential is staggering: a woman who can take pride in her *bisexual* feminist life could do far more than reclaim the full range of her sexual options as a woman. She could affirm that women can make choices to assert our power and visions rather than just react to oppression. She could affirm that we can move about in the dominant culture even while questioning it and challenging it from within, without giving up our freedom or lesbian-feminist values. She could show that we can be strong and brave and happy whether within the "women's community" or outside of it—an orientation that could make that community truly a home, not a fortress; truly a community, not a ghetto.

This is why it is so frustrating to see any lesbian (the noun) who is bisexual (the adjective) feel she must deny her bisexuality to affirm her lesbianism: she defines limits on her options for a feminist life when she could be shattering those limits.

A Matter of Labeling

Ironically, there is little difference in behavior between women who say they are lesbians and women who say they are lesbian *and* bisexual. A 1987 Kinsey Institute survey[5] taken at an unnamed "annual women's event which regularly attracts 7,000 women"[6] found that seventy-five percent of women currently calling themselves lesbians (and attending this event) had had sex with men since age eighteen, forty-six percent within the preceding seven years.

It should be noted that some of this sexual activity may have been attempts to do the socially "appropriate" thing or to avoid acting on feelings for women prior to accepting those feelings. Heterosexual behavior by women who self-label as bi may more likely have been purposefully chosen—though many bi women, especially those who have considered themselves lesbians, have gone through that same coming-out process and may have had the same ambiguous feelings about sex with women during that process. And yet, of the twenty-eight percent who had always called themselves lesbians, forty-three percent had had sex with men since age eighteen and twenty-one percent within the preceding seven years.

In other words, there may be very little difference in the amount or frequency of sex with men between a cross section of the lesbian community and those bisexual feminists who identify with the lesbian community. And among lesbian-identified women who do have sex with men, there is very little difference between those who deny and those who acknowledge that this makes us bisexual (the adjective) when it comes to our participation in the women's community and to the importance we place on our lesbianism. In fact, some of their statements about the relation between our lesbianism and our bisexuality are indistinguishable.

Louise Sloan speaks of being a 4.5+ on the Kinsey scale and wearing a shirt that reads, "Bisexual by luck, queer by choice."[7] The "queer" advocacy/presentation style aside, this would seem to articulate a political stance similar to Near's, but without the non-bisexual disclaimer. Rachel Kaplan can say, along with Near,[8] that "when I was with women I felt like a lesbian and when I was with men I still felt like a lesbian."[9] Kaplan, however, rejects the notion that a bisexual identity is inherently devoid of political content: she goes on to assert that calling herself bisexual in the nineties is "the closest approximation of freedom I can find . . . my inner child saying NO to a world where gender determines my desire and my behavior . . . I want to be able to do what I want to, to feel what I feel." If that isn't a strong (lesbian feminist) political statement, what is?

One can argue, then, that many of us "4.5+" bisexual feminists have the same "passion for women and . . . objection to male domination"[10] that makes some women avoid the "B-word" and call themselves lesbians—and many of us are much more queer, as well. To "4.5+" bisexual feminists, our love for women is anything but a casual matter, and our desire for and commitment to a community of women who love and support women is most serious, as can be seen in the way we agonize over self-identification. There are those who will say, proudly, that they are bisexual, but who identify as lesbian for the strongest possible confrontation with homophobia. There are those who call themselves bisexual lesbians. Then there are those who, when asked whether they are lesbian or bisexual, gleefully answer, "Yes!"[11]

The same agony over self-identification also arises for us over the very question of "identity politics." Is promoting the adoption of the bisexual label (or any other label) useful in promoting liberation, or is it a distraction from empowering people to choose their own range of behavior? In her essay in *Bi Any Other Name*, Rebecca Shuster defines identity as a set of beliefs about ourselves that we internalize, beliefs that may or may not correspond logically with our sexual behavior. [12] She believes it is possible to be bisexual in terms of sexual relations while genuinely and authentically identifying as a lesbian. Many "lesbian-identified bisexual" feminists agree with this idea, because it describes our lives.

On the other hand, many of us diverge from Shuster's analysis when she says the bi movement's goal should be the elimination of sexual identities as a way to effect total freedom of behavior. We value our lives as lesbians, because a lesbian identity celebrates our love for women, our appreciation for how women interact with each other and the world, and our commitment to women's liberation. Many of us are living what are basically lesbian lives. Some simply refuse to deny ourselves an enjoyable interaction with a man, should one come along who strikes our fancy, even while preferring women, especially for a serious relationship. Others insist upon the freedom to choose involvements with quality people regardless of gender. One woman, in a discussion at the first National Bisexual Conference, practically apologized for being so woman-oriented that she wondered if she technically might not really be bi since she had yet to be involved with a man—a Kinsey 5.9 if ever there was one.[13]

At the same time, bi-lesbian feminists use the articulation of a bisexual identity as a tool for liberation (even though our actual heterosexual involvement may be token), both to promote freedom of behavior and to confront bi- and heterophobia in the lesbian community. Many of us take part in bisexual *women's* groups without necessarily feeling part of a larger (and co-ed) bisexual community. I suspect we see bisexual feminism as affording us the best features of lesbianism, and a women's community, without the pressures of being expected to conform to political correctness. (In fact, one might wonder whether these groups could become one of the best places to meet quality woman-loving women—but that's really another essay.)

Bisexual women's groups are implicitly feminist, because they form on the assumption that women coming together in women's space is both necessary and desirable. Within these groups, an ongoing discussion topic has been how to live non-exclusively lesbian lives in a way that honors and promotes lesbian community and liberation. And so, bisexual-lesbian feminists see our groups as part of the women's community. They could even be part of the next wave of the lesbian feminist movement, because bisexual feminists could lead a transition from an oppression-based lesbian/feminist paradigm to a freedom- and power-based paradigm.

As I use the term in this essay, "oppression-based feminism" is essentially reactive, in the sense of moving away from anything that may have had an oppressive effect on any woman, whether this oppression was inherent in a particular practice or related to a particular set of circumstances. Freedom- and/or power-based feminism is essentially proactive, in the sense of individual women, or groups of women, defining for themselves the content of a particular practice based on intent and context.

A textbook question of oppression paradigm versus freedom paradigm would be the propriety of strip shows in lesbian bars: are they oppressive because they make a woman a sexual object, or are they liberating because they celebrating women's sexuality without male viewers? Should they be banned because they may have painful associations for some women, or should women be able to attend if they so choose?

Beyond the Womb

To some lesbians, the women's community is intended to be "safe (woman) space," not only oppression-free but also gentle and non-challenging enough to enable women to heal from patriarchal abuses.

Thus, they place an emphasis on the absence of oppression, even theo-retical oppression. Lesbians who dare to be bisexual obviously have a different point of view: we see feminism as something that has suffi-ciently empowered women and affected society to where we feel we can hold our own in, and gain rewards from, situations other lesbians might consider too unsafe or threatening. Because women are still our family, we see ourselves as living and moving in two worlds: we can be *in* the heterosexual world even as we decline to be *of* that world. Any-thing that gives us the freedom and power to explore and enjoy the entire world, rather than one "safe" corner of it, is of value to us— such as our claiming our bisexual potential.

There is one segment of the lesbian community that shows hints of a freedom-based lesbian way of living: the "posties," the twenty-some-thing post-baby-boomers of "Generation X" who have come of age taking a liberated (and sexually liberated) lesbian community for granted. To some extent, many of them are still reacting to the less sexually-explorative ways of their "elders" and thus have not yet ar-ticulated what bonds and commonalities of life they experience as women (rather than as queers). Perhaps as more non-conforming "boomer" lesbians speak out about the pride in sexuality that did in-form early post-Stonewall lesbian communities, these young women will realize that woman-identification and sexual exploration (and celebration) can indeed go hand in hand.

Nonetheless, many lesbians continue to reject the notion that bi-sexual feminists (and our pro-choice philosophy of sex) are part of the women's community. Partly because they believe the heterosexual re-lationships we might engage in are something that can be dangerous to women and thus make the community less safe, no matter to what standards we hold those heterosexual relationships. They would also argue that we have a different place in a kind of hierarchy of oppres-sion. This oppression-based analysis, by eclipsing our erotic variety and invalidating our strategies for empowerment and liberation, alien-ates us from a community and movement we believe we are a part of.

Unfortunately, our alternatives in terms of community and move-ment, even though they attempt to build upon a paradigm of claiming freedom, also pose problems. The emerging co-sexual lesbian/gay/bisexual (when this community deigns to include us by name) com-munity and the "queer" community very often ask lesbians and bi feminists to forsake our cherished woman-identification and define ourselves as gay/ queer first and women second. Not only do they expect us to put co-sexual (or even men's) issues before fighting sexism, but they also often pressure us to buy into negative "post-feminist" stereotyping of feminist and woman-identified lesbians as repressive and anti-sexual.

A New Feminist Perspective

Bi-feminists are the women most likely to pioneer a new, inclusive feminist perspective beyond the dualism that lesbian feminism has not yet transcended. After all, we must resolve the duality of gay versus straight within ourselves to come out as bi. And so, just as the bisexual movement does the important work of calling both heterosexuals and homosexuals to question their intolerance, bisexual feminists can call on the women's community to deal with rigidity and political correctness and call on the co-sexual "queer" community to deal with its issues about lesbians and feminism.

Moreover, it would seem it is left to bisexual-lesbian feminists to resist a campaign to get lesbians to abandon woman-identification in favor of participation in a "co-sexual" gay community whose culture, sexuality and politics are defined by urban gay men. (This process begins with pressure on lesbians to repudiate our distinct culture and agenda because they were supposedly inimical to fighting AIDS. It has continued with the stereotyping of lesbian feminists as being anti-sexual, and the encouragement of women to define the essence of lesbianism as marginalized sexual acts, preferably with some amount of public display thereof or allusion thereto, which has led me to refer to this process on occasion as the "bimbo-ization" of lesbianism.[14])

From a bi-feminist point of view, I would like to compare and contrast these oppression-based (that is, lesbian-feminist) and freedom-based (that is, radical co-sexual gay) movements, then show what bisexual feminists have to offer the women's community, in terms of both revitalizing a woman-identified women's community and leading the way to a new and powerful stage in the continuing process of women's liberation.

The realization that the personal is political was a stroke of genius. It empowered countless women to recognize and name our oppression instead of blaming ourselves for it (or accepting it as "normal") and gave us an incisive analysis of the power dynamics of male-dominated societies. It birthed a community that both fought our oppression and made space for us to heal from that oppression. Nonetheless, when we said the personal *is* political, we did not give ourselves enough room to fine-tune this aphorism in case of success: to be able to say the personal *is often* political or the personal *can be* political. As a result, our feminist analysis sometimes gets so theoretical that it can misrepresent what is actually going on in real women's lives.

Consider, for example, Andrea Dworkin's take on hetsex. She has devoted an entire book to the proposition that heterosexual vaginal intercourse is inherently demeaning to women because of the semiotics of penetration: being penetrated automatically demeans women, making us vulnerable and therefore subordinate.[15] Now, undoubtedly, such has been the experience of quite a number of women, even above and beyond rape survivors. On the other hand, many heterosexual and bisexual women will insist that they engage in and enjoy sex with men on their own terms, in a way that gratifies them without putting them one down.

In all likelihood, feminism has made this redefinition of hetsex by women possible—but we have not yet explored the political implications of this personal progress. Too often, when contradicting viewpoints (out of theory versus out of practice) are discussed, there is no way for them to end up reconciled—no way to explore Dworkin's metaphors and still be empowered by knowing some women can "sleep with the enemy" and emerge unscathed. Too often, a straight or bisexual woman will be told she can't really be in control of her sexuality. That her subjective successful experience diverges from what should be true in theory is taken as a sign that she is deluding herself and needs her consciousness raised. In real-life terms, the result may be our losing a woman highly motivated to dedicate time and energy to the feminist movement, all because she feels invalidated where she expected to find support.

The same kind of absolutism has been applied to another insight. Because so much—and such basic—privilege has been created by one group elevating itself at another's expense, some of us assume, almost by reflex, that a woman less thoroughly oppressed or disadvantaged than others is herself an oppressor if she does not renounce whatever this difference may be. For example, there are women who claim that because they are readily identifiable as dykes and incapable of appearing otherwise, women whose appearance is more socially acceptable (that is, "straight-looking") are oppressing their more butch sisters if they do not dress and act in an "identifiably lesbian" manner.

This attitude is confusing equality with reduction to the lowest common denominator; this is bringing a few women down rather than bringing many women up. We have gotten so good at naming oppression that we look for it everywhere, even where women have made gains we might otherwise want to celebrate and build upon. We have given ourselves so much praise and support for identifying victimization that we are in danger of not knowing how to be anything but victims. No wonder some lesbian feminists think of bisexuality as giving in to patriarchal expectations of women.

Feminism Is the Theory, Bisexual Feminism Is the Practice

Bisexual feminists define our bisexuality as staking out more safe space for women, thus expanding our options and affirming the choices we make as women, and doing the work it takes to make this so. Because this work is about taking the "compulsory" and "institutionalized" out of heterosexuality, any lesbian icon who does have some sexual involvement with men (and there are more than one) could be an incredibly powerful role model as an out bisexual feminist. In a world in which heterosexuality can be a dangerous thing for women, it would be empowering to know that someone could essay it and emerge centered and empowered; that someone could explore it on her own terms to get the reward she sought, while maintaining her feminist perspective and commitment; that yes, indeed, feminism is, however slowly and arduously, making the world a safer place for women to live whatever lives we wish to live.

Staking out safe space in which women can love each other may shelter individual women, but it does not in and of itself transform the world from which they are escaping. Bi feminists have in common with lesbian feminists our woman-centeredness; we have made a choice in a male-dominated culture to acknowledge women's importance to us and act upon it. We take that consciousness out into the world in order to transform the world. I believe our relationships with men are different from those of heterosexual women; I believe we do ask for (and often get, despite the odds) different things in those relationships. All the women who say they can't be bisexual because they "feel like a lesbian being with a man" describe what we out bi feminists feel: our woman-identification and interconnection with women are a significant part of who we are, something to which heterosexual relationships must adapt.

So which view of the *fact* of bisexuality is more empowering of women? Bi feminists, by venturing out beyond the boundaries of the women's community into the larger world (and dealing with the people and situations we encounter there in an honorable and feminist way), force ourselves to test out lesbian-feminist theories and identities empirically and determine to what extent they are in touch with real experience—to what extent the political is still personal. We have to analyze the *presentation* of lesbian-feminist theory in terms of its *relevance* to the majority of lesbians outside the core women's community, as well as to women in general. This is all extremely important for a group as invisible as lesbians—and it is a process undermined by the kind of lesbian biphobia that stems from an identity and politics based on who is more oppressed rather than on how we claim our freedom.

We're Here, We're Feminists, Get Used to It

But what of political groups composed of and doing advocacy for the other-than-heterosexual that claim to be based on taking freedom (for example, ACT UP, Queer Nation)? In theory, they should have much to offer the bisexual lesbian feminist, especially with their strong pro-sex (and pro-choice regarding sexuality) stances. In practice, however, they participate in a major fault of the advocates of a co-sexual gay community: the stereotyping of any lesbian-oriented feminism, if not feminism itself, as part and parcel of the abuses of "political correctness" of which some radical lesbian feminists have been guilty.

Take, for example, Queer Nation. Queer Nation San Francisco is, at least in theory, both concerned with women's issues and bi-positive. Its primary women's focus group is called LABIA (Lesbians and Biwomyn in Action), and among the stickers with which it has plastered the city are those reading "rape is a men's issue." Some women say simply being a part of the group/tribe makes them feel "much more self-assured in being an out lesbian," and some are comfortable enough in Queer Nation that they do not feel a need to belong to LA-

BIA.[16] Their concept of "vibes watchers" who sniff out "discomfort, and watch for silenced dissent, sexism and racism"[17] is empowerment-oriented rather than oppression-oriented because it is concerned with acting for immediate results rather than with political breast-beating.

On the other hand, Queer Nation presents both ideological and practical problems for lesbian and bisexual women. On the practical side, some women and people of color believe Queer Nation's practice has not kept up with its stated goals around sexism and racism.[18] On the ideological side, Queer Nation stands for an identity and a relationship with the dominant culture that leave women very little room for self-definition *as women* or for a primarily feminist analysis of our lives. This is because "queer" identity and culture are, to a large extent, an extension of identities and lifestyles developed by gay men, and, historically, there has been some resentment of lesbians' failure to align ourselves with those identities and lifestyles and to exempt gay men from our feminist critiques of a male-dominated society.

The concept that male and female "queers" share a culture, identity and struggle stemming from our being marginalized for our sexuality addresses only part of our experience as women-loving women and undercuts any kind of lesbian/ bisexual-feminist perspective. The ideology that "queerness" transcends any lesbian and bisexual women's culture, identity and politics cuts us off from the side of ourselves focused on our lives as women, and thus from a vital support network, no matter how flawed that network might be. The perspective that queer ideology would supersede is centered around the very basic feminist notion that lesbian relationships and community are essentially about female bonding, not just a set of sexual practices (wonderful as those are), and that this is what makes us such a threat to the hetero*patriarchy.*

A writer in the *Village Voice*[19] noted (very perceptively) that Queer Nation dykes "were just trying to look like fags."[19] Indeed, many queer-identified women act as though they want to prove to gay men how unlike pc-lesbians they can be, and that they, too, are into cutting-edge (that is, like gay men's) sexuality—and the results can be disastrous.

In its 1991 Freedom Day issue, the San Francisco *Sentinel* honored twenty-two "gay heroes" (some of them heterosexual AIDS activists), one for each year since Stonewall. One of the honored was Madonna, for popularizing gay imagery and sensibility. But while this feature was no doubt being worked on, *Rolling Stone* ran a two-part conversation between Madonna and Carrie Fisher (accompanied by a photo spread of Madonna that overflows with overt lesbian imagery) in which the two of them articulated the standard straight male put-down of lesbian sex:

> CF: So why don't you go out with women? I have the answer from my end.
> M: Because after they give me head [which she had identified as a major "like"] I want them to stick it inside me.
> CF: My answer is, because there's no payoff.
> M: Although, I guess a woman could strap on a dildo.
> CF: Not really. There's no way to look at somebody who has strapped on a dildo and still think that they're a human. Their dignity levels are frighteningly low.
> M: I've never had one inside of me, but for a joke I asked a friend of mine to put one on. I just couldn't stop laughing, so I don't see how anyone could look at them with a straight face.[20]

There you have it in a nutshell: women can't really have fulfilling sex together (even women who like "getting head for a day and a half"[21]) because there's no penis involved, and their attempts to approximate "the real thing" with dildos not only fall short but make them ridiculous as well.

In falling all over themselves to prove how sexually hip and liberated they are, queer-identified lesbians can end up sucking up to those who oppose lesbians and feminism politically, like pop academic Camille Paglia. Paglia, who fancies herself one of the "Sixties people [who] were defeated, but we wised up and we're returning"—in her case as a neoconservative feminist- and pc-basher—has the "post-feminist" crowd lapping up her put-downs of lesbian sex and feminists as sexuality-killers. She believes "American feminism's nosedive began when Kate Millett . . . declared Freud a sexist," and in a 1991 essay and interview, she espoused the right-wing line that feminism is a fascist, dissent-stifling plague on our campuses.[22] In this interview, Paglia praised gay men for their "outstanding cultural contributions . . . to beauty and pleasure" and praised their (pre-Stonewall) "revolutionary *philosophe*-like iconoclasm," but called women's studies programs "institutionalized sexism" and said lesbians have a Norman Bates-type

246 Closer to Home

attachment to our mothers. She further claimed that lesbian sex is inherently not as "hot" or "passionate" as heterosexual coupling.

Responding to this article, linguistics professor and author Robin Lakoff noted this was the "same old [neoconservative] harangue, albeit . . . in the mouth of a self-styled 'feminist.'"[23] Another writer, noting that she and many other feminists are "both pro-pleasure and anti-rape," cited Paglia's "standard fag-hag misogyny" and said, "men must be thrilled to find a smart woman preaching their line for them (Daddy is better than Mommy; women who get raped deserve it)."[24] On the other hand, a nouveau queer lesbian writing in *Image* magazine (identifiable as such by her buzz word-laden proclamation that she "has always enjoyed hot sex"), said she was not at all offended by Paglia's remarks on the inherent boredom of lesbian sex: "She is obviously a woman of passion and power, and I say, 'Right on!'"[25] Is this the bimbo-ization of lesbianism personified, or what?

To further the goal of repositioning lesbianism as a sexually "hot" post-feminist identity and culture, the co-ed gay media regularly portrays women who are not going along with the program as selfish shrews ideologically opposed to a long-overdue male-female cooperation and joint culture. A rather striking indication that the partisans of co-sexuality have lost any understanding of lesbians being feminists because we are women was a March 1991 editorial in the San Francisco *Sentinel* decrying the denial of press credentials to the male *Sentinel* reporter assigned to cover the National Lesbian Conference in Atlanta. The most shocking and extreme consequence may be the case of the Boston gay man who, upon learning a new feminist book and crafts store was making two of its first ten evening events women-only, filed a complaint with that city's Human Rights Commission. "This is the nineties," he said, "we [*sic*] don't do that kind of thing anymore."[26]

Another concept/catch phrase comes up over and over in talk of the purpose of Queer Nation: anti-assimilationism. This has the potential of joining political correctness as a paradigm that denies women's own definitions of the realities of our lives. In Queer Nation's essentialist[27] metaphor of lesbians, gays and bisexuals as something akin to an ethnic minority, anything "queers" do that replicates any aspect of heterosexual life can be viewed as selling out to gain straight acceptance—even if it involves lesbian culture or lesbian issues of long standing. In an atmosphere in which even the appropriateness of forming couples can be called into question,[28] what do we do with the Sharon Kowalski-Karen Thompson case, the crux of which was our right to form our own families and have them respected *just like straight families?* When wanting children is called "tokenism"[29] or "a sheepish but almost relieved dash for normalcy,"[30] what do we do with the one lesbian in three who is a mother—a mother whose custody of her children may be tenuous, a mother who may "assimilate" into the PTA to promote her children's education?

If the idea of separating ourselves out into Lesbian Nation never worked for more than a small number of women, what would make a Queer Nation any more successful or relevant to the average woman-loving woman? What we have is a vast number of women caught in a squeeze play. A co-sexual gay community attempts to entice them with the siren song of relief from the occasional excesses of lesbian feminism (that is, politically correct rigidity in the place of diversity and empowerment), excesses that it plays up for all they're worth. The price of validation for these women, however, is their feminism.

If the women's community were a place where women were wanted and appreciated, where our differences were nowhere near as important as our commitment to working for women's rights, as each of us understood that process to be, these disaffected women would flock to it in droves. They could be drawn to such a community even more readily by an attractive role model—by someone who dared to define her own life, a life that embraced a multitude of options, yet who still had impeccable political credentials—a role model like . . . well, you know. Instead, all that these disaffected women hear or read are ominous rumblings of PC enforcement—or the co-sexual community's stereotypes of lesbian feminists, especially the stereotype that lesbian feminism stifles our sexuality.

New Community, Old Stereotypes

Major dilemma, eh? And a source of grief and frustration for bi lesbian feminists to whom the concept of a true women's community is so very dear, especially when our presence in that community, and our commitment to it, could be a powerful force for its transformation and growth. I see bisexual lesbian feminists as capable of playing an important role in women's liberation, period, above and beyond resisting the campaign to get lesbians to abandon woman-identification. We can challenge the dualistic paradigm of privilege/political correctness because our lives demonstrate that real life is complex and calls for personal creativity and responsibility. Our lives take feminism out of the realm of an almost-academic discipline to reaffirm its goal of concrete gains of freedom in the real world.

And in that real world, it is, perhaps, bi feminist women who can best hold heterosexual relationships to feminist standards. We can analyze what happens when "queer" women are involved with men because we acknowledge that many of us are, sometimes in fairly deep ways, involved with men, and that these are, indeed, heterosexual relationships. Lesbians who have affairs with men are often too much in denial about what that means to talk about it. Bisexual lesbians do talk about it, if only to understand what such involvements mean to our lives, identities and politics (especially if we have significant lesbian backgrounds). And unlike straight women, we need not ease up on our feminist analysis of relationships with men for lack of alternatives. Silence bisexual women, and you silence a very important feminist voice.

We are also in the process of creating an alternative community for those woman-loving women who, in rejecting lesbian-feminist community political correctness, have only gay men's political correctness—or sexual correctness—left to adopt. By bridging the gulf between lesbian and heterosexual feminists (as does the East Bay National Organization for Women chapter and its Lesbian Rights Task Force in Northern California), bisexual feminists can take the "women's community" from being a euphemism for lesbian community to a true community of women working together for our rights and claiming our freedom and autonomy.

We are ready to catch the wave, too. Bi visibility is rising, thanks to anthologies like *Bi Any Other Name* (and this one) and "'zines" like *Anything That Moves*. And gay/lesbian publications are beginning to address the emergence of a bisexual movement, if only to report on the alleged "hetero-dyke" scare. Indeed, it is the lesbian community that feels most challenged by our emergence.

Kim Corsaro, publisher of the San Francisco *Bay Times*, wrote an extremely cogent editorial on the intense reaction among lesbians to the addition of the word "bisexual" to the paper, the printing of special "forum" sections of responses and counter-responses to a column about dialogues between bisexuals and lesbians and gays, and the accusation that lesbians had been purged from her staff. Noting that all the counter-responses to letters from bisexuals were written by women (a first), she speculated that "bisexual women can bring up our worst fears and insecurities, and that relates directly to the powerlessness we often feel as women and as lesbians, individually and as a community."[31]

Many of the letters, alas, repeated too-familiar lesbian stereotypes of bisexual women. One writer seemed particularly stung by a letter of mine that had pointed out the similarities in behavior between lesbians who call themselves lesbians and lesbians who acknowledge their bisexuality; she, like others, attached a great deal of significance to labeling oneself lesbian rather than bisexual. My letter had pointed out that women critical in print of bi-lesbians seem to have little if anything to say when women who self-label as lesbian talk of lesbians having sex with men.

Indeed, I had hit upon the utter irony of lesbians stereotyping bi women: the type of behavior they complain about runs rampant—and unquestioned—among the most publically visible lesbians, that is, those who have a high profile in the co-sexual press. Lesbian stereotypes of bisexual women stigmatize us and make it more difficult for bisexual *feminists* to define bisexuality (especially the lesbian exploration thereof). Instead, female bisexuality ends up being defined for the lesbian/gay community by default, by the actions and utterances of women in denial about their bisexuality, women who may also be conflicted about feminism. The examples are seemingly never-ending.

Do lesbians worry that bisexual women will give the message that lesbians can be wooed away by men? The "lesbians" of ACT UP/New York say, "There are more obvious [political] reasons now for lesbians to both be involved with men [sexually] and also to acknowledge it."[32] Do lesbians worry that "bi-dykes" will devalue the meaning of a lesbian identity?[33] Those same ACT UP women say lesbians can be involved in heterosexual relationships—not as lesbians who acknowledge this as bisexuality, but as women demanding validation of their lesbian identity: "If I'm celibate for two years, am I still a lesbian? I think yes. If I sleep with a man for two years I can still be a lesbian."[34] This is purportedly because being with women has transformed their heterosexual relationships into something not really heterosexual; that is, they are not really "straight" people. And yes, these women, too, insist, "I don't feel like a bisexual."[35]

And do lesbians worry that bisexual women will share women's intimacies and sexual secrets with straight men? Well, don't look now, but *On Our Backs* advertises access to these secrets in everything from the *Yellow Pages* to fairly mainstream magazines like the *Utne Reader* with the slogan, "The most intelligent sex magazine just happens to be lesbian!" Editor Susie Bright will win no awards for political correctness and "hates" being asked the one question that leaves her "unnerved": whether, based on her behavior, she is lesbian or bisexual.[36] Nonetheless, she is acknowledged in the lesbian/gay and women's media as a *lesbian* sex expert and presents herself and her magazine as representing *lesbian* sexuality. So what makes self-acknowledged *bisexual* women the ones said to betray lesbian secrets?

The reporting of the *fact* of bisexuality among lesbians has thus been left, by default, to those whose agenda includes stigmatizing the woman-identified and the feminist-identified as hypocrites for our commitment to female bonding, in order to herd women into co-sexual activism, identity, sexuality and culture in a brave, new "post-feminist world." Why? Because the bisexual feminists who could combat this trend are going unheard. So, too, are all our acts of acknowledging our bisexuality as something that exists *in addition to* our lesbian feminism, as opposed to the "not really bisexual" bisexuality described previously: the incorporation of heterosexuality into lesbian sexuality and identity.

"I am a happily married woman," says Dodie Bellamy, who nonetheless takes great offense at being mistaken for straight by gay people. "But I'm married to gay novelist Kevin Killian, which isn't exactly the same as being married to a regular straight man. [This is better.]"[37] Bellamy goes on to talk of her lesbian past always being a part of her— and presumably ensuring her queer credentials. Never does she state the obvious: this must be bisexuality. That would resolve all her conflict. Instead, she implies that having heterosexual relationships (even marriages) is something lesbians do—whereas bi lesbians say that if and when we do it, it is something specifically bisexual rather than lesbian.

*

Sisters Are Sisters

In these times, when the politicized subgroup of those stigmatized for non-heterosexual behavior (for example, the co-sexual "queer" community) is increasingly becoming a hostile place for woman-identified women, our politics and our culture, the lesbian community needs its bisexual feminists more than ever. And yet, many lesbians insist that any lesbian who acknowledges her bisexuality—no matter how tenuous or latent—must really belong to a community different and separate from the lesbian community. Although some of these women are "willing" to engage in dialogue with this theoretically distinct bisexual community, the very idea strikes me as being incongruous: too many women fall into both groups, and too many bisexual feminists do too much for the lesbian community to be regarded as separate from that community.

Amanda Udis-Kessler writes of how those committed to a "lesbian-feminist monoculture" could feel betrayed by women involved (and invested) in women's communities but not the entire belief and lifestyle system of this monoculture.[38] While pondering her ideas, I thought of my own activities of the recent past: publicizing events for a lesbian social group (one of them in my own home), working out lobbying tactics for East Bay NOW's Lesbian Rights Task Force and negotiating rebuttal space from a magazine editor and writing copy explaining the inappropriateness of a "parental advisory" heading for an interview with a gay man. For someone supposedly a threat to the lesbian community, this bisexual certainly spends enough time and energy supporting that community and *being* that community.

And maybe that's the answer. Perhaps it is up to us lesbians (the noun) who are bisexual (the adjective) to be the role models for women like Holly Near. Perhaps it is up to us to live life on our own terms, exercise our passions to the fullest and reject the limits anyone would place on our lives. Doing these things proudly, as woman-identified women who will love and fight for women, is the purest lesbian-feminist value I can think of. Following the feminist tradition of speaking the truth about our lives, our bisexual-lesbian-feminist lives, we can build the kind of loving women's community that lesbian dreams are made of.

And, Holly, you can come on home to this community any time!

Endnotes

1. Holly Near, *Fire in the Rain, Singer in the Storm* (New York : William Morrow, 1990).

2. Quotes are from an untitled interview in the *Advocate*, September 11, 1990; Near's book and the Advocate interview were discussed further in the *Los Angeles Lesbian News*, November 1990.

3. *Fire in the Rain*, and quoted in just about every article, review or interview about the book.

4. Interviewed by Carol Stocker, "So Near, Yet So Far," *Boston Globe*, Aug. 27, 1990.

5. June Reinisch, Stephanie Sanders and Mary Ziemba-Davis, "Self-Labeled Sexual Orientation, Sexual Behavior and Knowledge about AIDS: Implications for Biomedical Research and Education Programs," in Blumenthal, Eichler and Weissman, *Proceedings of NIMH/NIDA Workshop on Women and AIDS: Promoting Healthy Behaviors* (Washington, D.C.: American Psychiatric Press).

6. Can you say, "Michigan Women's Music Festival"? I knew you could.

7. In one of her 1990 "Gay Matters" columns for the *San Francisco Bay Guardian.*

8. Op.cit. Near, *Fire in the Rain, Singer in the Storm.*

9. Rachel Kaplan, "Another Coming Out Manifesto Disguised as a Letter to My Mother," *North Bi Northwest* (October/November 1990).

10. Holly Near, quoted in the "B-Word" controversy in the *Los Angeles Lesbian News*, November 1990.

11. And then there are the bisexual softball dykes who refer to themselves as "switch hitters."

12. Rebecca Shuster, "Beyond Defense: Considering Next Steps for Bisexual Liberation," in *Bi Any Other Name*, eds. Loraine Hutchins and Lani Kaahumanu (Boston: Alyson Publications, 1991), pp. 266-74.

13. But the Eastern European judges only gave her a 4.7.

14. Cf. Beth Elliott, Bethania Gonzales and Charlotte Wilkins, "The Lesbian Agenda and the AIDS Crisis: Are We Taking Care of Ourselves?" a workshop at the National Organization for Women 1990 Conference.

15. Andrea Dworkin, *Intercourse* (New York: Macmillan/Free Press, 1987).

16. Tim Kingston, "In Your Face: Queer Nation," *San Francisco Bay Times*, December 1990.

17. Ibid.

18. See ibid. and Maria Maggenti, "Women as Queer Nationals, *Out/Look* (Winter

1991).

19. *Village Voice*, July 2, 1991.

20. Carrie Fisher, "True Confessions: The Rolling Stone Interview with Madonna," *Rolling Stone*, June 13, 1991, p. 40.

21. Ibid.

22. Camille Paglia, "A Scholar and Not-So-Gentle Woman" *Image* magazine, *Sunday San Francisco Examiner and Chronicle*, July 7, 1991.

23. Letters, *Image* magazine, *San Francisco Sunday Examiner & Chronicle*, August 4, 1991.

24. Ibid.

25. Ibid.

26. *Gay Community News*, January 7-13, 1990.

27. As in the great "Essentialism vs. Constructionism Debate" dominating the field of lesbian/gay studies. Is homosexuality something innate (that is, essential) to the point where a gay identity exists that crosses cultural lines, or do sexual identities vary (that is, are constructed differently) from culture to culture to the point that extrapolating a North American gay culture and identity from other cultural systems would be misleading? Heated stuff, this, believe it or not. For an excellent—and sane—introduction, especially as this debate relates to bisexual politics, see Amanda Udis-Kessler in Hutchins and Kaahumanu, *Bi Any Other Name*, pp. 22-23.

28. See Maggenti, "Women as Queer Nationals," pp. 16-29.

29. Justin Bond, "Queer Interviews," *Out/Look* (Winter 1991), p. 14-16.

30. Op. cit. Maggenti, "Women as Queer Nationals," pp. 22-23.

31. Kim Corsaro, "Bisexuality in the Gay/Lesbian Community: The Controversy Continues," *San Francisco Bay Times*, May 1991.

32. Jorjet Harper, quoting Alexis Danzig: "Lesbians Who Sleep with Men: Only Her Hairdresser Knows for Sure," *Outweek*, February 11, 1990.

33. See, for example, "Community Forum" *San Francisco Bay Times*, May 1991.

34. Op. cit. Harper, "Lesbians Who Sleep with Men."

35. Ibid.

36. Patricia Yollin, "Painting the Town Lavender," *Image* magazine, *San Francisco Sunday Examiner & Chronicle*, March 10, 1991.

37. "Mrs. America at the Congress of Dreams: Writing Identity and Desire Between Dennis Cooper and Erica Jong, *Out/Look* (Summer 1991), p. 47.

38. Amanda Udis-Kessler, "Culture and Community: Thoughts on Lesbian-Bisexual Relations After the 1990 Bisexuality Conference", *North Bi Northwest*, (January/February 1991), quoting a character from Alison Bechdel's comic strip, "Dykes to Watch Out For."

Karin Baker

Bisexual Feminist Politics:
Because Bisexuality Is Not Enough

I was one of hundreds of people who attended the now historic March 15, 1990 meeting of the Northampton Massachusetts queer community, called to create a public forum to discuss the controversial exclusion of bisexuals from the name and organizing committee of our pride march. All the fears I initially felt were confirmed as the meeting progressed and person after person expressed ignorant and hostile attitudes toward bisexuals and bisexuality.

Soon after coming out as bisexual I experienced the rejecting attitudes of lesbians and gay men. I was slow to understand why gay men and lesbians felt this way, since to me my bisexuality was not just a trendy image, a phase or a compromise with compulsory heterosexuality. On the contrary, I was proud of my bisexual identity. I considered it personally right for me and politically revolutionary.

The move to exclude bisexuals from the Northampton march (except in the role of "allies, along with straight supporters," as they had the gall to say) was initiated by a group of local lesbian feminists who had gained control of the march committee. Among the first steps they took was to close the committee to bisexuals; it included no gay men, and to my knowledge, all the lesbian members agreed with the policy of exclusion of bisexuals. This composition of the committee, as a result, did not reflect the community as a whole; at the meeting, for example, there were large numbers of lesbians and gay men who thought bisexuals should be included in all aspects of the march.

Still, I was not particularly surprised by the position of the march committee, which represented a strong trend in the local "women's" community. What did surprise me was the discovery that although some statements made at the meeting by the pro-exclusion people offended and hurt me, there were many times when I agreed with more of what they said than with the arguments of those who supported bi-sexual inclusion.

Don't mistake me, my sympathies were with my bisexual counter-parts as we demanded validation within the community where so many of us have long participated as de facto members. The problem I had lay with the apolitical nature of the arguments for inclusion, from the bisexuals who spoke. The lesbian feminists who spoke, on the other hand, had a political vision and, specifically, a feminist analy-sis.

Political Bisexuality

This started me thinking about exactly how bisexuals fit into a feminist vision. As with the march committee, I believe that the struggles for queer liberation and women's liberation are intimately connected. Unlike the march committee, I believe that bisexuals have a particular role to play in these struggles, a role that both overlaps and diverges from that of lesbians and gay men. I believe that, as a group, bisexu-als need to focus more attention on examining what this role might be.

For example, bisexuals clearly challenge compulsory heterosexual-ity, as do lesbians and gay men, to the degree to which they relate sexu-ally to the same sex. At the same time, bisexuals are not limited in their sexuality to a specific sex, and thus bisexuality challenges the gen-der system, which we associate with biological sex, in a way that lesbi-ans and gay men do not. Gender is as much, if not more, a tool of women's and queer oppression as compulsory heterosexuality. Thus, the role that bisexuals can potentially play in subverting the gender system is indispensable to a radical social transformation. However, this potential can only come from a bisexuality that is consciously feminist.

The Social Construction of Sexuality and Gender

Systems of oppression are often justified by an oppressor as being rooted in biology, as based in something buologically inherent to hu-man nature. Feminists confront the deeply held cultural belief that women are inherently (biologically) inferior to men. The institution of compulsory heterosexuality rests on the concept that only heterosexual sex is "natural," leading to queer oppression.

In fact, it is clear that the traditional ideas described above, and

others like them, are not biologically based, but rather are socially constructed, and any claims as to their biological basis are attempts to
demonstrate their legitimacy.

Not only the concept of women's inferiority but our very category
of gender itself is a social construction. Gender is a dual category system in which certain human traits are assigned to one biological sex,
and certain traits to the other. Women and men are actually more
alike than different, and most of our differences are social creations.
The concept of the social construction of sexuality and gender plays a
central role in the ideas I put forward here. By deconstructing these
socially held attitudes, we can get at the basis of women's oppression
and lesbian, bisexual and gay oppression, and work out a strategy for
challenging them.

Scientifically Proven or Socially Imposed Concepts?

Gender is the social construct applied to biological sex. Even where
gender is recognized as socially variable, biological sex is often assumed
to be a fixed and entirely definable category. This is not the case. One
way to show this is to demonstrate how rigid the framework of this
dual category system is compared to the biological realities. Women,
for example, are recognized as physically smaller and weaker than
men, and exceptions to this, cases in which women are larger and
stronger, are ignored. Our system of categorization is not able to encompass the breadth of variation here.

Even chromosomes and hormones, seen as the basis for gendered
behavior, can be demonstrated to have less to do with gender than social upbringing does. For example, individuals with male chromosomes will display social traits associated with females if they are raised
to belong to that gender. Furthermore, it has been shown that perhaps
as much as hormones govern behavior, behavior may influence hor-
mone production. As one author on the subject has concluded, "no
matter how detailed an investigation science has thus far made, it is still
not possible to draw a clear dividing line between male and female."[1]

My point is not that there are not differences between groups our
culture presently divides according to gender. Rather, these differences
have been fetishized and made to fit into categories that are not as easily delineable as our usual culture framework makes them appear. Men
are aggressive, it is said, so an aggressive woman is "mannish," because

the categories must be maintained in spite of apparent contradictions.

I am not saying it is possible, or desirable, to go beyond any recognition of difference. My object is rather to point out that there are other ways of viewing difference, and an alternative I would advocate is a more flexible *continuum*, rather than forcing human traits into one or two opposing and inflexible categories.

Where does this all lead? Just as class oppression did not exist before human communities had divided into classes, women's separation and subordination make them appear inferior and this perception becomes a justification for their subordination, or economically, once women lose access to economic power they do not have the means to be economically powerful. Thus, the perception of women and men as belonging to separate and opposing genders is both a tool and a product of women's oppression.

Tools of Oppression: Gender and Compulsory Heterosexuality

My position contrasts with much of lesbian feminist analysis which views *compulsory heterosexuality* as the basis for women's oppression. Heterosexual pairing is seen as a mechanism for the domination of women because it forces individual women into dependence on individual men while isolating women from each other. Given such a premise, the belief of some lesbian feminists is that lesbians are the true revolutionaries in the struggle for women's liberation. Lesbianism confronts the coercion of heterosexuality, avoids the domination within heterosexual pairing and, at the same time, brings women together.

There is no doubt that compulsory heterosexuality serves all the functions described above, and lesbianism most directly challenges this institution. My resistance is not to the conclusions of this analysis, but to what it leaves out.

Compulsory heterosexuality is composed of its own component building block, gender, and thus is an inadequate basis for women's oppression. Its very name reflects its basis in the gender system: compulsory "hetero"sexuality, "hetero" referring to "other" gender. Heterosexuality couldn't exist without the gender system.

True, compulsory heterosexuality is clearly the particular mechanism by which the gendering of the sexes is perpetuated and enforced. However, as a tool for analysis, gender has broader relevance. Basing feminist analysis on a gender framework is more revealing because many aspects of women's oppression go beyond the realm of intimate relationship, without, granted, ever being totally unconnected from these.

For example, women's economic oppression takes place inside, and outside, the bedroom and family. Gender is more directly relevant than compulsory heterosexuality when considering why the boss is more likely to be male than female. Thus, I would substitute gender for compulsory heterosexuality as the basic building block of women's oppression.

Bisexuality, Gender and Women's Oppression

Lesbianism *is* a challenge to compulsory heterosexuality. Bisexuality, however, has the potential to challenge the dual gender system, which oppresses women and queer people insofar as it is a foundation of compulsory heterosexuality.

Bisexuality fits in here in two ways, but the principle in both cases is the same: bisexuals blur the lines between categories often regarded as fixed and definable. First the strict dichotomy between homosexuality and heterosexuality gets blown. Bisexuals don't even fit into a clear-cut category because of the obvious variety of bisexual experience. Thus, bisexuality blurs the supposed duality of sexuality in a manner that is itself a challenge to other dual category systems, such as that of gender.[2]

In addition to this, bisexuality is not based on gender. Compulsory heterosexuality assumes a strictly defined gender system. Lesbian and gay relationships challenge gender by avoiding traditional gender roles. However, lesbian and gay sexuality is based on attraction to a specific gender to the same degree that heterosexuality is. By definition, both heterosexuality and homosexuality rely equally on a strictly defined gender system. Thus both uphold the present gender system, although compulsory heterosexuality has more to do with its perpetuation.

I believe that bisexuality has the potential to go beyond gender. True, there are bisexuals whose experience contradicts this to some extent. I have known some bis to say that they are attracted to women for the qualities culturally associated with this gender and to men for qualities identified as masculine. Even in such cases, however, sexual connections are possible with either gender and thus, to this degree, the gender system is challenged.

However, in many cases, including my own, bisexual people recognize that most, if not all, of which they find attractive in another has little to do with gender. In my case, I am attracted to people whose gender it is impossible for me to ignore, but my attraction for them involves many factors, none of which break down simply according to gender. I am attracted to people around whom I feel safe, individuals who seem to understand me better than most, who are straightforward, who can be supportive and nurturing, who are physically active and who "have some flesh on them." A few of these characteristics are more common with one gender, but they certainly aren't limited to that gender.

Gender and Sexism: The Current Realities

If one of the lesbian feminists from the Northampton march committee were reading this article, and were still with us at this point, she would undoubtedly have at least one very valid critique. Gender exists, sexism is a reality, and any political analysis or sexual lifestyle that does not take those facts into account perpetuates these institutions. A bisexual politics that does not acknowledge the inevitable differences between the social and personal consequences of relationships with women and relationships with men, that is, one that pretends it is presently possible to "go beyond gender," is misguided.

When I was first exploring these types of questions, I was hoping for insight from other bisexual women, particularly older women, who I believed would be likely to have thought about and discussed these things. During this time I attended a panel in which three or four bisexual people told their coming-out stories. I posed the question to the two women panelists: what do you think it means for bisexual women to remain open to relationships with women and men, the latter being members of a group that oppresses us as women?

I didn't want my question to lead the whole room into a discussion of feminism and sexuality, but I had expected to hear a bit of background on the debate and the opinions of the panelists. Instead, the woman who answered looked uncomfortable and avoided the question by reassuring me that I shouldn't let politics interfere with my personal feelings and should allow myself to do what felt good without guilt. I agreed with her as far as it went, but I thought the question was of fundamental importance to bisexuals.

It is the case that gender-blind bisexuality, if it lacks a feminist political analysis, is not a direct challenge to women's oppression. Bisexuality attacks sexism by subverting gender, but since the very manner in which it subverts gender is by ignoring it, it also ignores sexism. Unfortunately, sexism will continue in our present society, with the institutions that support it in place, even if we ignore it—more so in fact.

That means two things. On a personal level, any bisexual woman who chooses to be with a man faces sexism. From the outside, her relationship will be perceived as heterosexual relationships are seen—she becomes "his" woman. Within the relationship, with sexism as deeply embedded in our society as it is, there will be times when she will experience sexist dynamics with her lover. There are few men who will never fall back on male privilege when they feel threatened—for example, they may dismiss their lover's criticisms as "nagging" or wait for her to do the emotional processing necessary to smooth out a snag in the relationship.

On the level of broad social change, without lesbians women's options would be heterosexuality and bisexuality. In our social system based on the concept that women need men, neither of these orientations allows for the option that women can create lives without men. Thus, that aspect of compulsory heterosexuality that says that women need men is not challenged.

But we need to challenge this. We cannot leap from our present system to a nongendered, polysexual system of sexuality. It is necessary to confront sexism in all its institutionalized forms before we can go past it. Thus bisexuality itself is not enough. With compulsory heterosexuality still in place, even bisexual women will face strong social influences to be in relationships with men, and their power to avoid domination within these relationships will be relatively weak. Both gender and compulsory heterosexuality must be fought at the same time.

The Central Role of Lesbians in Women's Liberation

We will not be able to say any woman has freely chosen to be with a man until all women are free not to be with men. For this reason, lesbianism must be an option. More directly than bisexuality, lesbianism is a challenge to compulsory heterosexuality. Thus, lesbians play a central role in the struggle for women's liberation and must remain a visible and distinct segment of this movement.

Lesbian identity and community challenge the notion that women "need" men and create a space in which women can focus exclusively on women. In the words of a lesbian quoted in an *Outweek* article on bisexuality: ". . . to not ever seek approval of men or turn your energy to men. There's tremendous power in being a lesbian."[3] Flourishing lesbian communities and sexual politics that promote this choice are necessary if women are to overcome this oppression.

Clearly, lesbians and gay men also challenge gender. Heterosexual relationships are one of the main arenas for playing out gender roles. In contrast, within a relationship between lesbians, or gay men, traditional gender roles cannot be played out. Even cases in which gay men or lesbians take on approximations of traditional roles can never be the same in same-sex relationships as they are in opposite-sex relationships. In general, societal perceptions of lesbians and gay men indicate that their existence is a challenge to the system of gender. Men who are gay are seen as "effeminate," whereas lesbians are "mannish."

It follows then that, aside from avoiding gender-specific sexuality, bisexuals also challenge gender in their same-sex relationships by avoiding traditional gender roles, as lesbians and gay men do. They also confront compulsory heterosexuality in their same-sex relationships, as lesbians and gay men do. Lesbians and gay men, however, are a more outright and complete challenge to compulsory heterosexuality at least insofar as they confront that aspect of the institution that compels opposite-sex relations.

To summarize the above: lesbians and gay men directly challenge compulsory heterosexuality through their same-sex relationships and indirectly challenge gender through avoiding traditional gender roles within their relationships. Lesbians, specifically, confront the male supremacist belief that all women need men. Bisexuals directly challenge gender by avoiding gender-specific attraction and indirectly challenge compulsory heterosexuality and the acting out of gender roles through their openness to same-sex relationships. All of the above are necessary elements in the struggle for women's liberation and queer liberation.

*

The Choices We Make

I don't believe, as some bisexuals do, that all people are bisexual, except on the most abstract of levels. Clearly some women are not attracted to men. Other lesbians may have some attraction to men, but their personal and political beliefs about sexism make it impossible for them to be comfortable in a relationship with a man. Sexism is intolerable for such women, even in the relatively minimal levels in which it is present in some men. Furthermore, the fact that a relationship with a man will be perceived as just another heterosexual relationship by most of society may be too repulsive an experience for some women.

I am open to being with men despite this because, to begin with, I am attracted to men. But this in itself would not necessarily be enough. The most important reason I am open to relationships with men is that I have had rewarding relationships with them. From my experience, relationships between women and men are workable, if sometimes difficult, depending to a great degree on the individual man. As a bisexual woman within a mixed-gender relationship, it also helps my position within the relationship that my male partner knows I have the option to end it in favor of a relationship with a woman.

Furthermore, I believe that there *are* men who have overcome their own sexism as much as is possible under present social conditions. My current lover is an example. His awareness of sexism is such that I don't have to do the work of challenging him; he rarely slips, and if he does he catches it himself. If it weren't for my experiences with him and other men like him, I would be much more tempted to identify as a lesbian.

Queer Men

Gay and bisexual men have a potential role in the struggle for women's liberation. I don't believe it's an accident that my current lover, who has confronted so much of his own sexism, is himself bisexual. Queer men are in a unique position in several ways. For one thing, they often experience social contempt for displaying traits perceived as feminine. The form of oppression they face gives them a particular interest in the abolition of the gender system and sexism, and specific insight into these institutions.

Also, gay and bisexual men are also more likely than heterosexual men to be emotionally intimate with other men and, along with this, to give and receive emotional support from each other. This challenges a major aspect of compulsory heterosexuality under which women are supposed to be the nurturers, mediators, ego-builders and support-systems for men, who are not expected to return in kind. The capacity of some bisexual and gay men to turn to other men for emotional support takes the burden off women, who traditionally "exist to do men's feeling for them," as Audre Lorde has put it.[4] Our brothers are learning to do it for themselves.

Bisexual Community

Where anything approaching a "bisexual community" exists, it is incomplete and tenuous. It is not surprising that lesbian and gay communities are more cohesive and visible. Because sexuality is seen in our culture as an either/or concept, lesbian and gay sex and culture are more identifiable, making it relatively easy for lesbians and gay men to recognize each other.

Clearly, the existence of lesbian and gay communities and the gains of their respective social movements and of the women's liberation movement have all been beneficial for bisexuals. (Of course, we have participated in all of the above, as well, and not simply been the beneficiaries.) The achievements of lesbian and gay struggles and feminist organizing are part of the reason so many people are now coming out as bisexual. At the same time, the present context, which has in part been created by these movements, is a challenge to bisexuals.

The existence of lesbian and gay communities has led to a situation in which we bisexuals often find ourselves asking to be accepted into these communities. Upon coming out, most bisexuals feel they have more in common with lesbians and gay men because we experience the most overt social rejection around our own same-sex relationships. Thus we find ourselves in contexts with lesbians and gay men where it is impossible to be fully recognized for "who we are."

To the degree that we have attempted to form our own communities, we have had mixed success. Perhaps this is because we are coming together because of a growing realization that we don't belong in either monosexual community—straight or lesbian and gay, rather than our of some common sense of our own identity drawing us together.

Our Uniqueness as Bisexual People

What is missing in such attempts at community is an understanding of why we belong together, of what gives us an identity as ourselves, as opposed to a negative identity of not x, not y. This is difficult to realize because, as mentioned, our most obvious divergence from the "norm" is our same-sex relationships. However, as long as our self-definition ends there, we will always tend to fall back on asking to be received among lesbian and gay men, instead of coalescing our own community.

In fact, as someone who is bisexual, I do see myself as a member of the queer community, if not the lesbian and gay community. A major hindrance to the recognition of our place there, however, is our own inability to define how we fit in. For this reason, among others, we need to work toward defining a bisexual politic, one based on our capacity as bisexuals to blur categories of sexuality and gender, on our role in the struggle for queer liberation and women's liberation and so on.

Returning to the Northampton, Massachusetts, pride march, the question of the uniqueness of the bisexual experience came up for me in a debate with a lesbian acquaintance as we discussed the march title. In her opinion, bisexuals need not be identified in the march title because we are oppressed only to the degree that we are perceived as lesbian or gay. This led me to question whether I believed that we are oppressed as *bisexuals*, and if so, how is that oppression experienced.

Bisexuals and Compulsory Heteromonosexuality

I eventually concluded that bisexuals are oppressed as bisexuals. One aspect of oppression, in my understanding, is when a specific group is denied legitimacy by a socially upheld institution.[5] The very invisibility of bisexual experience, which led my lesbian acquaintance to see bisexuals as sometimes a subset of the category "lesbian and gay," and sometimes part of the straight world, is the basis for bisexual oppression.

In the process of exploring this idea, I developed a new perspective on the institution of compulsory heterosexuality, which I had previously conceived of as oppressive *in its compulsion to other-sex relations and prohibition of same-sex relations.* Thus far in this paper I have written as though that were my underlying assumption. In fact, compulsory heterosexuality has two components (to do my own dichotomizing): "hetero," and hidden within that, "mono." Bisexuals are sometimes affected by the first, and always by the latter. Without compulsory heterosexuality there would be no such thing as straight or queer. It is responsible for our current framework, which leaves no room for a sexuality that is not monosexual, no room for bisexuality.

If bisexuals are not bi-bashed, denied housing as bisexuals or subjected to overt forms of oppression, this is in fact a result of our invisibility, and that invisibility is, for the present, how we experience oppression. As we become more visible, our experiences of oppression will become more overt. A recent example of this is the scapegoating of bis in the AIDS crisis, which resulted from the fear of this murky category of people who blur the lines between "them" and "us," those who are innocent. This dynamic is clearly different from the type of stigma experienced by gay men as a result of AIDS.

Bisexual Liberation

A bisexual politic as foundation for a bisexual liberation movement can confront the social framework that only allows for either/or. If explicitly feminist, it has a role to play in challenging gender, the basis for women's oppression. In a general sense, bisexuality challenges our system of categorization, which provides the basis for other forms of oppression: the division between "of color" and "white," as well as "woman" and "man," "queer" and "straight" and so on.

In the shorter term a bisexual feminist politic can form the basis for a group identity upon which a bisexual community can be formed. Such a politic would create a framework for our common individual experiences. For the present, that which we have in common is harder to recognize than the shared experiences within each monosexual community. But, in fact, there are common threads within the bisexual experience. The achievement of a vibrant bisexual community would pose a significant and unique challenge to the dual gender system and the limitations inherent in compulsory heteromonosexuality. Our contribution might even go beyond this to challenge our entire oppressive social system, helping to break down the categories of identity on which much of it is based.

Endnotes

This essay is an expanded version of an article I wrote with Helen Harrison, who has been very involved in the development of the ideas found here.

1.   Holly Devor, *Gender Blending: Confronting the Limits of Duality* (Bloomington, Indiana: Indiana University Press, 1989), p. 1.

2.   One problem with the label "bisexual" is that the prefix "bi" assumes a dual gender system.

3.   Carrie Wofford, "The Bisexual Revolution: Deluded Closet Cases or Vanguards of the Movement?" *OutWeek,* Feb. 6, 1990, p. 3.

4.   Audre Lorde, *Sister Outsider: Essays and Speeches* by Audre Lorde (Trumansburg, NY: The Crossing Press, 1984).

5.   Economic oppression, where present, is something other than this, but it is not unrelated.

Rebecca Kaplan

Compulsory Heterosexuality and the Bisexual Existence: Toward a Bisexual Feminist Understanding of Heterosexism

Can bisexuality help us form a more complete feminist vision? Can feminism help us construct more empowering identities as bisexual women? I believe the answer to both questions is yes, that great potential lies in the formation of a feminist bisexuality and a bisexual feminism.

One of the underlying principles in a bisexual-feminist ideology is that of sexual choice. The primary focus is on the right to choose male or female lovers, but the concept of sexual choice can be expanded to include other issues, such as the right to choose nonmonogamy, to choose lovers of traditionally "inappropriate" sociocultural groups and to choose *not* to have sex. The issue of sexual choice is one that lesbian, heterosexual and bisexual feminists should be able to embrace. Bisexual women have not explored or adopted this issue, at least not to as great extent as possible. The ideology of sexual choice has been explored by lesbian-feminist writings, but unfortunately, many lesbian-feminist supporters of this ideology have not seen bisexual women as allies.

One work that I feel has much to say to bisexual women about the issues of sexual choice is "Compulsory Heterosexuality and Lesbian Existence" by Adrienne Rich.[1]

Rich's essay is often misinterpreted as a call for universal lesbianism, despite her assertion that this was not her intent.[2] I believe it is a call for women, and particularly heterosexual women, to challenge the forces of heteropatriarchy in general and compulsory heterosexuality in particular. Rich suggests that lesbianism provides examples of radical resistance to heteropatriarchy and alternative vantage points that heterosexual women ought to consider. Her essay is a challenge to heterosexual women, that they might not continue to go through life

269

in a state of, as she puts it, "unexamined heterocentricity." Rich's article examines the institutions by which compulsory heterosexuality is enforced and calls on all feminists to challenge those institutions. That thesis is best summarized in Rich's own words:

> The assumption that "most women are innately heterosexual" stands as a theoretical and political stumbling block for many women. It remains a tenable assumption, partly because lesbian existence has been written out of history or catalogued under disease; partly because it has been treated as exceptional rather than intrinsic; partly because to acknowledge that for women heterosexuality may not be a "preference" at all but something that has had to be imposed, managed, organized, propagandized, and maintained by force, is an immense step to take if you consider yourself freely and "innately" heterosexual. Yet the failure to examine heterosexuality as an institution is like failing to admit that the economic system called capitalism or the caste system called racism is maintained by a variety of forces, including both physical violence and false consciousness. To take the step of questioning heterosexuality as a "preference" or "choice" for women—and to do the intellectual and emotional work that follows—will call for a special quality of courage in heterosexually identified feminists but I think the rewards will be great: a freeing-up of thinking, the exploring of new paths, the shattering of another great silence, new clarity in personal relationships.   (p. 20)

Not surprisingly, this essay gained most of its popularity in lesbian circles rather than heterosexual ones. I have often heard lesbians refer to Rich's essay to support their assertions that heterosexual relationships are inevitably damaging to women. Although it is important to see this article as validating and affirming lesbian existence, I believe that some of the more powerful and perhaps more radical ideas in the article—ideas that are often overlooked—lie in its message to women who are not exclusively lesbian.

I think there has been a misreading of Rich's article on two sides. The lesbian-feminist movement has taken the essay as part of a philosophy that asserts that lesbianism is the ideal expression of feminism. By the same token, many bisexual and heterosexual women have taken offense to the article, claiming that Rich does not attribute any "free will" to women who are involved with men and that she unfairly damns all heterosexual relationships. Perhaps many of the women who do have involvements with men are offended by this article, in part, out of defensiveness and an unwillingness to examine the sociopolitical implications of their heterosexual relationships.

Much of what has been called "heterosexual privilege" would be more accurately called male privilege. Women are not privileged for identifying as heterosexual, but rather, for being connected to a man (or men). This examination can help us understand how bisexual women can be a force of resistance to heteropatriarchy, by not guaranteeing our accessibility to men.[3]

Many of Rich's statements seem based on an unstated belief in biological determinism.[4] As a feminist, I find deterministic arguments terrifying when advocated by the religious Right, and they are no less dangerous when supported by feminists. If we wish to deny that women are "innately weak," we cannot also say that women are "innately peaceful." One place where Rich asserts a deterministic stance is in a footnote:

> Linda Gordon notes *accurately* that: "It is not that feminism has produced more lesbians. There have always been many lesbians, despite high levels of repression; and most lesbians experience their sexual preference as *innate*." (emphasis added)

Obviously, it is politically dangerous for feminists to believe that feminism causes lesbianism. If this belief were publicly espoused by feminists, the backlash would be (and has been) great. Nonetheless, asserting the innateness of sexual orientation is equally problematic. How can we say that heterosexuality is a product of cultural force, but lesbianism is an innate orientation?[5] If living under a heteropatriarchal culture that values only men can impel women to be heterosexual, then it seems plausible that entering into a philosophy of valuing women first and foremost could, in some instances, encourage lesbianism. In order to attain an accurate model of the ways in which cultural forces shape human sexuality, it is necessary to look at all sexualities in terms of potentially being influenced by culture. It is important for feminists to explore how conscious choice influences our sexual relationships, and then enhance our ability to make such choices.[6]

One problem common to most lesbian writing is the ongoing question of the meaning of the word "lesbian." In some ways, Rich exacerbates this problem by broadening the use of the word beyond its usual scope. Rich does distinguish between "lesbian existence" and the "lesbian continuum" (p. 20). The term "lesbian existence" refers to the more common usage of women who have emotional/erotic relationships primarily or exclusively with women. "Lesbian continuum" is a broader term and refers to a range of woman-oriented acts, a range of resistance to heteropatriarchy.

In her use of the term "lesbian continuum," Rich conflates woman-oriented behavior with resistance to heteropatriarchy. This can be a problematic definition. One example Rich gives of behavior that is on a lesbian continuum is that of a mother enjoying nursing her daughter. Another example is of the Chinese marriage resisters; two examples which seem quite different. It is not entirely implausible to say that under conditions of heteropatriarchy, all acts that are woman-oriented are a form of resistance. Nonetheless, I fear that this makes the idea of resistance broad to the point of losing its meaning. Is a woman nursing her daughter resisting heteropatriarchy? Is a woman who refuses to bow to men's rules, but never does anything for/with women contributing to building a more woman-oriented culture? Is the lesbian continuum a continuum of pro-woman acts or a continuum of anti-patriarchal acts? Are these the same things? This conflation can increase confusion to the bisexual reader who is uncertain whether her own behavior is considered a form of resistance.

Not all woman-oriented acts are a resistance to heteropatriarchy. Resistance involves being aware of our choices, making our choices consciously. Both acts that are pro-woman and acts that assert women's independence from men can be ways to resist a heteropatriarchal imperative which posits men as the focus of women's existence.

For bisexual women reading "Compulsory Heterosexuality," it can be unclear whether we are supposed to consider ourselves included in the category of "lesbians".[7] An ongoing debate within lesbian communities has been whether a lesbian is a woman who relates emotionally and erotically with women, or a woman who does not relate emotionally and erotically with men. Or, for that matter, whether a woman must fit both criteria to be considered a lesbian.

Rich does not address this question of the definition of lesbianism. That may be primarily because her article was written before the majority of the discourse on this issue arose. Rich says, "Lesbian existence comprises both the breaking of a taboo and the rejection of a compulsory way of life" (p. 21). This definition could apply to bisexual women. However, some lesbians do now object to the inclusion of behaviorally bisexual women in their communities.[8] Perhaps earlier in the development of contemporary lesbian communities, organizers were more eager to have any woman who wanted to join. As lesbian communities have grown, the position of bisexual women in them has become a more controversial issue.

Another issue that is often raised by lesbians, is that by using the word "lesbian" to refer to women's resistance to heteropatriarchy in general, we are in danger of erasing lesbian existence yet again. Whenever discussing the inclusion of bisexual and heterosexual women in feminist resistance to patriarchy, it is important that we not forget, neglect or erase the reality and power of lesbian existence, and value the ways in which that experience may differ from our own. Bisexual women should commit to respecting lesbian space and lesbian existence, not only for its similarities to our own experience, but also for its uniqueness.

The fact that Rich's essay does not directly address bisexual women is one of the barriers preventing bisexual women from learning from the essay. It is important not to lose track of the time at which it was written. In 1977 there was not much of an organized bisexual community, and certainly not a bisexual feminist one.[9] Many of the things I now take for granted did not exist, such as huge womyn's music festivals and wide selections of lesbian fiction, analysis and other literature. Discussions about whether or not bisexual women were welcome in lesbian communities were less common than they are now. Many authors also did not differentiate between lesbians and bi women; any woman who was ever in a relationship with a woman might have been called a lesbian.

Rich does address bisexuality indirectly. She uses the word "bisexuality" once:

> The extension of this assumption is the frequently heard assertion that in a world of genuine equality, where men were nonoppressive and nurturing, everyone would be bisexual. Such a notion blurs and sen-

timentalizes the actualities within which women have experienced sexuality; it is the old liberal leap across the tasks and struggles of the here and now, the continuing process of sexual definition which will generate its own possibilities and choices. (p. 9)

It is often claimed that Rich is "dodging" the bisexual question. I believe the question is incorrectly phrased. The very existence of the word "*bi*sexual" is based on a false belief in sexual dichotomy. If gender was not the most salient social category in our culture and was not differentially valued, then why would people who had relationships with both men and women be called *bi*sexual? The word implies being sexual with both groups, but it also implies that there are two (and only two) groups, groups that are discrete, discontinuous and mutually exclusive. It also indicates that this particular method of grouping people is the single most important form of categorization. Why aren't people who date lefties and righties called bisexual? Obviously the question of people's sexual orientation as we currently conceive it is relevant only in the context of a society that uses gender as the primary division.

Rich says that the statement "in a world of equality, all people would be bisexual" is not a valid one. In the past, when I read this article, I was under the impression that Rich was asserting that this statement was wrong. But she never brings any evidence to the contrary. It seems, in rereading the piece, that Rich is really saying that this statement is irrelevant, and its truth or falsehood does not even need to be discussed, and perhaps cannot be discussed. We do not live in a world of equality between men and women. And perhaps we cannot even accurately conceptualize what such a world would be. In fact, in a world of true equality between women and men, there would be no categories of heterosexual, homosexual and bisexual, because the gender of someone's sexual object choice would not be a salient social category if gender categories did not have a priori value differences associated with them.

By understanding that the categories of gay, straight and bi are artifacts of our culture and, specifically, artifacts of a culture based on a gender hierarchy, I think we can grasp why the question "what would your sexual orientation be in a world free of sexism?" is unanswerable.

Another statement by Rich often viewed as problematic for bisexuals follows:

The question inevitably will arise: Are we then to condemn all heterosexual relationships, including those which are least oppressive? I believe this question, though often heartfelt, is the wrong question here.... Within the institution exist, of course, qualitative differences of experience; but the absence of choice remains the great unacknowledged reality, and in the absence of choice, women will remain dependent upon the chance or luck of particular relationships and will have no collective power to determine the meaning and place of sexuality in their lives. (p. 31)

I do not want to assert that this statement is unproblematic. Particularly the line "women will remain dependent upon the chance or luck" implies that women are not active agents in our own destiny and that we lack volition to make choices that will positively impact on our lives. Certainly the belief that women are mere "victims of chance" is something that many feminists do not want to accept. However, the key issue here is the lack of *choice*—women having relationships with men in the absence of a conscious realization that other options exist—which is oppressive. The quest is not necessarily for women to abandon relationships with men, but rather, to be free from the requirement to be with men and to be self-conscious of our motivations when we are with men.

In her additional comments, written in letters after "Compulsory Heterosexuality" was published, Rich clarifies her views by adding, "I was trying to ask heterosexual feminists to refuse to settle for the personal privilege and solution of the individual 'good relationship' within the institution of heterosexuality."[10] The relevant clarification is found in the word "privilege." Upon being told of the mechanisms of compulsory heterosexuality, some women respond with "but my relationship is not like that." This response misses the point and is irrelevant in the context of discussing heteropatriarchy. Upon being told of the existence of any form of systematic oppression, to respond with "but that is not happening to me" is antithetical to a feminist vision. Women who are in "good" relationships with men have perhaps the greatest obligation to examine their relationships critically and the ways in which they are privileged through their heterosexuality.

A bisexual-feminist analysis offers a unique opportunity to bring fresh perspectives to feminist discussions. Bisexuality can provide a new vantage point from which to examine gender relations. Having intimate relationships with both sexes can allow us to bring valuable knowledge to all of our relationships. In our relationships with women we often learn that we have no obligation to put up with patriarchal behavior and attitudes in any of our intimate relationships. We learn that we do not need men to have full, rich lives. We learn to appreciate women, and in doing so, we learn to value ourselves. When, as feminists, we are involved with men, we work on addressing issues of differential power and privilege. Perhaps through our work on building egalitarian and nonoppressive relationships with men we can learn the valuable and vital lesson that good relationships do not happen automatically. Just because two people in a relationship are both female does not mean that they understand each other innately, does not guarantee compatibility and does not preclude violence, oppression and abuse.[11] Perhaps by experiencing that nonoppressive heterosexual relationships take work, we can learn that we need to put that kind of effort into *all* of our relationships. Rich does acknowledge that such efforts may be necessary:

> It [lesbian existence] has of course included role-playing, self-hatred, breakdown, alcoholism, suicide, and intrawoman violence; we romanticize at our peril what it means to love and act against the grain... (p. 21)

It is important that we, as feminists, create a paradigm in which it is possible for all women to resist oppressive structures. There are many ways in which bisexual women can participate in this struggle.

Bisexual women can struggle for queer liberation, together with gay men and lesbians. We can be feminist activists, working with both lesbian and heterosexual women. And some forms of resistance, or breaking down of existing ideologies, are uniquely suited to bisexual women. When a bisexual woman is involved with a woman, it becomes less possible for heterocentric men to believe she's in the relationship only because she hates men, wishes she were a man or can't get a man. Perhaps the ultimate threat to the heteropatriarchy is a woman who has had "a good fuck" and still isn't "cured." When assholes hit on me on the street, I am often tempted to say "fuck off, I'm a dyke." But then, it occurs to me that that is not the point. Perhaps it would be more appropriate to say, "fuck off, you're a jerk."

After all, doesn't the first response imply that his behavior would be acceptable, if not for the fact that something is wrong with me? I would be implying that it is my lesbianism alone that prevents my receiving his advances positively and that his behavior is not at fault. By asserting our bisexuality, we can say that we will date men, but only on our own terms. Thus we shift more of the burden of building viable sexual relationships toward men.

That possibility is raised in Rich's work, in a statement that alludes to the ways in which women who do relate to men can be a force of change:

> It seems more probable that men really fear, not that they will have women's sexual appetites forced on them, or that women want to smother and devour them, but that women could be indifferent to them altogether, that men could be allowed sexual and emotional—therefore economic—access to women only on women's terms, otherwise being left on the periphery of the matrix. (p. 15)

Bisexual women can help make it clear to men that they must treat women as equals and that they have an obligation to help end our oppression if they wish to be part of our lives. We can choose not to take various heterosexual privileges (such as legal marriage) when in relationships with men and discuss why we are doing so with our friends. In this way, we make it clear that we *can* be with men, but do not *have* to be. We can do so out of choice, making our choices conscious ones and our consciousness public. We can discuss the ways in which we are treated differently when we are in a heterosexual relationship as opposed to a same-sex one and challenge those differences.

One of the reasons that the "individual good relationship" is not a good enough solution is the ways in which others respond to us. Even if a bisexual woman is in an entirely egalitarian and nonoppressive relationship with a man, the treatment from the rest of the world is not egalitarian. Compulsory heterosexuality influences the ways in which we are diminished and the ways in which we are treated better when we are seen with men. Both the insults and the so-called compliments must be challenged. We and the men we are with can confront people on their heterocentric assumptions when we encounter them. By doing so, we shake up those assumptions, since people do not expect to have their homophobia confronted by apparent heterosexuals.

We can also work toward creating a vision of alternative relationship structures for everyone. This is one form of radical revision it was hoped the "gay liberation" movement could bring about. Unfortunately, much of the power (that is, rich, white males) in the gay liberation movement is no longer pushing for expanded definitions of human relationships, but rather is fighting for inclusion under the current restrictive model.[12] The current relationship model (under mainstream Western values) states that you must be with only one other person for life. Furthermore, nonmonogamy, autosexuality and asexuality are seen as flaws—as symptoms of psychological immaturity or indications of transience or indecision. These are the same judgments often made about bisexuality.

We women are taught not to value ourselves. Simply choosing not to be in an emotional/erotic relationship at all is a choice that is invalidated in our society, perhaps even more condemned than being in a same-sex relationship. Being "single" and being "nonmonogamous" are tolerated under the same constraints as bisexuality. If you are single, nonmonogamous or bisexual it can be grudgingly accepted if it's interpreted as a sign of indecision or of having not yet reached your full potential. By the same token, all three ways of being are viewed as marginally acceptable if we espouse the attitude that they are transitional. It is okay to be single between relationships, nonmonogamous between periods of monogamy and bisexual as a "stage" in youth that precedes a "real" sexual orientation. All three situations are also treated as being indicative of indecision.

Bisexual people and nonmonogamous people are treated as having not *yet* made up their minds. If someone is not in any committed relationship, it is assumed that they do want to be in a couple, but have not met the right person yet. The assumption underlying these stereotypes is that the goal state of all people must be a monogamous relationship with a person of the other sex. All other alternatives, when they are tolerated at all, are viewed as occurring simply because the person(s) involved have not yet achieved her or his goal state. It is important to work for acceptance of more options, both within individuals and populations. We must acknowledge that people may have varied ways of devising relationships and that individuals may desire different ways of relating at different points in their lives.

By challenging these assumptions, a bisexual-feminist perspective can help build new ways of constructing our relationships that allow for a greater fluidity and a greater range in the accepted forms of human interaction.

The imperatives to be heterosexual, monogamous and male-focused all force women into constrained roles. By challenging these imperatives, we allow for *all* people to see how their identities and relationships have been constructed and we facilitate thinking about changing those constructs, in the context of wider possibilities.

What we as feminists ought to be doing is valuing the different vantage points of women with a range of experiences so that we can better explore the possibility of a resistance to heteropatriarchy from *all* women.

Endnotes

I would like to thank the other wonderful bisexual feminist who assisted me with this piece; Robyn Ochs, Annie Senghas and A. J. Babineau.

1. Adrienne Rich, "Compulsory Heterosexuality and Lesbian Existence," originally published in *Signs: Journal of Women in Culture and Society* 5, no. 4 (1980): pp. 631-60.

2. In her foreword to the 1982 reprint of "Compulsory Heterosexuality," Rich writes, "It was not written to widen divisions but to encourage heterosexual feminists to examine heterosexuality as a political institution which disempowers women—and to change it" (Rich, p. 1).

3. Another useful distinction to draw may be between compulsory heterosexuality and compulsory *hommosexuality*, from the root word "hommo," meaning male (the concept of hommosexuality is explored in Teresa de Lauretis, "Sexual Indifference and Lesbian Repression, *Theatre Journal* 40, no. 2 (1980): 155-77). The belief under *hommosexuality* is that the purpose of all sex is male gratification and that the locus of sexuality is male. Compulsory heterosexuality, on the other hand, states that sexual relationships may occur only with members of the other sex. Some of the examples discussed by Rich seem to be compulsory *hommosexuality* rather than compulsory heterosexuality, though clearly the two forces interact in our culture. Under *hommosexuality*, women are never agents of sexuality. Sex is something that is performed on women by men, for men's gain. This is one of the forces that feminists should be, and are, fighting against. By looking at a paradigm of *hommosexuality*, it becomes more clear why female masturbation is a radical resistance to heteropatriarchy and male masturbation is not. If heteropatriarchy were enforcing only heterosexuality, male masturbation would also be a resistance. This clarification can also help us understand the differential relevance of lesbians and gay men.

Since under compulsory *hommosexuality* all sex must be male focused, lesbianism is a drastic form of resistance, yet male homosexuality can remain irrelevant to Rich's analysis.

4. Biological determinism is an ideology that states that a variety of human behavioral traits arise as a result of biological phenomena, such as hormones or genetics. Determinism often, but not always, includes the belief that such traits are immutable.

5. Additionally, arguing that we should be allowed to be homosexual because we "can't help it" implies that we agree that there is something wrong with homosexuality. For more on this, see Lindsy Van Gelder, "The 'Born That Way' Trap," *Ms.* 1, no. 6 (1991): pp. 86-87.

6. Carla Golden, in "Our Politics and Our Choices: The Feminist Movement and Sexual Orientation" (presented at the American Psychological Association's annual meeting, Boston, 1990) points out the high incidence of political and conscious choice in the formation of lesbian identity.

7. Meaning, it is unclear whether we are to be included in the category "lesbian existence." It is clear that we are included in the category "lesbian continuum."

8. In Northampton, Massachusetts, some lesbians have been pressing for the exclusion of bisexuals from the "lesbian and gay" pride march, and this issue has become a matter of contention in recent times. *Bi Women,* August/September 1991.

9. Those bisexual organizations that did exist in the 1970s appear to have focused on sex and "swinging," with most of the members being in married heterosexual relationships. These were not environments that would have encouraged women to question their mandatory commitment to men. See the chapter on bisexual organizations in Fritz Klein and Timothy Wolf, *Two Lives to Lead: Bisexuality in Men and Women* (New York: Harrington Press, 1985).

10. Adrienne Rich, *Blood, Bread and Poetry: Selected Prose, 1979-1985* (New York: W. W. Norton, 1986), p. 72.

11. It is important to move away from an essentialist view of gender, which assigns all violence by definition to men. As long as a dominant feminist paradigm assigns the locus of all evil to men, intrawoman violence will continue to go unaddressed.

12. For example, the "gay rights" movement is currently pushing for "gay marriage" in several cities. This approach does not question the notion that one must be in a monogamous, committed relationship. One of the reasons given for supporting "gay marriage" bills is that same-sex couples will have the same access to "family health plans" that opposite-sex couples have. I propose that we, as feminists, ought to oppose the notion that health care access should be dependent on whom one is sexually involved with.

Paula C. Rust

WHO ARE WE AND WHERE DO WE GO FROM HERE?
CONCEPTUALIZING BISEXUALITY

In the 1970s, critics of the women's liberation movement charged that feminists were destroying the natural order of man and woman. In the 1980s, Jerry Falwell charged that homosexual behavior is a rejection of God that "not only destroys individual lives but also destroys national life," and accused the gay men's movement of corrupting children and damaging "the home."[1] Change is often seen as threatening because it means the destruction of familiar ways of life. Those who find the familiar ways of life comfortable and satisfying see no need for change and can only envision the breakdown of society. To those who find the familiar ways of life oppressive, however, change is necessary and signals not the breakdown, but the evolution of society.

Today, as we approach the turn of the century, the fabric of our society faces another "threat"—the bisexual movement. Like the feminist, gay and lesbian movements that preceded it, however, what the bisexual movement promises is not destruction, but evolution. But evolution in which direction? The answer to this question depends upon the ideological groundwork being laid now. During this early stage of the movement, critical questions are being debated. What is bisexuality? Who is a bisexual? What are the goals of the bisexual movement? The answers we give to these questions now will determine the course of the bisexual movement in the years to come. If we follow the lead of the black, women's, gay and lesbian movements in adopting a liberationist ideology, the bisexual movement might succeed in adding one more group of people to a growing list of oppressed minorities. If we break with recent political tradition, however, the bisexual movement has the potential to radically alter the way we think about gender and sexuality. Is such a change possible in the current political climate, or would it doom the bisexual movement to failure?

If we seek to transform the pie rather than to demand our share of it, what foundation do we need to build for ourselves now?

At the heart of ideology is the concept of bisexuality. We must decide who "we" are before we can describe the nature of our oppression, determine the reasons for our oppression, and decide upon the best strategy for ending this oppression. In short, our goals depend upon who we conceive ourselves to be. For bisexuals, defining who we are is particularly problematic because according to current sexual ideology we do not even exist, much less have an identity. By the same token, however, starting without a predetermined identity seems to allow us unlimited possibilities for defining who we are and what we are about.

But ideology—and therefore identity—does not develop in a vacuum. Ideology develops within a historical, cultural and political context that is already organized by an existing ideology. In fact, it is our dissatisfaction with existing ideology that motivates us to generate new ideology, thus new ideology owes its very existence to the context in which it developed. But more important, it is unavoidably shaped by that context. Just like the child of an alcoholic who resolves never to become an alcoholic and therefore teetotals, new ideology is molded by the need to be different from the ideology it is designed to replace.

Why can't we break free from our context altogether and reorganize the world along entirely new lines? Although this would seem to be an easy way to eliminate all the problems with the current system altogether, it is neither possible nor would it be politically effective. It is not possible because it is impossible to produce a truly and completely original thought; creative thought involves novel combinations or mutations of ideas, not completely new ideas. Like it or not, our thoughts are organized according to deep cognitive structures we ourselves are rarely aware of. Many of these structures are established by our language itself and cannot be eradicated without eliminating language, hence eliminating our capacity for the type of abstract thought necessary to produce political ideology. Even if it were possible for human intelligence to produce a truly original ideology, this ideology would be politically ineffective because it would be unintelligible to other people. It would, in effect, be written in a language they could not understand. In order to discuss the possibilities for bisexual identity we must first understand the context within which the bisexual movement is developing. Only then can we examine the diverse ways in which we conceptualize bisexuality, and only then can we answer the question, where do we go from here?

The Context

Throughout history, human beings have engaged in sexual activity with other human beings of both genders. Different cultures have organized this activity in different ways. For example, the Etoro of New Guinea believe that men become virile by receiving the sperm of other men; men therefore spend their teen and young adult years engaging in homosexual activity with older men before they marry a woman and commence heterosexual activity.[2] In ancient Greece, sexual relations between an adult male teacher and a male pupil as well as romantic relationships among men in the army were normative and did not preclude simultaneous heterosexual involvements; in fact, exclusive homosexuality was discouraged among the ancient Greeks.[3] Although different cultures have established different rules regarding the timing and meaning of homosexual and heterosexual behavior, the fact remains that both forms of behavior have always been part of the human sexual repertoire.

In the mid-nineteenth century, however, a change occurred in the way this behavior was viewed in the Western world. This change can be described as the birth of the homosexual person.[4] Prior to this time, people who participated in homosexual activity were simply engaging in one of the many forms of behavior that were possible. With the birth of the homosexual person, however, homosexual behavior became the basis of identity. Homosexuality is now no longer something that one *does*; it is something that one *is*. One no longer simply engages in sexual relations with members of one's own sex; now, one is a homosexual.

But if people who engage in homosexual relations are homosexuals, then who is everyone else? Well, if these other people are not engaging in homosexual relations (otherwise, they would be homosexual), then they must be engaging in heterosexual relations. If they are engaging in heterosexual relations, they must be heterosexuals. We now have two types of people in the world—homosexuals and heterosexuals. This is all very neat and tidy and quite comfortable for those individuals who find that they are attracted only to members of their own sex or only to members of the other sex.

But some of us were left along the wayside during this transformation. Those of us who recognize that we are attracted to members of both sexes do not find this new sexual ideology comfortable. Our heterosexual experiences have been separated from our homosexual experiences, and two different people have been created from these different experiences. Sexuality is now the basis for identity, and our sexuality has been split in two and stolen to create two separate identities, leaving us with no identity of our own. We have, in effect, been defined out of existence. In order to claim our sexual existence, we must challenge the notion that sexuality consists of a homosexual/heterosexual dichotomy.

But challenging the homosexual-heterosexual dichotomy is not easy. If the appeal of this dichotomous conception of sexuality were merely that it is neat, tidy and comfortable for some people, it might not be so difficult to dismantle. The appeal of dichotomous sexuality goes much deeper than that. First, it is compatible with traditional Western thought and found a friendly audience among those of Cartesian and Judeo-Christian heritage.[5,6] Second, over a century after its birth, it has become embedded in a network of social and political institutions. Uprooting the conception of dichotomous sexuality now would disturb the social and political institutions that have been built upon it. Bisexuality threatens to do exactly that. By challenging the dichotomous conception of sexuality at this juncture in history, bisexuality places itself at odds with traditional Western thought and threatens to destroy powerful social and political institutions. It is no wonder that bisexuality is perceived as a threat, and it is no wonder that we find it difficult to convince both heterosexuals and homosexuals that we really exist.[7] Since these, then, are the reasons for our difficulty, they deserve a closer look.

In the Cartesian and Judeo-Christian West, concepts are clearly defined and distinguishable. Unlike things are kept separate from each other and not mixed. If something is not right, it is wrong. If something is not black, it is white. Birds, plants and chemicals are carefully classified and typologized. When we ask, "What is this?" we mean, "To what class of object does this belong?" Things that do not fit into categories are disturbing because we do not know what they are. Such things must be destroyed, stigmatized or ignored because they threaten the clarity of the distinctions that organize our world. Like the pig, they are impure and must not be allowed to contaminate us.[8] The fact that reality is not always as discrete as we wish it were leads us not to reject our neat categories, but rather to reject reality.

If classification schemes are nice because they simplify and organize the world, then dichotomies are the ultimate classification scheme: two categories are the height of simplicity and organization. One of the most important areas of our lives—sexuality—is organized entirely in terms of dichotomies, and the homosexual/heterosexual dichotomy fits right into this conceptual scheme. The fact that none of the dichotomies in this conceptual scheme accurately reflect the complex reality of human sexuality does not lead us to reject the scheme, but rather to ignore the troublesome reality of our own sexuality.

The fundamental dichotomy in this conceptual scheme is biological sex. We conceive of biological sex as composed of two categories: female and male. Despite the existence of hermaphrodites and considerable variation in the degree to which individuals possess primary and secondary sex characteristics within both female and male categories, we continue to insist that people be either female or male. Hermaphroditic children are "assigned" to one sex or the other and given hormonal and surgical treatment to "correct" their biological "abnormalities." If the result of such treatment were the production of fertile human beings, then such procedures would at least be defensible on the basis of biological normality. But the result is usually a person who is still unable to reproduce; what has been produced is not biological normality, but social normality. In other words, the goal of such treatment is not to produce conformity to "natural" biological prescriptions, but rather to produce conformity to social prescriptions. It is not the physical health of these individuals that concerns us but rather the health of our society, which cannot deal with people who are neither clearly female nor clearly male.

Based upon biological sex are the concepts of gender identity (psychological sex) and gender role (social sex). Like biological sex, gender identity and gender roles are dichotomous: one perceives oneself as either female or male, and one is either feminine or masculine. These two gender dichotomies persist despite the existence of a variety of transgender phenomena such as cross-dressing and gender dysphoria, not to mention the wide variability of the content of individual gender identity and conceptions of the feminine and masculine roles.

Dichotomous sexual orientation also follows from dichotomous sex: if one must be biologically either female or male and choose a sexual partner who must also be either female or male, then it follows that the relationship is either other-sexed or same-sexed, that is, heterosexual or homosexual. The heterosexual/homosexual dichotomy is so familiar to us today that we may fail to recognize the absurdity of this conclusion. By what precedent do we justify referring to a physical trait that belongs to one person (for example, my *partner's* biological sex) in order to describe the emotional, psychological or behavioral traits of another person (for example, *my* sexual identity, *my* feelings of sexual attraction and *my* sexual behavior)?

This series of neat dichotomies, which I call the "sex-gender edifice," provides the simplest possible conceptual scheme within which experience may be organized, and it is not easily dislodged in favor of more complex schemes. Moreover, since these dichotomies are intimately related to each other, a change in any one would necessitate adjustment among all the others. Hence each dichotomy is preserved by the inertia of the whole edifice. Any attack upon the heterosexual/homosexual dichotomy must confront the entire conservative force of socially constructed sex, gender and sexuality.

But the problem goes even deeper still. The sex-gender edifice is maintained not only by its own inertia, but also by the fact that much of modern Western social structure has been built upon sex-gender distinctions.[9] The fact that our society is organized along gender lines is self-evident and well documented and hardly needs to be proven again here.[10] One need only look at the ratio of women to men among our elected political "representatives," at the disparity between women's and men's incomes, and at the content of commercial advertising to recognize the importance of gender in organizing our social, political and economic lives. The maintenance of our social structure thus not only depends upon preserving a clear distinction between the genders, but also magnifies the consequences and therefore the importance of biological sex which underlies gender. One's biological sex becomes a prime determinant of one's life chances. Any attempt to de-emphasize the distinction between women and men constitutes a threat to our social, political and economic systems. This threat is likely to be resisted by chauvinists and many feminists alike; by chauvinists who recognize that the maintenance of patriarchy depends upon the assertion that women are "naturally" different from men, and by feminists who argue that gender-blind policies will not produce gender-blind results until the persistent effects of past discrimination have been corrected by programs such as affirmative action.

Just as social and political institutions have been built around sex and gender since the dawn of human society, so have they been build around the homosexual/heterosexual dichotomy since its inception more than a century ago. This build-up has accelerated in the past two decades as a result of the growth of the modern lesbian and gay movement. Early homophile organizations preferred to minimize the implications of the distinction between heterosexuals and homosexuals. Members of these organizations chose to seek acceptance within heterosexual society by hiding their sexual orientation or by self-conscious conformity to mainstream values in all other areas of their lives. Early activists, for example, took care to adopt traditional gendered dress styles in an attempt to gain acceptance through assimilation. With the advent of the modern liberation movement, however, such strategies were replaced by a more radical style involving the emphasis of differences and pride in distinct lesbian and gay male lifestyles.

The ideology and form of this modern liberation movement were borrowed from the black and women's liberation movements of the 1950s, 1960s and 1970s. Liberation movements belonging to this tradition are built around the belief that the route to liberation consists of a struggle on the part of the oppressed to overthrow the oppressor. Liberation thus requires that a clear distinction be drawn between the oppressor and the oppressed so that the oppressed can identify and struggle against the oppressor. The ensuing conflict serves to sharpen the lines of demarcation between conflicting parties.[11] In the heat of battle, those who are not identifiable as allies must be assumed to be enemies; neither side can afford to trust those who claim to be neutral. Neutral ground thus disappears as participants are forced to choose sides, and those who continue to claim neutrality are perceived as lacking commitment or courage. Neutrality becomes a sign of political backwardness as radicalism becomes defined as political progressivism.

288   *Closer to Home*

Thus, the rise of the lesbian and gay liberation movement in the 1970s and 1980s drew the battle lines on the territory of sexual orientation. This new movement has been built upon the bedrock of the homosexual/heterosexual dichotomy and today constitutes a powerful political institution with an interest in preserving its own foundation, that is, the concept of dichotomous sexuality. As the struggle for liberation has grown more heated, the grey area that is neither heterosexuality nor homosexuality has become politically suspect, and those who claim to inhabit this area are accused of harboring loyalty to the enemy, or worse, of being traitors. Bisexuality thus becomes the badge of political cowardice, and social pressure is brought to bear upon those who identify as bisexuals to "make up their minds." Within this atmosphere, claims of bisexual existence are defined as illegitimate and politically regressive. The homosexual/heterosexual dichotomy becomes a self-fulfilling prophecy as individuals succumb to the pressure to abandon bisexual identity and pledge allegiance to one of the politically legitimate categories.

Yet, despite the mounting social pressure to abandon bisexual identity, some of us stubbornly hold onto our bisexual identities. Faced with a world in which only heterosexuals and homosexuals are allowed to exist as legitimate social and political beings, how do we conceptualize our own bisexuality? And how do lesbian-identified women, many of whom gave up a bisexual identity to adopt lesbian identity, conceptualize the bisexuality they have rejected? It is to this question that I now turn.

Who Are We?

We cannot look to biologists, historians or philosophers to answer this question. To discover how we conceptualize bisexuality, we must ask each other. As part of a larger study of the beliefs and opinions of bisexual-identified and lesbian-identified women,[12] I asked more than four hundred women, "What is your opinion of bisexuality?" These women's answers revealed that we have many ways of defining ourselves and others as bisexual, and that these definitions reflect fundamental differences in the ways we conceptualize sexuality itself. In fact, four very different ways of conceptualizing sexuality and bisexuality emerged from this study.

One way in which women conceptualize sexuality is as a dichotomy in which heterosexuality and homosexuality are clearly distinct and exhaustive categories and bisexuality is nonexistent. Of course no bisexual-identified women conceptualize sexuality in this way, but one out of three of the lesbian-identified women who took part in this study do. These women made comments such as:

> "I think either you are a lesbian or you're straight."
> "I was born [homosexual]; some are born heterosexual. I find it hard to believe that people can be bisexual."
> "It does not exist."

Some of these lesbian-identified women acknowledge that there are people who call themselves bisexual or who engage in both homosexual and heterosexual behavior, but they proceed to explain that these women are "really" lesbians who are just confused, afraid, and so on, that they are women in transition to lesbianism, or that they are mentally ill as evidenced by their delusions of bisexuality. The following are typical quotes from these women:

> "I feel people who think they are bisexual are confused about it, or in transition."
> "Bisexuality is for the undecided.... Or someone afraid to totally commit themselves to just one lifestyle."
> "Bisexuality is a term used to escape dealing with one's own homophobia."
> "I see it as an interim stage and that most people vacillate toward being straight or gay."
> "My experience of women who define themselves as bisexual suggests that bisexual women are either (a) really "lesbian" but using the bisexual label to preserve their heterosexual privilege in society, or (b) on their way to becoming lesbian and using the bisexual label as a "safe" transition stage, or (c) experimenting with lesbianism but not in a serious way ['sexual tourists']."
> "It would be possible but would be better described as schizophrenic."
> "Bisexual is still heterosexual unless it is pathological."

The second way of conceptualizing sexuality is also dichotomous, but in this case bisexuality does exist and is defined as a combination of heterosexuality and homosexuality. This dualistic conception of bisexuality is popular among both bisexual-identified and lesbian-identified women and takes a variety of forms: some women conceive of bisexuality as a combination of attractions to women and men, whereas others refer to a combination of abilities to love women and men, to a combination of heterosexual and homosexual "lifestyles" or to a dual membership in both heterosexual and homosexual societies. Both the belief that bisexuality exists and the dualistic conception of bisexuality are evident in the following quotes:

> "I think that it would be a very hard way of life. I could not juggle the two."
> "I think it is very possible to be attracted to both sexes."
> "In general, I think bisexuals get to obtain privileges from being members of both groups."
> "I have met some bisexuals, and I don't understand how they juggle two different lives."
> "A person whose affectional preference includes both men and women. And/or a person who is sexually involved with both men and women."

In contrast to the dichotomous conceptualizations of sexuality maintained by most bisexual and lesbian women, a small number of women referred to a "continuum," a "spectrum" or a "continuous scale" of sexuality. Some respondents elaborated upon this concept, explaining that some women are attracted to "both sexes to differing degrees" or emphasizing that there are "not clear distinctions between straight, bisexual or gay." Respondents who endorse this model typically do, however, draw lines between straight, bisexual and lesbian/gay somewhere along the continuum. The location of these lines varies: some respondents would define everyone as bisexual except those few who fall at the extreme endpoints of the continuum, whereas others would call bisexual only those who fall at the exact midpoint. For example:

> "I feel it is one aspect of the wide spectrum of human sexual identity. Just as there are women who are attracted to women, men to men, and women and men to each other to varying degrees, so there are also women and men who are attracted to both sexes to differing degrees."

"I feel that most people, women and men, are to a certain extent bisexual—but this constitutes a continuous scale, not clear distinctions between straight, bisexual, or gay."

"Everyone is inherently bisexual. Even among bisexuals there is a continuum, and bisexuals can prefer heterosexuality or homosexuality."

"Everyone is bisexual, but most feel more strongly toward one sex."

"I believe sexuality is on a continuum and that people can fall anywhere on that continuum. If someone falls in the middle, then they are bisexual and that's just the way it is."

Finally, some women conceptualize bisexuality as qualitatively different from heterosexuality and homosexuality. Rather than defining bisexuality as a variation on heterosexuality and homosexuality, these women define bisexuality as a third, distinct sexual orientation; in effect, they conceptualize sexuality as a trichotomy. Some state merely that bisexuality is a third form of sexuality, for example:

"I do believe that this category exists legitimately."

"It's a valid orientation."

However, others provide details regarding the criteria with which they define bisexuality; these criteria are qualitatively different from those they use to distinguish heterosexuality and homosexuality from each other. These distinctions often place either a negative or positive evaluation on bisexuality. For example, some respondents characterized bisexuals as "indiscriminate" lovers, in apparent contrast to the "discrimination" practiced by heterosexuals and homosexuals, who are distinguished from each other by the direction of their discrimination. Others define bisexuality as the ability to love a person regardless of gender, in apparent contrast to heterosexuality and homosexuality, which are defined in terms of the gender of potential romantic or sexual partners.

"Bisexuals are into 'gay decadence'—sex with anybody just for a thrill."

"Bisexuals are indiscriminate—they just sleep with anybody."

"One who is truly 'bisexual' allows themself to fall in love with a person and not a gender."

"It represents a feeling that the sexuality of the individual doesn't matter but rather the important aspect is the personality."

"I think that bisexuality is a recognition that sexuality is not necessarily gender-specific."

"People who love people regardless of sex."

Even as they describe sexuality as dichotomous, continuous or trichotomous, however, some women argue that most or all people are "really" bisexual. The difference is one of human potential versus social reality; for example, all people might have the potential to be bisexual, but factors such as the imbalance of power between men and women, condemnation of homosexual relationships, ostracism of bisexuals by both heterosexual society and the gay and lesbian communities, and dichotomous or either/or thinking patterns prevent most people from realizing this potential.

Are there differences between bisexual-identified and lesbian-identified women in the way they conceptualize sexuality? There appear to be.[13] As mentioned, the concept of sexuality as a dichotomy in which bisexuality does not exist is confined to lesbians. Many bisexuals do agree that sexuality is basically dichotomous but argue that bisexuality exists as a combination of homosexuality and heterosexuality; more than half of the bisexual-identified women who participated in this study have dualistic definitions of bisexuality. Conversely, the idea that sexuality is trichotomous is twice as popular among bisexual women than it is among lesbians: four out of ten bisexuals and two out of ten lesbians define bisexuality as a third distinct form of sexuality.

Bisexuals are also twice as likely as lesbians to state that most or all people are theoretically or potentially bisexual: thirty percent of bisexual women and fifteen percent of lesbians express this belief.

It is not surprising to find that lesbians commonly think of sexuality as dichotomous and believe that bisexuality is either nonexistent or a combination of heterosexuality and homosexuality. After all, women who identify themselves as lesbians apparently find the prevailing dichotomous conception of sexuality comfortable enough to fit themselves into; they have no reason to question its validity. They recognize that there are women who call themselves bisexual, but conclude either that these women are simply mistaken, or that they somehow contrive to be both heterosexual and homosexual at the same time.

What is noteworthy, however, is that a number of bisexual women also conceive of sexuality as dichotomous. Although none of these women go so far as to believe that bisexuality is nonexistent, neither do they assert that bisexuality has an existence independent of heterosexuality and homosexuality. Instead, they conceive of bisexuality as a combination of the two legitimate forms of sexuality rather than as a legitimate form of sexuality in and of itself. In other words, these women fragment their own inner experiences: the distinction between what one does experience and what one does not experience takes a back seat to an externally constructed distinction which runs straight through the middle of one's own experience. Such a conception only serves to reinforce the hegemony of the homosexual/heterosexual dichotomy, a dichotomy that ultimately denies the legitimacy of bisexuality.

That some bisexual women would conceive of bisexuality as such is certainly understandable. We develop our bisexual identities within a context in which the homosexual/heterosexual dichotomy is institutionalized and enforced socially, politically and linguistically.[14] We all build our identities out of the raw materials made available to us; the fact that we consider sexuality to be a legitimate basis of identity at all is evidence of this. Therefore, if the only materials we find at hand are labeled "heterosexual" and "homosexual," then we are not to be blamed if we try to use them to build an identity.

If these materials were completely insufficient for the construction of bisexual identity, then we might be motivated to look for better building materials. Ironically, however, these materials are adequate for the task. It is possible to successfully describe one's own bisexuality as a combination of heterosexuality and homosexuality; the number of bisexual-identified women who do so attests to this. What has in effect happened is that the bisexual experience that would ordinarily demand independent conceptual existence has been co-opted by the construction of heterosexuality and homosexuality. There is no single experience a bisexual can have that cannot be described by reference to either heterosexuality or homosexuality; hence, there is no leftover experience that demands to be represented in some other way.

For example, a bisexual person might have a partner of either gender, but a given partner must be of one gender or the other. As soon as the gender of this partner is discovered, the relationship can be classified as either heterosexual or homosexual, and the experience is co-opted. The bisexual woman finds that she can adequately describe this particular relationship as either heterosexual or homosexual, and that other people understand her when she does. If she persists in claiming that this does not mean that she herself is either heterosexual or homosexual, she will find that her protests elicit not comprehension, but social sanction for her presumed adultery. Since it is difficult for her to explain exactly what it is about her that is not either heterosexual or homosexual but purely bisexual, she may give up the effort and concede that her bisexuality is a combination of heterosexuality and homosexuality.

What is missing in her identity, of course, is not the recognition of any particular experience, but rather a recognition of the holism of her experience. Each of her experiences can be accounted for, but all of her experiences cannot be accounted for simultaneously. She is, in effect, two people rather than one; a fragmented person rather than a whole sexual being.

Whether an individual should strive to build a holistic conception of her own bisexuality is not for others to say. We can, however, discuss the implications of a dualistic conception of bisexuality for the future of the bisexual movement. The implications are quite simple: a dualistic conception of bisexuality will not support a bisexual movement at all, and particularly not within the current political climate. At a superficial level, this implication seems apparent; after all, dualistic bisexuality incorporates the homosexual/heterosexual dichotomy that ultimately denies the independent existence of bisexuality. Trying to build a bisexual movement upon a dualistic conception of bisexuality is therefore self-defeating. But this point is philosophical; it might work in the political ivory tower, but what about the streets of Greenwich Village?

As noted at the beginning of this essay, identity is the core of ideology. We must know who we are before we can describe our oppression, determine the reasons for our oppression and decide upon the best strategy for ending this oppression. Once we have decided what our political goals are, we can then build a movement that is designed to accomplish these goals; a movement without goals is not a movement. What, then, would a bisexual movement based upon the dualistic conception of bisexuality look like? How would it describe bisexual oppression, how would it explain this oppression and what strategies would it adopt to accomplish what goals?

We run into trouble immediately. If bisexuality is merely a combination of heterosexuality and homosexuality, then the oppression bisexuals experience is merely a combination of the oppression experienced by heterosexuals and homosexuals. Since heterosexuals are the oppressor and not the oppressed, heterosexuals do not experience oppression for being heterosexual. Therefore, the only oppression experienced by bisexuals is the oppression experienced by homosexuals. In fact, it is only the "homosexual side" of bisexuals that is oppressed. So the nature of bisexual oppression is identical to the nature of homosexual oppression; if anything, bisexuals experience quantitatively less oppression, since only half of themselves experiences this oppression. In this case, bisexual women should simply join forces with lesbians; since there is no qualitative difference in the nature of their oppression, there can be no difference in their political interests or movement goals. Therefore developing an independent movement would succeed only in weakening the numerical strength of the combined efforts of bisexuals and lesbians. In short, if bisexuality is conceptualized as a combination of heterosexuality and homosexuality, the bisexual movement is left without any unique goals of its own and, hence, without a reason for independent existence.[15]

At this point, you might comment that it is all well and good to argue that if bisexuals have the same political interests and goals as lesbians, then there is no justification for a separate bisexual movement, but the practical fact remains that many lesbians do not accept bisexuals and will not welcome them as political partners despite the identical nature of their interests.[16] Is this lack of acceptance not a sufficient motivation for the development of a separate bisexual movement? I would reply that intolerance by lesbians might be enough to drive bisexuals out of the lesbian movement, but it would not motivate the development of an independent bisexual movement. Once outside the lesbian movement, the very motivation for developing a bisexual movement would evaporate, having been left behind when the lesbian movement was left behind. All that would remain would be individual dualistic bisexuals who are outcasts of the lesbian movement and who lack a platform of their own around which to build an independent movement.

Moreover, underlying some lesbians' rejection of bisexuals is the belief that bisexuals are fence-sitters who cannot make up their minds or take a political stand. This belief is only reinforced by the conception of bisexuals as half-heterosexual, half-homosexual. So, by conceptualizing bisexuality in dualistic terms, we not only rob ourselves of the potential for a unique bisexual political agenda, we also encourage the belief that our politics are no more than watered-down lesbian politics, and that we ourselves are, politically speaking, "uncommitted lesbians." Thus, we define our politics as derivative of lesbian politics at the same time we grant lesbians permission to reject us on the basis of our lack of commitment to lesbian politics. We slight ourselves coming and going.

Leaving dichotomous sexuality behind, we turn to the next alternative—the sexual continuum. The concept of a sexual continuum was made famous by the Kinsey reports *Sexual Behavior in the Human Male* and *Sexual Behavior in the Human Female*.[17] In these reports, Kinsey and his associates shocked both scientists and laypeople alike with findings such as "37 per cent of the total male population has at least some overt homosexual experience to the point of orgasm between adolescence and old age" and an additional "13 per cent of the males (approximately) react erotically to other males without having overt sexual contact after the onset of adolescence."[18] In order to model human sexual behavior, the authors developed the 7-point Kinsey scale based on sexual fantasies and behaviors, on which a score of "0" (zero) indicated complete heterosexuality, a score of "6" indicated complete homosexuality, and intervening scores indicated intermediate gradations of bisexuality. Since then, perhaps no other model of sexuality has received as much attention in theoretical discussions of sexuality in the scientific literature.

Despite this theoretical lip service, however, scientists have very rarely made full use of the scale in actual research. A typical practice on the part of researchers is to collect extensive information about subjects' fantasies and behaviors and assign a Kinsey score to each subject, only to divide subjects into two categories "heterosexual" and "homosexual" on the basis of their scores, thus destroying the purpose of the scale. One possible reason for researchers' reluctance to leave the scale intact might be that, statistically speaking, continuous variables are slightly more complex to handle than are categorical variables. The former are by no means difficult to handle, however, and researchers' preference for categorical variables may be traced to the same factor that underlies our cultural preference for categorical analysis: our Cartesian heritage. Scientists grew up in the same culture as did the heterosexuals and homosexuals they study, and like everyone else they prefer to stick with the comfortable and familiar. Since their subjects usually identify themselves as either heterosexual or homosexual, scientists are under no great pressure to do otherwise.

That very few bisexual and lesbian-identified women conceptualize sexuality as a continuum likewise reflects the cultural awkwardness of the concept of a sexual scale. For lesbians, the concept of a sexual scale not only is more complex than necessary, it is also politically compromising because it calls into question the distinction between homosexuality and heterosexuality. For bisexuals, the concept of a sexual continuum is not very satisfying: locating oneself at a particular point on a continuum does not provide a very solid basis for personal identity. It is much easier to draw identity from one's membership in a group than from one's position on a scale; hence, "I am a bisexual" is a more effective means of self-identification than "I am a Kinsey 4.35," even if bisexuality is dualistically conceptualized.

But can the conception of bisexuality as lying between heterosexuality and homosexuality on a continuum support a bisexual movement? The answer is clear: if such a conception of bisexuality is unable to support personal identity, it can hardly be expected to support a political movement of individuals who are so identified.

The concept of a sexual scale does have one attractive feature. It is unidimensional and as such emphasizes the similarities rather than the differences between people. The implication is that there is an underlying thread linking all humanity and that bisexuality is the link that connects heterosexuality to homosexuality. Since we experience both heterosexuality and homosexuality, we are the ultimate expression of human sexual potential, and both heterosexuals and homosexuals could learn from our example to express their full potential as well. This idea is very tempting, but self-defeating in the current political climate. As wonderful as it sounds to us, we can have little hope of selling this idea to heterosexuals and homosexuals; they are not going to be won over by the argument that they, too, could be bisexual if only they would be honest with themselves. If we wish to challenge

the hegemonic homosexual/heterosexual dichotomy, assert the existence of bisexuality and emphasize the commonality of all people, we
must communicate this message in a language that is intelligible and
effective in the current political climate. Conceptualizing bisexuality
as a qualitatively different form of sexuality—not as a combination of
heterosexuality and homosexuality, and not as halfway between heterosexuality and homosexuality, but as a distinct, qualitatively different form of sexuality—offers us the opportunity to do exactly that.

But qualitatively different in what way? There are many ways to
define a qualitatively distinct form of sexuality: the women who participated in the survey provided a variety of suggestions, ranging from
"bisexuals are indiscriminate" to "bisexuals fall in love with a person,
not a gender." Obviously, we need to choose a positive definition. We
are not indiscriminate, sleeping with whoever is available. We do make
choices about whom we will love, have sex with and spend our time
with. We might make these choices on the basis of a variety of criteria,
and some of these criteria are more important to us than others. In
this respect, we are no different from heterosexuals and homosexuals;
that is, most heterosexuals choose their partners on the basis of a
number of criteria as well; they do not indiscriminately sleep with any
member of the other sex any more than we indiscriminately sleep with
any member of either sex.

Where we do differ from heterosexuals and homosexuals is in the
way we treat one particular criterion—biological sex. Heterosexuals
and homosexuals treat biological sex as a necessary criterion; another
person must be of a particular sex in order to be eligible as a romantic
partner.[19] After this criterion is met, other criteria of varying importance may be brought to bear on the problem of identifying those
people who are in fact the most attractive potential romantic partners.[20] Bisexuals do exactly the same thing, the only difference being
that we do not treat a person's sex as a primary and necessary criterion.
This does not mean that we necessarily consider a person's sex to be irrelevant: some of us do feel that biological sex is irrelevant, but some
of us feel differently toward men than we do toward women, others of
us prefer one sex over the other and many of us develop different kinds
of relationships with people of the two sexes primarily because of the
gender differences which are superimposed upon the biological. Biological sex, then, is for us merely one of a number of criteria we might

use to choose our romantic partners. We can consider it to be important or not, just as we might consider any other personal characteristic to be important or not. In short, we do not differ from heterosexuals and homosexuals in the way we choose our partners; we merely decline to place biological sex or, in its stead, gender, at the top of the list as a necessary criterion.

That bisexuals do not practice exclusion on the basis of biological sex or gender is a negative definition of bisexuality, however; it states what we do not do instead of what we do. The point is not that we choose not to practice sex/gender exclusion, but that we open ourselves up to the possibility of consciously choosing our own criteria. This, then, is the aspect of bisexuality which must be emphasized.

In recognition of this, we sometimes refer to heterosexuals and homosexuals as "monosexuals," those who permit themselves to be attracted to persons of only one sex, in contrast to "bisexuals," who allow themselves to be attracted to persons of either sex. The term "bisexual," however, embodies the negative definition of ourselves just discussed: the emphasis remains upon the biological sex characteristics of potential romantic partners. Although we argue that we do not choose our partners based upon their biological sex, we still define ourselves with a word that refers to the biological sex of our partners. This is self-defeating; what we need to do instead is to remove the characteristic of partner sex from its privileged position altogether so that we are free to choose our own ways of defining ourselves and choosing our partners. Moreover, the term "*bi*sexual" is dualistic, implying that we as individuals are two halves rather than one whole. We need to choose a name that emphasizes our holism and that points out the freedom we claim, not the societal restrictions we reject.

New words sometimes take root and sometimes do not. Whether a new word takes root or not depends upon many factors, for example whether it is needed and whether the word itself is attractive and able to take on the meaning it is given. It is particularly difficult to use a new word to describe oneself, because until the word becomes familiar enough to embody the meaning it is given, it seems artificial and mechanical; objectively, the word might have the meaning needed, but subjectively it does not yet serve to express that meaning, and so it is an unsatisfying way to describe oneself. Satisfaction comes with time, however; all words are artificial, and they seem so until they become so familiar that we forget they are mere symbols and begin to feel that the meaning is inherent in the word itself. This is similar to learning a foreign language, or using foreign currency: at first, we experience a persistent feeling that the foreign currency is play money and that the foreign language is symbolic, whereas our money and language are real. But with time, words become familiar and they come to embody the meanings they are given, and then they become satisfying to use.

There is clearly a need for a new word that will more effectively describe who we are. The word "bisexual" might be familiar and comfortable to us now, but we will soon outgrow it, and without an alternative which defines us in our own positive terms, we will find it difficult to rally the like-minded under our banner. Just as we are challenging constructions that are comfortable for heterosexuals and homosexuals, so must we be willing to examine our own familiar terminology and make a conscious choice about whether we should keep or reject it.

We have already begun this work.   In his book *Bisexuality: A Reader and Sourcebook*, Thomas Geller includes a "bi-lexicon" of alternatives to the word "bisexual."[21]   Some suggestions, for example "bigenderist" or "equal opportunity lover," are as dualistic as the term "bisexual." Others, such as "pansexual," are more holistic. Pansexual, meaning "all-sexual," could convey the unfortunate impression that we are obsessed with sex or that we sleep with anything that moves, but should be understood to mean that we open ourselves up to all sexual possibilities.   Personally, I think that words like "idiosexual," which means "individual-sexual," or "autosexual," which means "self-sexual," would be more accurate, since our uniqueness lies in our determination to define our own individual sexualities, whether we choose to be open to all possibilities or not. But at the same time I cannot imagine telling people that I am an "idiosexual" or an "autosexual," because I immediately imagine the response, "You mean you are a masturbating sexual idiot?"

The term "pansexual" has two different meanings according to Geller. These two meanings appear to arise out of disagreement over the meaning of "sexual." Does "sexual" refer to the *sex* of one's partner, or does it refer to one's own *sexuality?* This same ambiguity surrounds words like "heterosexual," "homosexual" and "bisexual," but it was not problematic until we decided to banish the concept of partner sex from our vocabulary of self-identity. If it does refer to partner sex, then we certainly want to eliminate it. But what if it refers to one's own sexuality? Do we want to question the concept of sexuality itself? Many of us already have; it is, after all, defined in male terms and described in male language.[22] The term "pan*sensual*," also found in Geller's bi-lexicon, solves both problems; "sensual" clearly refers to one's own experience and avoids imposing narrow male-defined limits upon that experience. It allows us to claim a wider range of our own emotional and physical capacity. I think I could get used to calling myself a "pansensual." Already, I prefer it to the dualistic implication of the word "bisexual," a word I have never felt comfortable with at all.

As pansensuals, we distinguish ourselves from heterosexuals and homosexuals. We do so by identifying that which is unique about ourselves—our determination to describe our personal sexualities in terms meaningful to us rather than in terms offered by the sexual culture surrounding us. By distinguishing ourselves from heterosexuals and homosexuals, we carve out our own piece of sexual territory on a field heretofore claimed by heterosexuals and homosexuals. No longer are we squatters trying to lay claim to a bit of heterosexual territory and a bit of homosexual territory in order to fashion a makeshift identity for ourselves. Instead, we have created new territory by defining it in our own terms, and it is legitimately ours by virtue of this fact. We enter the battle of sexual meanings as contenders in our own right.

By the same token, we allow heterosexuals and homosexuals to remain legitimate contenders in this battle of sexual meanings. Since we are now creating our own territory instead of laying claim to the territory they have already claimed, we are no longer a threat to them. Instead, we grant them sovereignty over their territory, which they occupy legitimately through the same right by which we occupy ours, that is, by virtue of the fact that it is defined in terms meaningful to them. The concept of pansensuality allows those who feel comfortable identifying themselves as heterosexual or homosexual to continue to do so, while asserting our right to do otherwise.

But what happened to the battle cry "everyone is really bisexual" and to the argument that those of us who have overcome our sexual hang-ups or learned to describe our sexuality in nondichotomous terms are the sexual vanguard of society? If everyone is potentially bisexual or pansensual,[23] then the task of our movement is to liberate all people from the repressive proscriptions and dichotomous constructions of society so that they, too, can enjoy the fulfillment of healthy, self-defined sexuality. Why should we reinforce the artificial sexual boundaries erected among us, and why should we create an "enemy" out of people who are essentially as bisexual or potentially as pansensual as we are, all for the selfish purpose of carving out an identity for ourselves?

The argument is very appealing. What more powerful movement could exist than one to which everyone belongs? Even if individuals do not yet realize that they are bisexual or do not yet think in pansensual terms, ultimately they cannot help but recognize their own true sexuality and the desirability of pansensual self-description once it is explained to them, and then we will have a movement to which everyone belongs. Talk about the strength of numbers—think of the marches on Washington we would have! Moreover, it is very tempting to think of ourselves in the role of the vanguard, shouldering the "bisexuals' burden" and undertaking the charitable task of helping others to recognize their own sexual potential so that they can learn to enjoy themselves fully as we have taught ourselves to do. How grateful they will be to us, once they understand what we are talking about and enter the age of personal enlightenment. This is one movement that is a sure-fire success—we can win by simply including everyone in our movement, thus defining the enemy out of existence.

"Inclusivity" has become a political buzz word. We bandy this word about, proud that we are willing to include everybody in our movement, as if this were a sign of open-mindedness.[24] Although inclusivity and open-mindedness are characteristics that often occur together, they are not the same thing, and this version of inclusivity totters dangerously on the edge of intolerance. The subtext of the call for inclusivity reads "we will accept anyone into *our* movement" rather than "we will accept everyone the way they are."

The unremitting fact is that many people do define themselves as either heterosexual or homosexual and are quite happy in doing so[25]. The question of whether or not these people had the potential to be bisexual is quite irrelevant, analogous to asking a person born without eyes to undergo a chromosome test to discover whether her eyes would have been blue or green if she had had eyes.[26] The question of whether self-proclaimed monosexuals might recognize bisexuality within themselves later in life is likewise irrelevant. We know that both sexual behavior and sexual identity vary greatly over the course of a lifetime[27]. That someone might be bisexual in the future does not discredit the fact that she considers herself monosexual now, nor would it indicate in hindsight that she was "really" bisexual all along. This is merely playing with words. Latent bisexuality, like latent homosexuality, is a political concept with no scientific basis or utility. If we are to be truly tolerant of others, we must give up the notion of including people who do not want to be included and learn instead to respect their self-definitions as we ask them to respect ours.

Even if we believe in our heart that monosexuals are really bisexual, we must acknowledge that trying to convince them of this is a waste of our political energy. Such a strategy would be akin to African Americans attempting to end their oppression by pointing out that the first human beings were African; therefore, we are all descended from African ancestors; therefore, all Americans are African-Americans; therefore, there is no Anglo enemy and no oppression.[28] It would be very convenient, but it doesn't work. Light-skinned people stubbornly persist in believing that they are "white," not "black," and some of these people continue to hold prejudices against people they consider black; trying to tell them that they are black, too, because their origins are also African does not eliminate their prejudice.[29] Whiteness and blackness are real because we believe they are real; racism is a product of our culture, not our genes. Likewise, heterosexuality and homosexuality are real because heterosexuals and homosexuals believe that they are real; the concepts are no less powerful simply because they are cultural.

Where Do We Go From Here?

If we are pansensuals, then, what kind of a movement can we build? What are our goals? What kinds of social change do we want to accomplish, and how can we accomplish it? Will we merely succeed in adding one more group of people to a growing list of oppressed minorities, or can we aim higher? Can we radically transform the way we think about gender and sexuality, or even politics?

Simply by naming ourselves pansensuals, we present a quadruple challenge to current ways of thinking about gender and sexuality.

First, we challenge the cultural emphasis on biological sex, particularly as a basis for sexual identity. Second, we challenge the assumption that everyone is either heterosexual or homosexual. Third, we challenge the notion of "sexuality" itself by introducing the broader concept of sensuality. Fourth, we challenge the current political landscape, a battlefield that heterosexuals and homosexuals have claimed as their own, and assert ourselves as a new political force.

I began this essay by pointing out that the dichotomy of biological sex is the cornerstone of our thinking about gender and sexuality, and I will end by exploring some of the implications of challenging this dichotomy. First of all, as discussed previously, we do not argue that biological sex is necessarily meaningless or irrelevant; we are willing to allow other people to continue to define themselves as heterosexual or homosexual depending upon the genitals between their partners' legs. We do, however, argue that the primacy of biological sex should not go unquestioned. By choosing alternative ways of defining our own sexualities, we demonstrate that personal sexuality can be defined without reference to others' genitalia, and we make this option available to others who might find the idea attractive. Our goal is not the impossible one of obliterating biological distinctions or asserting that they are inconsequential, but the vital one of encouraging an examination of the role played by biological sex in our society.

In this way, we allow the existing sex-gender edifice to stand, while building up an alternative edifice that we construct with the bricks beginning to fall out of it. If the edifice constructed atop biological sex continues to stand, so be it. This edifice has many inhabitants, and they like the shelter they have found. Meanwhile, however, we can build our own house. Our house may be small at first, but as we continue to gather up the bricks that have fallen out of the original edifice, it will grow larger. As it grows larger, it will become more visible. Those inhabitants of the original edifice who are not happy with their current accommodations may move into our new house. We do not need to destroy the original edifice in order to build our new house, nor do we need to destroy it in order to begin to make its inhabitants aware of the new house being constructed next door. When they look out the window, they will see it. We become visible.

Visibility is an important issue. One complaint frequently voiced by bisexuals is that heterosexuality and homosexuality are visible while bisexuality is not. Of course, the quality of being heterosexual or homosexual is invisible; if one woman walks down the street, other people cannot "see" her sexuality. The fact is, however, that the manifestations of heterosexuality and homosexuality are visible. If the same woman stands on the street corner kissing her female lover, then other people will "see" lesbianism, and if she walks down the street holding hands with her male lover, then other people will "see" heterosexuality. The fact that she may be bisexual will never be "seen" in the same way; bisexuality is, in effect, invisible.

But bisexuality is only invisible because it is not seen. The truth is, of course, that bisexuality per se is no less visible than heterosexuality and homosexuality. The failure to see bisexuality lies in the observer, not the observed. The only reason we "see" heterosexuality and homosexuality in the first place is because we unquestioningly define sexuality in terms of partner sex. If we begin to throw this definition of sexuality into question, observers would no longer be able to see heterosexuality and homosexuality any more than they can now see bisexuality. If they can no longer rely upon their observations of partner sex as an indication of others' sexuality, they will be forced to acknowledge that sexuality is a personal characteristic that can only be determined through self-observation and self-description. In other words, they will learn to perceive pansensuality, and heterosexuality and homosexuality will then become as invisible as bisexuality is now.

In order to make ourselves visible, then, we do not need to prohibit others from defining their own sexuality in terms of the biological sex of their partners. All we need to do is introduce an element of doubt about the universality of this manner of defining sexuality. Once others can no longer take sexuality based upon partner sex for granted, they will no longer be able to "see" heterosexuality and homosexuality in others with any degree of certainty, even if they continue to see heterosexuality or homosexuality within themselves. Thus we become visible without annihilating them. In terms of the edifice metaphor, we do not need to destroy the sex-gender edifice next door to us. All we need to do is to build our own house, large enough to be seen. Once our house is built, the inhabitants of the original edifice will no longer be able to take others' addresses for granted, but will have to ask which house they live in.

What kind of a political movement is this that challenges simply by naming? In one sense, all political movements challenge the status quo by naming themselves: feminists reject the term "girls," lesbians and gay men reject the term "invert" and reclaim words like "dyke" and "faggot." Changes like these are important because they reflect changes in political awareness. But "pansensual" is more than another word for the politically correct to remember; it is a new meaning, and it is the beginning of a new language of human relations that does not oppress us by imposing artificial dichotomies and narrow limits on our experience. This is a new kind of political movement in this age of liberationism; it is not a struggle against an oppressive enemy but a struggle to change an oppressive system of meanings. Although we are all subject to the power of this oppressive system, we also hold the power in our own hands because we are the ones who use the language and we are the ones who can change it. Our weapon is visibility, not destruction. Our potential is to radically alter the way we think about not only gender and sexuality, but also the nature of power itself.

Endnotes

The author wishes to thank Elizabeth·Reba Weise for her comments on an earlier draft of this paper. The research reported in the essay was supported in part by a grant from the Horace H. Rackham Scholl of Graduate Studies at the University of Michigan, Ann Arbor.

1. Jerry Falwell, *Listen, America!* (Garden City, N.Y.: Doubleday, 1980), p. 184.

2. R. Kelly, "Witchcraft and Sexual Relations: An Exploration in the Social and Semantic Implications of the Structure of Belief," in *Man and Woman in the New Guinea Highlands* (Washington,·D.C.: American Anthropological Association, 1976).

3. Vern L. Bullough, *Sexual Variance in Society and History* (Chicago: The University of Chicago Press, 1976), p. 101; and *Homosexuality: A History From Ancient Greece to Gay Liberation* (New York: New American Library, 1979), p. 53.

4. Karl Heinrichs Ulrichs was the first to propose nonderogatory terms for the type of person who was attracted to members of her or his own sex. He used the term "urning." The word "homosexual" was coined in 1869 by Karoly Maria Benkert, under the pseudonym Kertbeny. The birth of the homosexual as a type of person is frequently credited to Benkert, although the concept was actually in existence at the time he suggested the use of the term "homosexual." (See Bullough, *Sexual Variance in Society and History*, p. 67; Bullough, *Homosexuality: A History*, p. 7; and Hubert Kennedy, *Ulrichs: The Life and Works of Karl Heinrich Ulrichs, Pioneer of the Modern Gay Movement* (Boston: Alyson Publications, 1988), pp. 50-59.

5. Descartes was not the first to draw the distinction between mind and body upon which our current preference for clearly distinct categories is patterned. He was, however, among the first to draw this distinction so sharply and clearly, and he has therefore become a popular symbolic target upon which to pin the blame for our current state of affairs.

6. Richard J. Hoffman, "Vices, Gods, and Virtues: Cosmology as a Mediating Factor in Attitudes Toward Male Homosexuality," *Journal of Homosexuality* 9, no. 2/3 (1983/84): pp. 27-43.

7. Using the word "homosexual" feels uncomfortable to me. I would prefer to use "lesbian" or "lesbian and gay," but I use "homosexual" frequently in this essay because it emphasizes the antithetical nature of these two forms of sexuality as they are historically defined.

8. Writing of Israelites, Hoffman notes that "all animals anomalous for their class, or which seem to fall between two classes, are abominations and forbidden to be eaten.... Thus, the pastoral model of the cloven-hoofed, cud-chewing ungulate was a standard for judging other animals.... The infamous pig has cloven hoofs, but does not chew its cud—hence it was forbidden."

9. Society is, of course, also organized along other lines, for example, racial and class lines. The assertion that society is organized along gender lines is in no way meant to imply that gender is the only such characteristic.

10. Since we usually take people's outside appearance (clothes, hair, voice, and so forth) as an indicator of their biological sex, we do not usually check to see if their breasts are real or if they have a penis before acknowledging them as male or female and treating them as such. But appearance does not always accurately reflect biological sex; culture dictates the proper appearance for each sex, and individuals who choose to pass as the other sex find that they are treated as if they were the other sex. In other words, we respond to a person's appearance, not to his or her biological sex per se. Thus, although sex usually is the basis for appearance, it is actually gendered appearance and not biological sex that directly underlies the social distinctions between men and women. Thus, it is customary to use the term "gender" rather than the term "sex" when referring to the different social positions of men and women.

11. Lewis Coser, *The Functions of Social Conflict* (New York: The Free Press, 1956).

12. A detailed description of the sample and method used in this study can be found in Paula C. Rust-Rodriguez, *When Does the Unity of a 'Common Oppression' Break Down? Reciprocal Attitudes Between Lesbian and Bisexual Women*, (Ph.D. diss., University of Michigan, Ann Arbor, 1989), available from University Microfilms International, 300 N. Zeeb Road, Ann Arbor, Mich. 48106, order #9001704; and Paula C. Rust, "Neutralizing the Political Threat of the Marginal Woman: Lesbians' Beliefs About Bisexual Women" (presented at the American Sociological Association 1991 annual meeting, Cincinnati, Ohio).

*

13. Since this is not a representative sample of the bisexual and lesbian populations, findings regarding the relative popularity of these various conceptualizations of sexuality among bisexual and lesbian women must be interpreted with extreme care.

14. An example of linguistic reinforcement of the homosexual/heterosexual dichotomy is the word "bisexual" itself, an issue that I address later in this essay.

15. Some of the ideas contained in this paper were originally presented at a session on Lesbian and Gay Studies at a meeting of the Canadian Sociology and Anthropology Association in 1987. As I began discussing the question of whether or not a bisexual movement is beginning, the attendees looked puzzled. Eventually, they asked, "But what would a bisexual movement *do*? What could bisexuals *want*?"

16. The primary focus of the larger study from which the information presented in this essay is drawn was lesbians' attitudes toward bisexual women. The larger study documents the extent to which lesbians hold the following beliefs: bisexual women experience less prejudice and discrimination than lesbians; bisexuals are really lesbians claiming to be bisexual; bisexuals are in the process of coming out as lesbians; bisexuals lack political loyalty to the lesbian movement and personal loyalty to female friends; bisexuals do not understand the problems lesbians face; and bisexuals are more likely to want to pass as heterosexual and find it easier to pass as heterosexual than do lesbians. It was found that although these beliefs are very popular among lesbians, they are not universal. Moreover, many of these beliefs are held by some bisexual women themselves, although not as strongly as they are held by lesbians. For a detailed description of lesbians' attitudes toward bisexual women, see Rust-Rodriquez, "When Does the Unity of a 'Common Oppression' Break Down?"; and Rust, "Neutralizing the Political Threat of the Marginal Woman."

17. Alfred Charles Kinsey, W. B. Pomeroy and C. E. Martin, *Sexual Behavior in the Human Male* (Philadelphia, Pa.: W. B. Saunders, 1948); Alfred Charles Kinsey, W. B. Pomeroy and C. E. Martin, *Sexual Behavior in the Human Female* (Philadelphia, Pa.: W. B. Saunders, 1953).

18. Kinsey, Pomeroy and Martin, *Sexual Behavior in the Human Male*, p. 650.

19. Since biological sex is generally visible only through the display of gender, these choices are actually made on the basis of gender rather than biological sex. This reliance upon gender is, however, based upon its assumed correspondence with bioligcal sex. Further exploration of the relationship between sex and gender is necessary, but outside the scope of this essay

20. For example, a heterosexual woman first narrows her field of view to men. Then she narrows her field of view further by specifying that she would also like to find a partner who is intelligent, feminist and brown-eyed. She may consider intelligence and feminism to be as necessary as male sex, while she considers brown eyes preferable but not necessary. In the center of her romantic field of view, then, she sees intelligent, feminist men with brown eyes. Just beyond these people, she sees intelligent, feminist men with other colored eyes. When she meets a new person for the

first time, she can determine immediately whether this person is male or female through observation of gender attributes which are assumed to reflect sex. If this person is female, she eliminates her from her romantic field of vision immediately and never thinks of her in romantic terms at all. If this person is male, she then has to discover whether he is intelligent and feminist, a process that will take some time. During this period of time, he is potentially within her romantic field of view; therefore, all men are initially seen in romantic terms. It is possible that during this brief introductory period, she may begin to feel romantic toward a man but then discover that he is either not intelligent or not feminist; thus, although she had considered intelligence and feminism to be as necessary as male sex, in practice she may find that intelligence and feminism are not in fact as necessary as male sex.

Thus, the primary role played by biological sex in mapping out the romantic field for heterosexuals and homosexuals has two sources. First, heterosexuals and homosexuals implicitly state at the outset that they will consider only people of a particular biological sex as potential romantic partners. The heterosexual-homosexual dichotomy encourages this kind of statement and provides the language with which to make such a statement. Second, the visibility of biological sex through gender allows people to effectively practice this exclusionary rule. If people of one sex are eliminated immediately from one's romantic field of view, they are never seen in romantic terms at all and there is little possibility that one will allow oneself to develop romantic feelings toward them.

21. Thomas Geller, *Bisexuality: A Reader and Sourcebook* (Ojai, Calif.: Times Change Press, 1990), pp. 105-108.

22. For example, our cultural model for sexuality is heterosexual intercourse, which we describe as "penetration" instead of "enveloping."

23. I intentionally refer to both bisexuality and pansensuality here because the concepts are not interchangeable. If we think in terms of pansensuality, the argument that "everyone is bisexual" becomes "everyone (even those who are accurately described as monosexual) could learn to describe their sexuality in pansensual terms." Phrased in terms of bisexuality, the argument asserts that people who have learned to repress feelings for one or the other sex could learn to express their sexuality more fully. Phrased in terms of pansexuality, the argument is that our ways of thinking about our sexuality have been constrained by current sexual ideology, and that everyone will be liberated by learning to think about their sexuality in a new way, whether that uncovers repressed feelings or not.

24. Our claim that bisexuals are inherently more "open-minded" or "inclusive" than monosexuals is itself based upon a dualistic conception of bisexuality. We believe that we are "inclusive" because we think of ourselves as people who are "open" to romantic involvement with both sexes. In other words, we are "inclusive" in our search for romantic involvement with both sexes. In other words, we are "inclusive" in our search for romantic partners. This appearance of inclusivity is only an artifact of our using partner sex to define personal sexuality in the first place; as discussed above,

pansensuals are not necessarily any more inclusive (read "indiscriminate") than monosexuals; we simply choose not to practice discrimination on the basis of the same criterion. Nevertheless, it is only a short jump from considering ourselves "inclusive" with regard to partner sex to considering ourselves fundamentally more "in of moral superiority upon our supposed open-mindedness, without realizing that the roots of this claim grow in dichotomous homosexual/heterosexual soil, a soil ultimately poisonous to us.

25. Personally, I happen to prefer the theory that we all begin life with the potential for an infinite variety of sexual responses. I also believe that we are products of our society and that our postpartum experiences determine how this potential will be manifested and how we choose to construct this manifestation linguistically. The result is no less "real" simply because it is the product of social experience; on the contrary, since we cannot grow up without social experience, perhaps it is our potential that is the less real of the two.

26. This analogy was made by "Toby," a guest on the "Oprah Winfrey Show." Toby has neither male nor female sexual organs and refuses to be placed in either the male or female category. Audience members and callers to the show had great difficulty accepting this refusal and persistently tried to find some basis for classifying Toby as male or female. Toby drew this analogy in response to a question about whether s/he had had her chromosomes tested to see "whether s/he was male or female."

27. Philip Blumstein and Pepper Schwartz, "Bisexuality: Some Social Psychological Issues," *Journal of Social Issues* 33, no. 2 (1977): pp.30-45; Philip Blumstein and Pepper Schwartz, "Lesbianism and Bisexuality," in *Sexual Deviance and Sexual Deviants*, ed. Erich Goode (New York: Morrow, 1974), pp. 278-95.

28. This argument is different from the argument that civilization began in Africa, an argument that attacks racism by emphasizing the contributions made by our black ancestors rather than by attempting to convince whites to identify with blacks; such an argument is effective in counteracting Eurocentric views of history.

29. In the United States, our white-defined racial categories are constructed such that a person with "one drop of black blood" is considered black even though most of her ancestors were white. See, for example F. James Davis, *Who is Black? One Nation's Definition*, University Park, Penn, Pennsylvania University Press, 1991, for an extended discussion of race and definitions in the U.S. This racist classification system is based upon the notion of whiteness as purity. Therefore, those who consider themselves white in the United States are generally immune to arguments regarding their African origins because they can see no blackness in their own ancestry. In other cultures where races are more mixed and defined in less racist terms, for example in Puerto Rico, this argument does have some persuasive power (this observation is from a personal communication with L. Rodriguez, 1991).

Amanda Udis-Kessler

APPENDIX:
NOTES ON THE KINSEY SCALE
AND
OTHER MEASURES OF SEXUALITY

The Kinsey scale is so well known among lesbians, gay men and bisexuals that it is commonly mentioned in writings on sexuality without further explanation. It is one of at least three scales that have been developed to measure sexuality; two other well known scales were created by Michael Storms and Fritz Klein.

Alfred Kinsey was a zoologist at the University of Indiana in the 1940s. He was tapped to teach the human sexuality course, so the story goes, because he was an extraordinarily boring man and the school administration, which did not want to offer the course at all, thought that if he taught it no one would attend. What they did not take into account was Kinsey's painstaking commitment to research; when he went to prepare material for the course, he found that no current research on human sexuality existed to teach and so set out to gather his own data. He developed an extensive questionnaire and interviewed over ten thousand people, publishing his data in *Sexual Behavior in the Human Male* and *Sexual Behavior in the Human Female.*[1]

The books received attention mainly for their "value-free" (read: nonjudgmental) approach to sexuality, unheard of at that time, but one set of findings in particular turned out to have a great deal of impact: Kinsey's discovery that one-third of the men he surveyed had had homosexual encounters to orgasm as adults, and that forty-six percent of the men surveyed were neither exclusively homosexual nor heterosexual. Although the sheer amount of homosexuality reported was entirely unexpected, the sexual range was at least as surprising and led Kinsey to draw up a scale in order to make sense of his data.

*

311

The Kinsey Heterosexual-Homosexual Scale

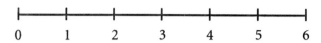

| 0 | 1 | 2 | 3 | 4 | 5 | 6 |

0. Exclusively heterosexual
1. Predominantly heterosexual, only incidentally homosexual.
2. Predominantly heterosexual, but more than incidentally homosexual.
3. Equally heterosexual and homosexual.
4. Predominantly homosexual, but more than incidentally heterosexual.
5. Predominantly homosexual, only incidentally heterosexual.
6. Exclusively homosexual.

Kinsey developed the scale to stress sexuality as a continuum, but it has generally been cited to prove that ten percent of the population is gay. This famous number, so useful to us since Kinsey's day, is almost undoubtedly wrong,[2] and it has since become clear that Kinsey's sample (the set of people who provided his data) was not representative of the country as a whole. Nonetheless, phrases such as "one in ten" and "Kinsey 6" are probably as ingrained in queer culture as Judy Garland, Oscar Wilde, leather, *Desert Hearts*, Provincetown and Ferron.

Kinsey's model went unchallenged until the 1970s. At that point, a debate began to occur among psychologists and social psychologists interested in gender roles, a debate that would ultimately lead to a second sexuality scale. Traditionally, gender roles had been understood as consisting largely of traits or attributes that could be labeled masculine or feminine (independence, aggression, empathy, gentleness and the like). Such traits had been measured on a single bipolar scale, with "masculine" traits at one end of the scale and "feminine" traits at the other; the standard masculinity-femininity scale thus looked very much like the Kinsey scale. The ends of the continuum were exclusive of each other: one was *either* feminine *or* masculine. Moreover, the middle of the scale was not well defined; it was unclear whether someone in the center would have attributes of both men and women, or few attributes of either men or women. During the 1970s, gender role researchers began to question whether the traditional scale was the most useful way of understanding gender role attributes. Psychologists such as Sandra Bem, Janet Spence and Robert Helmreich proposed an alternative approach: two separate scales, one measuring "feminine" attributes, one measuring "masculine" attributes.[3] This new method of measurement cleared up a number of problems. A person could score high on both scales, or low on both scales, or high on one and low on the other; the first two possibilities were no longer blurred into one confusing "middle range."

Given that the Kinsey scale operated on the same bipolar format as the earlier gender role scale, it was only a matter of time before the same problems that had been raised with regard to gender would be focused on sexuality. The Kinsey scale presented homosexuality and heterosexuality as exclusive of each other and failed to clarify what was measured by the middle section. Kinsey surely intended the continuum to show degrees of bisexuality, but—like the early gender role scale—falling between the two extremes could mean that one was both homosexual and heterosexual, or that one was neither one nor the other. (Someone with little sex drive and few sexual desires for anyone might show up at "3" on the Kinsey scale, as would someone with strong sexual desires for both men and women. The former person would be considered asexual, whereas the latter would be considered bisexual.)

Michael Storms, a psychologist at the University of Kansas, had been studying sexuality and erotic fantasies, and his research seemed to point to some of these conceptual problems with the Kinsey scale. He found that bisexuals engaged in as much heterosexual fantasizing as heterosexuals, and as much homosexual fantasizing as their lesbian and gay counterparts.[4] He ascertained from this that bisexuality seemed to somehow incorporate total heterosexuality and total homosexuality in a way not indicated by the Kinsey scale (in which bisexuality is between the two "extremes," rather than encompassing them). Storms was also bothered by the issue of asexuality described above. In 1980, he proposed a new sexuality scale, similar to Bem, Spence and Helmreich's work on gender roles, but using an x-y axis rather than two separate continua.[5]

The Storms Sexuality Axis

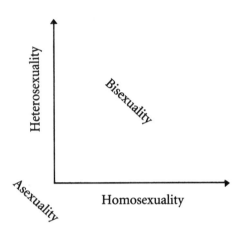

Few people of any sexuality seem to be aware of this model; Kinsey's and Fritz Klein's models are cited far more frequently. This may be because Storms published in a psychology journal, while Kinsey produced two books and Klein published in the *Journal of Homosexuality*. Or it may be because Storms's model does not translate into catchy phrases like Kinsey 6, or because the subtlety of his argument differentiating bisexuality and asexuality was lost on most of the people who did encounter his articles, or even because of social trends in lesbian and gay communities, in which the Kinsey scale has been especially valued.[6] Regardless of the reason, Storms's model did not set off a new debate about the conceptualization of sexuality, and Klein's model, created several years later, does not appear to have been a response to Storms.

Psychiatrist Fritz Klein developed the Klein Sexual Orientation Grid (KSOG) "in an attempt to better demarcate and understand the complexities of human sexual attitudes, emotions and behaviors."[7] Klein found prior definitions of homosexuality, heterosexuality and bisexuality to be hopelessly vague and inconsistent. He thought that Kinsey's original scale was useful to a degree, but was concerned that the different factors that make up sexual identity—attraction, fantasies, behavior and the like——be taken into account, and that the variance of these factors over time be duly acknowledged. Klein created the KSOG to rectify these problems and, in one of the most interesting sampling strategies I have ever heard of, tested its usefulness by having *Forum* (a *Playboy* clone) readers fill it out.[8]

The Klein Sexual Orientation Grid

In order to ascertain your sexual orientation, add the numbers in the twenty-one boxes and divide by twenty-one in order to see where you place on the Kinsey scale. If you have a dash in any box, divide by one less for each dash. You can then ask yourself if this grid is a fairly accurate indicator of your sexual orientation.

	Past	Present (in past year)	Ideal Future Goal
Sexual attraction			
Sexual behavior			
Sexual fantasies			
Emotional preference			
Social preference			
Self-identification			
Lifestyle			

Sexual attraction. Who turns you on? Who do you find attractive as a real or potential partner?

Sexual behavior. Who are your sexual contacts (partners)?

Sexual fantasies. Who do you enjoy fantasizing about in erotic daydreams?

Emotional preference. With whom do you prefer to establish strong emotional bonds?

Social preference. Which sex do you prefer to spend your leisure time with, and with which sex do you feel most comfortable?

The Kinsey scale offered a range of numbers correlating with different degrees of heterosexuality and homosexuality; the Klein grid is filled out by using Kinsey's number system. A "Kinsey number" between 0 and 6 is placed in each box of the grid. Thus, a woman who has only slept with men but who only wants to sleep with women in the future would fill out the "sexual behavior" boxes "0" (completely heterosexual), "0", and "6" (completely homosexual) respectively. A man who currently socializes only with men would fill in "social preference--present" with a "6," but if he is equally sexually active with men and women, he would fill in the number "3" (equally homosexual and heterosexual) in the "sexual behavior—present" box.

Klein's model seems to have found many fans among sex educators and among bisexuals in general. Its multidimensional focus is certainly a step forward in precision from the conceptual vagueness of Kinsey and Storms, but Storms might complain that, like Kinsey, Klein blurs the asexual-bisexual distinction—twenty-one times per subject!

Because sexuality measures, especially Kinsey's, have appeared to be so useful for so many people, it may seem odd to raise objections to them. Yet feminist social scientists and others concerned with research methodology have pointed out that it is problematic to abstract any one aspect of a person, sexuality included, and hold it up as useful data on its own terms. Moreover, surveys, questionnaires and other self-reporting methods tell us only about someone's self-perception,[9] not necessarily about her behavior, motivations or unconscious influences. At a more basic level, the research methods generally used by the social sciences have been developed within a larger philosophical perspective that some feminists find problematic, because of its unquestioning valuation of male gender-stereotyped attributes as normative. Claims about scientific objectivity (both the possibility of it and the value of it), emotional distance from the subjects of study, and the "neutral" character of science are among the many areas of research contested by feminist thinkers. This is not the place to delve into a feminist critique of science or methodology, but I think it is important to mention that such a critique exists.[10] Another critical line of thought, influenced (ironically) by both ethics and postmodernism, sees sexuality scales as part of the trend of technologizing sex.[11]

Criticisms notwithstanding, sexuality scales are not likely to disappear in the near future; if anything, they may be continually redesigned to take sexual styles (such as s/m) into account or to reexamine sexuality-gender dynamics.

Postscript: As this book was going to press, I learned about a new sexuality scale.[12] Created in order to "validate and to contrast six proposed categories of bisexuality, as well as categories related to heterosexuality, homosexuality and asexuality" (p. 67), the Multidimensional Scale of Sexuality represents a recasting of some of Klein's ideas, while taking Storms's concerns into account. The six categories of bisexuality encompass those people who have switched from exclusive heterosexuality to exclusive homosexuality or the reverse; those people who are primarily attracted to one sex—whichever one it may be—but who have infrequent desires for, or sexual contacts with, the other sex; and those people who are equally oriented toward both sexes, but who are either always focused on one sex at a time or always attracted to, and active with, both sexes. If this scale becomes well-known, I predict that bisexuals will find it extremely interesting if complex (one ascertains one's score by filling out a forty-five item questionnaire), and that the new jargon associated with it ("sequential" versus "concurrent" bisexuality) will find its way into many a bi circle.

Endnotes

1. Alfred Kinsey, et al. *Sexual Behavior in the Human Male* (Philadelphia, Pa.: W. B. Saunders, 1948); Alfred Kinsey, et. al., *Sexual Behavior in the Human Female* (Philadelphia, Pa.: W. B. Saunders, 1953).

2. There is, ironically, conflicting data on whether "ten percent" is too high or low a figure. Part of the problem is that Kinsey's designation of sexuality by "counting orgasms" (an exaggeration, but not an unrealistic description, of his methodology with male subjects) is culturally far removed from the identity and subjectivity of the contemporary self-designated "queer," and as such cannot speak to lesbian, gay or bi life post-Stonewall very effectively.

3. See Sandra Bem, "The Measurement of Psychological Androgyny," *Journal of Consulting and Clinical Psychology* (1974) 42, pp.155-62; and Janet T. Spence and Robert Helmreich, *Masculinity and Femininity: Their Psychological Dimensions, Correlates, and Antecedents* (Austin, Texas: University of Texas Press, 1978).

4. Storms did not focus on the heterosexual fantasizing of self-identified lesbians and gay men, or on the homosexual fantasizing of self-identified heterosexuals. He took people's self-definitions at face value and did not "redefine" people by discrepancies in their fantasy lives. Whether such an exercise would have been more interesting must thus remain open to question until someone else researches this area.

5. Michael S. Storms, "Theories of Sexual Orientation," *Journal of Personality and Social Psychology* 38, No. 5 (1980): 783-92. It should be noted that Storms's sample was quite small as compared to Kinsey's (several dozen people as opposed to several thousand), and that his thesis about the best way to conceptualize sexuality has not really been tested. I believe that the greatest value of his model is its stimulation to our thinking; at this point, it is difficult to make any claims about its accuracy in describing human sexual experience.

6. This is not the place to discuss the political implications of the different sexuality scales or the ways in which they have been used historically by different groups. However, it is interesting that of the few people I know who are conversant with all three scales, bisexuals seem to be more fond of the Storms scale than are lesbians and gay men. The extent to which this is tied to social and cultural trends among the different groups is unclear, but I think some connection quite likely exists.

7. Fritz Klein, et al. "Sexual Orientation: A Multivariable Dynamic Process," *Journal of Homosexuality* 11, No. 1/2 (1985): pp. 35-49.

8. Klein did not focus on the breakdown of sexuality revealed by his sample—and with good methodological reason, given the nonrepresentativeness of his sample. He merely tested it for validity and reliability. To my knowledge, no one has used it on a large, diverse population to discover sexuality breakdown yet.

9. Or at least that part of her self-perception that she is willing to reveal.

10. See Susan Bordo, "The Cartesian Masculinization of Thought," *Signs: Journal of Women in Culture and Society* 11 (1986): 439-56; Sandra Harding, *The Science Question in Feminism* (Ithaca, NY: Cornell University Press, 1986); Dorothy E. Smith, *The Everyday World as Problematic: A Feminist Sociology* (Boston: Northeastern University Press, 1987); and *The Conceptual Practices of Power: A Feminist Sociology of Knowledge* (Boston: Northeastern University Press, 1990).

11. Other aspects of this trend include sexual technique manuals, sex therapy and in some versions, sex toys and books. An interesting socialist-feminist treatment of this topic can be found in Edwin Schur, *The Americanization of Sex* (Philadelphia, Pa.: Temple University Press, 1988), pp. 48-52, 63-66, 90-95, 135-138.

12. See Branden Robert Berkey et al, "The Multidimensional Scale of Sexuality," *Journal of Homosexuality* 19, No. 4 (1990): pp. 67-87.

Resource List

United States

Bi-Net
The Bisexual Network of the
United States
584 Castro St. #441
San Francisco, CA 94114-2588

Publishes a quarterly national
newsletter.

Bay Area Bisexual Network
2404 California St., Box 24
San Francisco, CA 94115
(415) 564-BABN

Publishes *Anything That Moves:
Beyond the Myths of
Bisexuality*, a quarterly magazine.

Boston Bisexual Women's
Network
Gay, Lesbian and Bisexual Commu-
nity Center
P.O. 639
Boston, MA 02140
(617)BIS-MOVE

Publishes *Bi-Women*, a bi-monthly
newsletter, the oldest newsletter on
bisexuality in the country and an
international directory of bisexual
groups.

Seattle Bisexual Women's
Network
P.O. Box 30645
Greenwood Station
Seattle, WA 98103-0645
(206) 783-7987

Publishes *North Bi Northwest*, a
bi-monthly newsletter with a
focus on feminist analysis of
bisexual issues.

United Kingdom

London Bisexual Women's
Group
BM LBWG
London WC1N 3XX
England

Netherlands

Landelijk Network
P.O. Box 5087
1007 AB Amsterdam
The Netherlands

Publishes *Bi Nieuws*, a quarterly
magazine.

New Zealand

Wellington Bisexual Women's
Group
P.O. Box 5145
Wellington, Aotearoa
New Zealand

Publishes *Bi-Lines* newsletter.

Bibliography

Off Pink Collective, *Bisexual Lives*, London: Off Pink Publishing, 1988.

Geller, Thomas, ed., *Bisexuality: A Reader and Sourcebook*, Times Change Press, 1990.

Hutchins, Loraine, and Lani Kaahumanu, eds., *Bi Any Other Name: Bisexual People Speak Out*, Alyson Publications, 1991.

Klein, Fritz and Timothy J. Wolf, eds., *Bisexualities: Theory and Research*, The Haworth Press, 1985.

Wolff, Charlotte, *Bisexuality: A Study*, Quartet Books, 1979.

Contributors

Diane Anderson, 23, has been a writer and a poet for fifteen years. She was editor of the *Crescent City Star*, New Orleans' largest gay and lesbian publication; worked as a reporter for Spectrum News network, a lesbian and gay television program in California, and as news editor for OUT! in Idaho. She is a civil-rights activist, animal-testing protester, and environmental proponent. She currently lives in New Orleans.

Karin Baker is a bus driver and activist who puts most of her energy into queer liberation and socialist politics. She is a member of Solidarity, a U.S. socialist group with branches across the country. She recently moved to San Francisco from western Massachusetts, to try organizing in a city environment, and in hopes of finding a more bi-positive environment.

Kathleen E. Bennett is a 26-year-old woman who saw herself first as a rabidly political lesbian, then as an uneasy pro-gay heterosexual, finally finding her epiphany at first contact with the bi movement. No longer confused, she now proudly identifies as emotionally bisexual, erotically lesbian and socio-politically queer. She has published her own poetry, and her essays and stories have appeared in several publications.

Brenda Marie Blasingame is an African-American, Jewish, bisexual woman who spent most of her childhood years growing up in a small agricultural town in Florida. She has been actively involved in social change work for the past ten years. She conducts oppression/liberation workshops focusing on issues of racism, sexism, heterosexism, anti-Semitism and adultism throughout the country. She loves to travel, laugh, dance and hang out with her friends and most of all spend time with her partner.

Margaret Mihee Choe is a second generation Korean-American. An ex-ex-patriot New Yorker, she has a B.A. in English Literature from Barnard College and an M.A. in Finland's Literature and Languages from Columbia University. She is currently considering ambicoastalism.

Beth Elliott comes from a long line of independent-minded California women of the dreaded white middle-class persuasion. A long-time lesbian feminist activist, she was a co-founder of the Alice B. Toklas Democratic Club and a member of the board of the lobbying organization which saw California's sodomy laws repealed in 1975—around the time she went down in flames in the lesbian PC wars. In 1982, she wrote (along with Lani Kaahumanu and others) materials for *Plexus'* groundbreaking bisexuality issue. A nine-time San Francisco Advertising Softball League all-star, she rather likes the designation "switch hitter."

Eridani is the computer account password of a chemist working for a very uptight large corporation. Bisexual for 20 years, she is currently working on reproductive freedom and fat liberation issues. An information junkie with five-dollar-a-day habit, she is a cyclist and weight lifter. She is a Zen druid avatar of Eris, goddess of quantum indeterminacy.

Ruth Gibian is a poet and social worker in Portland, Oregon. Her poems have appeared in *Poetry Northwest, The Seattle Review* and *Nimrod*, and she has taught writing at various colleges and rural public schools. She currently works with sexual minority youth.

Sharon Gonsalves is a thirty two-year-old woman who is awesome. She is an electronics technician who repairs computers for money. She is helping to form an intentional community with men and women of all sexual orientations based on a shared political, spiritual and personal growth philosophy. In her spare time she produces videos for a local cable TV station. She lives in Somerville, Mass. with her beloved cat, Ida.

Rebecca Kaplan is someone who believes that labels are an appropriate means of communication when well chosen, and is having difficulty deciding which labels to use to describe herself for this publication. She is a feminist, dyke, bisexual, left-handed, rugby-playing student. She has been involved in feminist and bisexual community activism for over three years. She recently helped organize a for-credit course on bisexuality at the Massachusetts Institute of Technology which was the first such course on the East Coast.

Elizabeth McKeon was born in 1963. She has been involved in several different women's groups and hopes to see socioeconomic class issues gain greater recognition within political coalitions. She plans to graduate from medical school in the spring of 1992.

Robyn Ochs is an escapee from New York City who now lives in Cambridge, Massachusetts. During the day, Robyn is a not-so-mild-mannered university administrator. In 1991 Robyn taught the (second-ever-anywhere) course on bisexuality at the Massachusetts Institute of Technology and in 1992 a (third-ever-anywhere) course on bisexuality at Tufts University. She is a founder and active member of the Boston Bisexual Women's Network and the East Coast Bisexual Network. She loves her cat, her friends, her mother, recycling and travelling.

Rebecca Ripley is monosexual and has naturally curly brains. Most of the people mentioned in this paper are her personal friends—an interesting bunch. All ideas not her own can be found in the last twenty years' lesbian, gay, bisexual, queer, women's and feminist publications, or (if you're lucky) your public library. She wishes to thank her many women friends of all sexualities for comments on earlier drafts. You know who you are.

Paula C. Rust is Assistant Professor of Sociology at Hamilton College where she teaches courses on gender and sexuality. She has done research on lesbians' attitudes toward bisexuality and is currently conducting research on the development of bisexual identity and bisexual politics.

Rebecca Shuster is a Boston-based psychotherapist, consultant, teacher, writer and support group leader. Her writings on bisexuality have appeared in *Lesbian Psychologies* (University of Illinois Press, 1987) and *Bi Any Other Name* (Alyson Publications, 1991).

Nina Silver is a therapist, Reichian bodyworker, singer and composer whose writing on feminism, sexuality, the natural sciences and metaphysics have appeared in *off our backs, Empathy, Gnosis, Green Egg, Jewish Currents, The New Internationalist* and the anthologies *Lesbian Bedtime Stories* and *Women's Glib*. She is currently working on book of essays called *The Visionary Feminist.*

Susanna Trnka is a junior at the University of California at Berkeley. She is majoring in women's studies and anthropology, with a particular interest in women's labor. Her writing has been published in the journal *Socialist Review,* at which she was an editorial intern, in *The Daily Californian* and in the feminist magazine *Broad Topics.* Her research has recently been cited by *Ms.*

Amanda Udis-Kessler is a writer, musician and bi educator in the greater Boston area. Her writings on bisexuality have appeared in a number of books, journals and newsletters. She loves cats, sociology, most kinds of music and Asian food, and has been known to have a sense of humor on occasion.

Amanda Yoshizaki, an educator, potter and reformer who lives in Philadelphia, hangs out with her bi-husband, and bi-cats. She has passions for chocolate, poetry and bubble baths.

Stacey Young has been active in feminism and lesbian/bisexual/gay politics since 1981. She currently teaches in the Department of Government in Skidmore College, and writes about sexuality, politics and community.

Vashti Zabatinsky believes in the power of words, music, closeness, chocolate, conscious choices, building alliances and being determined. She tries to avoid and occasionally heal single issue agendas, rigid or sloppy thinking, and all forms of toxic waste. In her spare time, she likes to sing, cook, exercise and write. She is thinking of buying her male lover a t-shirt that says, "I'm not a lesbian, but my girlfriend is."

Dvora Zipkin is a Jewish "bisexual-lesbian" feminist who has been and/or continues to be, at various stages of her life, a teacher, gardener, baker, political activist, stress management and assertiveness instructor, photographer, writer, traveller, explorer, seeker and general student of life. She is currently working on a doctorate in creativity.

Index

About the Editor

Elizabeth Reba Weise was one of the founding members of the Seattle Bisexual Women's Network and a long time editor of their newsletter, *North Bi Northwest*. She works as a writer and journalist and lives in Seattle.